THE

TRANSFER HANDBOOK

PROMOTING
STUDENT
SUCCESS

AACRAO®
1 · 9 · 1 · 0

American Association of Collegiate
Registrars and Admissions Officers
One Dupont Circle, NW, Suite 520
Washington, DC 20036–1135

Tel: (202) 293–9161 | Fax: (202) 872–8857 | www.aacrao.org

For a complete listing of AACRAO publications, visit www.aacrao.org/bookstore.

The American Association of Collegiate Registrars and Admissions Officers, founded
in 1910, is a nonprofit, voluntary, professional association of more than 11,000 higher
education administrators who represent more than 2,600 institutions and agencies in the
United States and in forty countries around the world. The mission of the Association
is to provide leadership in policy initiation, interpretation, and implementation in the
global educational community. This is accomplished through the identification and
promotion of standards and best practices in enrollment management, information
technology, instructional management, and student services.

AACRAO adheres to the principles of non-discrimination without regard to age,
color, handicap or disability, ethnic or national origin, race, religion, gender (including
discrimination taking the form of sexual harassment), marital, parental or veteran status,
or sexual orientation.

LIBRARY OF CONGRESS CATALOGING-IN-PUBLICATION DATA

The transfer handbook : promoting student success.

   pages cm

Includes bibliographical references.

ISBN 978-1-57858-110-8

1. College registrars—United States—Handbooks, manuals, etc.
2. College admissions officers—United States—Handbooks, manuals, etc.
3. Students, Transfer of—United States—Handbooks, manuals, etc.
4. Transfer students—United States—Handbooks, manuals, etc.
I. American Association of Collegiate Registrars and Admissions Officers, issuing body.

LB2360.T7355 2015
371.2′91—dc23
2015009453

CONTENTS

Deciphering the Data

CHAPTER ONE
BY BRUCE CLEMETSON, LEE FURBECK,
AND ALICIA MOORE

*Understanding the Data and Best Practices
for Supporting Transfer Students* 3

CHAPTER TWO
BY PAUL ATTEWELL AND DAVID MONAGHAN

*Lost Credits: The Community College Route
to the Bachelor's Degree* 15

Enrollment Management

CHAPTER THREE
BY NORA MANZ

Transfer Student Success and Retention 23

CHAPTER FOUR
BY SUSAN DAVIES, JANE REX,
AND LORI STEWART GONZALEZ

*Creating Institutional Teamwork for
Transfer Student Success* 37

CHAPTER FIVE
BY SHANEE R. CREWS AND JOANNE E. JENSEN

Recruiting Transfer Students 51

Regulations

Partnerships

Case Studies

Appendices

ABOUT THE AUTHORS

Paul Attewell teaches in the Ph.D. program in sociology at the Graduate Center of the City University of New York. His research focuses on the intersection of social stratification and education, and especially on processes affecting undergraduates from low-income backgrounds in non-elite colleges. His latest book, co-authored with David Monaghan, is titled *"Data Mining for the Social Sciences: An Introduction."*

E. Michelle Blackwell is the Director of Reverse Transfer at the University of North Carolina–General Administration. She previously served as Director of Transfer Student Services at Middle Tennessee State University, where she established one of the first reverse transfer agreements in the state with Nashville State Community College. She earned her bachelor's degree in psychology and master's degree in child and family studies from the University of Tennessee (UT), Knoxville. She served as Assistant Director

of the University Honors Program at UT for eight and half years. She has presented at national and regional AACRAO conferences on reverse transfer and the National Summit on Reverse Transfer sponsored by the National Student Clearing House.

Shawn Brick is Associate Director of Undergraduate Admissions at the University of California–Office of the President (UCOP). He has worked on admissions policy issues for the 10-university UC system for five years. Shawn also serves as the UC representative and Chair of the www.assist.org Executive Management and Oversight Committee. Prior to his work in admissions, Shawn was a financial aid policy expert for UCOP and a financial aid director at the California College of the Arts. He holds a B.A. in History and Anthropology from the University of Wisconsin at Madison and will complete his master's degree in public policy at UC Berkeley in 2015.

i

Kelly L. Brooks, MPA, is Registrar at Capella University in Minneapolis, Minnesota. Her higher education career spans more than 20 years, including positions at the University of Minnesota–Twin Cities campus as the School of Nursing's Undergraduate Enrollment Manager, as well as Medical School Registrar. Brooks has also served as Degree Audit Coordinator, Registrar's Office Supervisor, and Admissions and Transfer Officer at Capella University. She holds an undergraduate degree in print journalism and a master's degree in public affairs in policy analysis and higher education administration.

Andrew Cardamone is an Associate Director of Academic and Membership Affairs at the National Collegiate Athletics Association. Andrew joined the NCAA in September 2008 and currently serves on the academic, interpretations, and operations teams. Specifically, Andrew serves as lead for academic, transfer, and academic integrity related interpretations. He is also an academic team lead for business performance management and technology initiatives.

Prior to joining the NCAA he was Assistant Registrar for Athletics Eligibility and Certifications at Georgetown University and the compliance coordinator at Temple University. He also worked as an academic counselor in the Prentice Gautt Academic Center at the University of Oklahoma.

Andrew holds his undergraduate degree in psychology from Saint Joseph's University where he was a member of the baseball team. He also holds a master's degree in counseling and psychological services from Springfield College.

Marie-Jose (M.J.) Caro is Registrar at Embry-Riddle Aeronautical University, Daytona Beach. She has 18 years of experience in higher education and higher education consulting, having served as a software consultant for Ellucian, Inc., Director of Student Affairs at the Pennsylvania Academy of the Fine Arts, Registrar and Associate Director of Admissions at Florida Gulf Coast University, and Assistant Director of Enrollment Services at Lehigh Carbon Community College. She holds a master's degree from Jones International University and bachelor's degrees from Moravian College and Embry-Riddle Aeronautical University.

Christine Carter is a Senior Evaluator in the Office of the Registrar at Thomas Edison State College, where she has worked for nine years. She earned her bachelor's degree at Georgetown University, and her M.Ed. at the University of Virginia. Christine has presented at the AACRAO Technology and Transfer conference, as well as the AACRAO Annual Meeting on topics including military and non-traditional transfer credit.

Dr. Bruce Clemetsen is currently Vice President for Student Affairs at Linn-Benton Community College in Albany, Oregon. Bruce earned degrees from Willamette University, Michigan State University and Bowling Green State University. Bruce has worked in various student affairs roles at multiple types of institutions. He is an adjunct faculty member at Oregon State University, teaching in the College Student Services Administration and the Community College Leadership programs. Bruce serves on the Oregon Community College Student Success Oversight committee. His areas of interest include institutional partnerships, equitable student success and completion, and student progression.

Angela M. Crawford is the Manager of Marketing and Communications for the National Association of Intercollegiate Athletics (NAIA). She earned her bachelor's degree in public administration and public communication at Truman State University in Kirksville, Missouri. and her master's degree in communications and quantitative research methods at the University of Kansas.

Angela was among the initial group hired by the NAIA to help develop the processes for the Association's new Eligibility Center, leading to its opening in 2010. For her first two years at the NAIA, she oversaw academic eligibility decisions for students transferring to NAIA schools and conducted the staff training for academic eligibility decisions. Currently, Angela coordinates the education and communication efforts of the NAIA Eligibility Center for all external groups.

Shaneé Crews is the Associate Director for Transfer Recruitment at Virginia Commonwealth University. She received her bachelor's degree in psychology from Hampton University, and her Master of Education in Counselor Education, with a concentration

in College Student Development and Counseling, from VCU's School of Education. She began her career in higher education at VCU in August 1999, and has served in various capacities: in the Office of Records and Registration, the VCU Transfer Center, the School of Business, and currently in the Office of Admissions. In her current role, she is responsible for leading the coordination of marketing and communications, recruitment, and the application review process for the VCU Office of Admissions' transfer admissions efforts.

Susan Davies earned her B.A. in English from Georgia Southern University and her M.A. in College Student Development from Bowling Green State University. She is currently writing her dissertation on student price responsiveness in college enrollment decisions to complete a Ph.D. in Educational Studies from the University of North Carolina at Greensboro. Susan has served as Associate Vice Chancellor of Enrollment Management at Appalachian State University since 2009 and created the Office of Transfer Articulation, which has now expanded to an Office of Transfer Services. Prior to her time at Appalachian, Susan held various positions that impacted transfer student recruitment and retention, including Coordinator of Orientation and Parent Programs and Director of Admissions, over eleven years at Georgia Southern University.

Ed Devlin is currently a foreign credential evaluator with AACRAO International Education Services and previously held the posi-

iii

tion of Director of Special Projects. He has worked in international education for more than 40 years, directing the International Student Program at Monterey Peninsula College (MPC), California, and directing English language and academic orientation programs at Stanford, MPC and the University of California Santa Cruz. He has also worked in international admissions at Golden Gate University in San Francisco and as a consultant for many schools and programs in the United States and abroad.

Mr. Devlin served on the AACRAO International Admissions Committee and several NAFSA committees. He has given presentations, workshops and training sessions at numerous AACRAO and NAFSA conferences, and has contributed many articles for publications from both associations. The author of the AACRAO publication *Australia: Education and Training* and co-author/editor of the PIER workshop reports on Poland and the Czech/Slovak Federated Republics, Ed developed the first model for the AACRAO EDGE (Electronic Database for Global Education). Ed Devlin is a Life Member of NAFSA.

Christy M. Fry is the Associate Director of International and Diversity Recruitment at Colby-Sawyer College where she is charged with all international and transfer enrollment initiatives. For the past four years, she was the lead international credential evaluator for both International Graduate and Undergraduate Admissions at Johnson & Wales University. Christy has been an international education practitioner for nearly fifteen years,

where she has held public, private and government positions in Malta, Sicily, Italy, and the United States. These positions have afforded her experience in immigration and compliance, credential and transfer evaluation, training and assessment, student services, and articulation agreement management. Christy's M.A. was obtained from SIT Graduate Institute in International Education and Advising; her B.A. was completed in Psychology. She enjoys presenting and facilitating sessions, especially on the topic of credential evaluation, having done so at AACRAO, NAFSA, and UK NARIC conferences.

Lee Furbeck, Ph.D., currently serves as Director of Undergraduate Admissions and Student Transition at Cleveland State University and directs the transfer program for AACRAO's Technology and Transfer Conference. She has published and presented extensively on transfer-related topics, student access and equity, and admissions recruitment. Lee previously served as chair of AACRAO's Transfer and Articulation Committee and has worked with transfer students and transfer credit policy at the institutional and state levels in multiple states. She has also served as chair of AACRAO's Professional Development Committee and in several regional leadership roles. Lee earned a doctorate in English at the University of Missouri in Columbia, Missouri, and master's and bachelor's degrees from the University of Kentucky.

Lori Stewart Gonzalez, Ph.D., obtained her B.A. from the University of Kentucky's Com-

About the Authors

iv

munication Sciences and Disorders program. She received her M.A. in Communication Disorders from Eastern Kentucky University, and her Ph.D. in Communication Disorders from the University of Florida. She began her academic career at Southern Illinois University at Carbondale in 1988. In 1991, she returned to the University of Kentucky as an assistant professor in the Communication Sciences and Disorders program. She spent twenty years at the University where she served on the faculty and also served as Associate Dean of Academic Affairs. In 2005, she was appointed UK's third Dean of the College of Health Sciences serving in that capacity for seven years. Dr. Gonzalez served as Provost and Executive Vice Chancellor at Appalachian State University in Boone, North Carolina from 2011 until 2014. During her time as provost, she focused on student success initiatives including transfer student programming. She currently serves as the Senior Advisor to the Senior Vice President for Academic Affairs at the University of North Carolina General Administration.

Stephen J. Handel is the Associate Vice President–Undergraduate Admissions for the University of California (UC) System. In this capacity, Handel provides leadership around freshman and community college transfer admissions policy and practice for the nine UC undergraduate campuses. Prior to this position, Steve served for nearly a decade as the Executive Director of the National Office of Community College Initiatives at the College Board. At the College Board, Handel advocated for and conducted research with community colleges nationally and internationally, with a special focus on initiatives that advance educational access and equity for all students. Handel is the author of the *Community College Counselor Sourcebook* as well as other publications focusing on higher education issues, including *Remediating Remediation* (with Ronald Williams), *Strengthening the Nation by Narrowing the Gap* (with James Montoya), and *Second Chance, Not Second Class: A Blueprint for Community College Transfer*. Handel holds a Ph.D. from UCLA and a bachelor's degree from California State University, Sacramento.

Charles Hannon is Associate Dean of the Faculty and Professor of Computing and Information Studies at Washington & Jefferson College in Washington, Pennsylvania. He teaches courses in human-computer interaction, the history of information technology, data presentation, project management, and gender and women's studies. He has recently published in *Smashing Magazine* and *Interactions,* and is the author of *Faulkner and the Discourses of Culture* (2005), which won the C. Hugh Holman prize in southern literary studies. He holds a B.A. in English and German from James Madison University; an M.A. in Modern Literature from the University of Kent at Canterbury; and a Ph.D. in English from West Virginia University.

Heidi Hoskinson is Interim Vice President of Academic Affairs at Friends University in Wichita, Kansas. A higher education professional for over 20 years, she has worked in the areas of student affairs, enrollment management, and academic affairs. Heidi is finishing a Ph.D. in Adult and Higher Education with an emphasis in Administration from the University of Oklahoma and previously earned a Master of Science in Educational Leadership from Central Connecticut State University and an undergraduate degree from Fort Lewis College, Durango, Colorado. Active in AACRAO, Heidi has served on the Small College Issues and Academic Progress and Graduation Committee and currently serves as the Vice President for Outreach for the Kansas Association of Collegiate Registrars and Admissions Officers (KACRAO). She has served as Chair of the NAIA Registrars Association for the past year as well as serving on the NAIA Competitive Experience Committee.

Joanne Jensen is the Director of Marketing and Communications for Virginia Commonwealth University's Division of Strategic Enrollment Management, which includes admissions, financial aid, military student services, new student and family programs, records and registration, student accounting, summer and intersession programs, the transfer center, and university academic advising. Jensen earned her bachelor's degree in English and her master's degree in English composition and rhetoric from VCU. Prior to her work in higher education, Jensen worked as an account coordinator and writer in the fields of advertising and public relations, and as an editor for a newspaper. Jensen has served in several roles during her tenure at the

university. She began her career in higher education as a teaching assistant and adjunct instructor in the VCU Department of English. In 1999, she joined the staff in undergraduate admissions where she was responsible for overseeing marketing and publications. In her current role, Jensen leads all marketing and communications activities and programming for SEM.

Ann M. Koenig is an Associate Director with AACRAO International Education Services. Her career in international education spans more than 25 years, including foreign credential evaluation with IES and other professional evaluation services, and campus-based work in international undergraduate and graduate admissions, student records management, academic advising, and transfer credit evaluation. She has worked with Cardinal Stritch University in Milwaukee, a University of Maryland University College program in Germany, Golden Gate University in San Francisco, and the University of California, Berkeley.

As a respected expert in academic document review and fraud detection, Ms. Koenig has contributed to several AACRAO publications on the topic and shared her insights and recommendations for best practice at numerous workshops and conference sessions. Her achievements in international education include in-depth research and writing on education in several countries. She has presented at professional development and training events sponsored by AACRAO, NAFSA, NAGAP, EAIE, and several other organizations in the U.S. and Europe. Ms. Koenig has served on the NAFSA national ADSEC committee and the AACRAO International Education Committee.

Nancy Krogh currently serves as a Senior Consultant for Sierra-Cedar Inc. She previously worked at the University of Idaho and the University of North Dakota as university registrar and at Rocky Mountain College as the registrar and director of institutional research. Nancy earned her Ed.D. and M.Ed from Montana State University and a B.A. from the University of North Dakota. She has 25 years of experience in higher education including in registration, transfer, admissions, institutional research, residence life, and the administration and implementation of technology.

Nancy served on AACRAO's Board of Directors as vice president for finance. She has also served on several committees and taskforces including as chair of the Institutional Research and Enrollment Planning and Information Systems and Technology Committees and as the co-chair of the AACRAO Task Force on Association Governance. Nancy was awarded AACRAO Honorary Membership in 2015.

Nora Manz is the Associate Director of Transfer and Articulation at Delaware County Community College. She has an M.A. in Counseling, an Ed.M. in Psychological Counseling from Teachers College, Columbia University, and a B.A. in Psychology from Alfred University. She has been with Delaware County Community College for almost nine years, where she is responsible for managing the Transfer Office.

Over the last 13 years, Nora has worked in various roles in higher education including admissions, counseling, advising, and student activities. In recent years she served on the Board of Directors of SSI at West Chester University, and was invited to serve on NACAC's Transfer Advisory Committee. Nora has presented at local and national conferences regarding transfer student transitions, advising and adjustment, as well as *Transfer-Check*. She is currently a member of the New York State Transfer and Articulation Association (NYSTAA), and is a founding member of the Transfer Advising and Admissions Committee of Pennsylvania (TAAC).

Jack Miner is Director of Registrar Operations at The Ohio State University. He holds a bachelor's degree in political science and a master's degree in public policy and management, both from The Ohio State University. In addition, Miner has been recognized with the University's Distinguished Alumni Award and a scholarship named in his honor.

Jack has served as president and treasurer of the Ohio Association of Collegiate Registrars and Admissions Officers and serves on the Articulation and Transfer Credit Steering Committee for the Ohio Board of Regents. He has also served as vice chair of Nominations and Elections, chair of the LGBT Caucus, and on various committees for the AACRAO. Jack is currently the Vice Chair of the Program Committee and will be chair for the annual meeting in Phoenix in 2016. Jack is a recipient of the 2015 Thomas A. Bilger Award for service and leadership within AACRAO.

David Monaghan is a Ph.D. candidate in Sociology at the Graduate Center of the City University of New York (CUNY), and completed his undergraduate education at Tufts University. His research focuses on non-traditional students and open-access higher educational institutions, and in particular on how the stratified structure of American higher education reproduces educational inequality among college entrants. His research has been published in *Educational Evaluation and Policy Analysis*, *Sociological Focus*, and *Social Science Research*. He is completing his dissertation, which explores college enrollment among working-aged adults.

Alicia Moore, Dean of Student and Enrollment Services for Central Oregon Community College (COCC) and Senior Consultant with AACRAO Consulting, bring more than 17 years of leadership experience in the field of student and enrollment services. Ms. Moore emphasizes the need for campus-wide leadership in strategic enrollment management and providing opportunities for individuals across the campus, regardless of their position, to engage with the planning and implementation process.

During her tenure at COCC, Ms. Moore helped the College navigate record-setting enrollment goals, including doubling institutional enrollment in five years. Through her collaborative efforts, she has helped the

campus develop a SEM plan and associated student success strategies initiative, partnerships between high schools and universities, as well as a new comprehensive one-stop service center that includes admissions, registration, placement testing, academic advising, student account/bursar, and financial aid. Ms. Moore has also played a key role in the design of COCC's new Campus Center and student housing, and coordinated the development of ongoing efforts towards a successful institution-wide strategic enrollment management plan.

Ms. Moore has presented at numerous conferences on topics including strategic enrollment management, assessment in student services, student engagement and retention, and institutional branding, and has written several articles for AACRAO's *College and University* journal. She has a bachelor's degree from Willamette University, a master's degree from Colorado State University, and is currently pursuing her doctorate in educational leadership from Oregon State University.

Adam Parker is a Policy and Program Analyst at the University of California, Office of the President. He has worked on higher education issues including admissions, financial aid, and student diversity, for the last fifteen years. As an independent consultant, Adam works with nonprofits and foundations on issues relating to education and poverty. Adam has an M.A. in Public Policy from UC Berkeley, an M.A. in History from the University of Wisconsin-Madison, and a B.A. in History from UC Berkeley. Adam also has written three books on California history for elementary school students.

Jane Rex received her Bachelor of Science in Health and Physical Education from Slippery Rock University in 1979 and a Master of Arts in Student Development from Appalachian State University in 1989. Jane was a 23-year veteran of the North Carolina Community College System before directing the Office of Transfer Articulation. Established by Appalachian State University in 2010 to address the needs of transfer students, particularly as it relates to the seamless transfer of credit, the office has evolved into a one-stop center for transfer students. In addition to the challenges of creating a new office, Jane serves on numerous committees on campus and across the state to advocate for transfer-friendly policies and practices that address transfer student needs. Jane is a frequent presenter at state, regional, and national conferences and was recently awarded the Bonita C. Jacobs Transfer Champion Award by the National Institute for the Study of Transfer Students.

Douglas T. Shapiro, Ph.D., is the Executive Research Director of the National Student Clearinghouse Research Center, where he is responsible for leveraging the nation's largest student-level longitudinal dataset of college enrollment and degree information to help improve institutional practice, inform policy and increase student success. The Research Center publishes annual reports detailing trends in student enrollment, persistence, transfer, mobility and completion. The

Center also provides data services that track student enrollment and progress in postsecondary education for high schools, districts, states, postsecondary institutions, researchers and other educational organizations.

Shapiro has 15 years of experience conducting and publishing research on students in higher education, including 11 years of building and managing student-level research datasets at the institution, state and national level. Prior to joining the Clearinghouse, he was the Director of Institutional Research at The New School. Before that, he served as Vice President for Research and Policy Development at the Minnesota Private College Council. Shapiro spent his early career managing alumni development campaigns, teaching mathematics, and leading one of the largest graduate student employee labor unions in the nation. He holds a Ph.D. from the University of Michigan's Center for the Study of Higher and Postsecondary Education, an M.A. in Mathematics from the University of Michigan, and a B.A. in History from the University of Chicago.

Patricia (Pat) Shea is the principal investigator for the Interstate Passport Initiative. She holds an M.Ed. in Educational Administration and Supervision from George Mason University. As the Director of Academic Leadership Initiatives for the Western Interstate Commission for Higher Education (WICHE) in Boulder, Colorado, Shea oversees the activities of three membership organizations based there: the WICHE Internet Course Exchange, the Western Academic

Leadership Forum, and the Western Alliance of Community College Academic Leaders. She also directs WICHE's involvement in two other regional collaborative projects: the North American Network of Science Labs Online (NANSLO) and the Consortium for Healthcare Education Online (CHEO).

Roland Squire is the University Registrar for Utah State University. He earned his bachelor's degree in computer science from Utah State University. He has had a career in information systems; first with Salt Lake City and then as the Management Information Services Director for the Utah Department of Public Safety. While at Public Safety Roland was named by the Governor as the Enterprise Executive for the information technology component of the state's homeland security efforts. He has worked for USU for ten years and has worked on the WICHE Passport project from the start of the project.

Roland served four years in the Air Force. After receiving electronics training he was assigned to the White House Communications Agency in Washington, D.C. where he served for over three years.

Jason L. Taylor is an Assistant Professor in the Department of Educational Leadership and Policy at the University of Utah. He received his Ph.D. in Higher Education from the University of Illinois at Urbana-Champaign with a research specialization in evaluation methods and concentration in public policy. His broad research interests are at the intersection of community college and higher education policy and educational and social inequality. He has conducted and led several quantitative and mixed methods studies on college access and college pathways, including topics such as college readiness, developmental education, adult pathways to college, dual credit/enrollment and early college experiences, reverse transfer and transfer policy, career and technical education, LGBTQ students, and educational access and equity.

Jason is the Co-Principal Investigator for the research associated with the Credit When It's Due initiative, and is investigating the implementation and impact of reverse transfer programs and policies in the 15 states participating in Credit When It's Due. He has published in journals such as *American Behavioral Scientist, Community College Review, Community College Journal of Research and Practice, Education Policy Analysis Archives*, and *New Directions for Community Colleges*. Prior to transitioning into academia, Jason was an academic advisor at Illinois State University and the Registrar at Chaparral College in Arizona.

Liz Terry is a Policy and Program Analyst at the University of California, Office of the President, focusing on Undergraduate Admissions. She holds a master's degree in public policy from the Harvard Kennedy School and a bachelor's degree in mathematics from Brown University.

Edward F. Trombley III is Registrar at Embry-Riddle Aeronautical University, Worldwide. With more than 25 years of experience in education, he has served as Senior Operations Manager of the Registrar's Office at Walden University; Registrar at DeVry University in the Philadelphia and Washington, D.C., metro regions; and Dean of Administration at Bryant & Stratton College. He holds a bachelor's degree and master's degree from the State University of New York at Oswego.

Catherine Walker is the project manager for the Interstate Passport Initiative, which is managed by Western Interstate Commission for Higher Education (WICHE). She holds a bachelor's degree in music history and a Master of Arts in Teaching from The Colorado College. Walker is also a founder and partner in The Third Mile Group, an education policy and research firm that conducts project management, program evaluation, research, writing, editing, and constituent communication and relations. Her work has focused on education leadership, alternative education, teacher preparation and compen-

sation, and expanded learning opportunities. Previously she held numerous positions at the Education Commission of the States and the State Higher Education Executive Officers.

Frank Yanchak is University Registrar at Franklin University in Columbus, Ohio. He has been in higher education for more than 20 years and earned a Bachelor of Arts from West Liberty University and a Master of Business Administration from Wheeling Jesuit University. He has served on AACRAO's Mentor Services Committee and the Transfer and Articulation Committee.

Frank has been very active in Ohio ACRAO as President, Vice President of Mentoring and Membership, member of the Records and Registration Committee and Professional Development Committee, and Co-Chair of the Local Arrangement Committee. He was also selected by his peers to serve on the Ohio Board of Regents Articulation and Transfer Credit Steering Committee.

PREFACE

LEE F. FURBECK

Director, AACRAO Transfer Conference
Director of Admissions and New Student Transition, Cleveland State University, Ohio

In January 2015, President Barack Obama announced an ambitious proposal to offer two years of community college tuition-free to qualifying students, including non-traditional and part-time students excluded from similar state initiatives. Community colleges are a relatively recent American invention, starting with Joliet Junior College in Chicago nearly 100 years ago. Since then, community colleges have established a proud tradition as open-access institutions educating a wide variety of students ranging from first-time college students and military veterans to adult learners and new immigrants. According to the College Board, many of the millions of students enrolled in credit-bearing programs in community colleges are doing so with the intention of transferring to a four-year college or university and earning a bachelor's degree.

With the recent recession and college costs continuing to increase, student transfer has become more prevalent and its patterns have become less traditional. More than one third of students transfer at least once before earn-

ing a bachelor's degree (Hossler *et al.* 2012). With more options available for where and when they can access and complete courses, these students engage in multiple patterns of attendance, moving between four-year and two-year schools, and between public and private institutions. Any transfer student may be at a greater risk of not completing a degree, but they don't have to be. Partnerships between institutions as well as college and university support services can help transfer students succeed and graduate.

AACRAO has a history of being at the forefront of transfer, and for over 80 years has published *Transfer Credit Practices of Designated Educational Institutions* (TCP), a voluntary exchange of information regarding practices for acceptance of transfer credit. The much-needed publication *The College Transfer Student in America: The Forgotten Student* was published in 2004 just as institutions and state and federal government were turning an eye toward transfer. This guide translates research into practical advice on attracting, retaining, and graduating transfer students, and addresses strategies for orientation and advising, curricular issues, articulation agreements, and particular types of transfer. Not long after, AACRAO's *Accreditation Mills* (2007) was released as the first publication of its kind to explore accreditation fraud. The book gives a historical perspective of the problem, explores the relationship between degree mills and accreditation mills, and defines tactics used by mills to deceive the public.

One year later, in 2008, the AACRAO Transfer Conference was born as the association recognized the need to bring professionals working with transfer students together to address common issues and to take a stance on proposed federal legislation which would have shifted transfer credit decision-making from institutional control to the federal government. Since then, 300 to 400 transfer professionals continue to meet each year to share challenges and successes and to provide a venue for collaboration. In 2012, AACRAO's Transfer and Technology Conferences officially co-located for the first time, creating opportunities for attendees to explore the connections between the two while retaining the original focus of the meeting.

Now, AACRAO has once again filled the void for admissions, advising, enrollment, financial aid, registrar, and retention professionals working with transfer students. Individual chapters in this book cover enduring topics such as trends, transfer of credit and articulation, transfer policy, two-year to four-year pathways, credential verification, recruitment, transfer student athletes, advising, partnerships, and regulations with a fresh and timely perspective. Other chapters address more recent phenomena such as adult learners, growing numbers of military veterans, reverse transfer, technology, and student swirl.

With so few resources devoted entirely to the topic, this publication stands alone as a comprehensive publication on all things transfer. The best thing about working with transfer students is that no two days are the same. Whether you are just beginning your journey with this fascinating student population or charting the course for transfer student success at your institution, you will find a valuable source of information here.

xiv

INTRODUCTION

DOUGLAS SHAPIRO

Executive Research Director, National Student Clearinghouse Research Center

Transfer is a large and growing part of students' experience of postsecondary education today, and thus it is increasingly important for student professionals, institutional registrars, admissions officers, and enrollment managers to understand. Student mobility, generally referring to any of the multiple-institution pathways that students follow in pursuit of their educational goals, can include all directions of transfer, such as "traditional" transfer from a two-year to four-year institution; "lateral" transfer from one two-year to another two-year institution or from a four-year to another four-year institution; "swirling" from one institution to another and back again to the starting point; "reverse" transfer from a four-year to a two-year institution; and concurrent and dual enrollment patterns that may include simultaneous enrollment in more than one institution, such as an on-line university, a local evening or weekend program, or even a high school. Understanding these patterns and their implications for student success is increasingly vital to institu-

tions as they seek to improve how they serve their students, how they meet increasing demands for accountability from state and federal policy makers, and how they meet their own institutional goals.

There are very few institutions remaining for which students arrive only as first-time freshmen and leave as newly-minted graduates (or dropouts). Trying to measure the scale of student transfer can present difficulties, however, because of the slipperiness of the phenomenon and the need for multi-institutional data to track individual student movements from campus to campus. Recent research by the National Student Clearinghouse Research Center has found that the numbers depend upon the vantage point for viewing the student pathways and the amount of time spent in observance. Tracking a cohort of students from their very first postsecondary enrollment, for example, shows that one-third of students will enroll at a different institution from where they started within their first five years and before earning any degree or certificate. This number is fairly consistent regardless of whether that first institution is a community college, public four-year, or private non-profit four-year institution (Hossler *et al.* 2012). These are the students who entered your campus as first-time freshmen. Add the ones who transferred in and, for the average institution, the proportion of mobile students reaches one-half. Looking at a graduating cohort instead of a starting cohort confirms that this is not just a matter of the struggling students trying to find their footing, but includes the successful ones as well; half of all students who earned their first degree or certificate between 2003 and 2013 had enrolled in more than one institution along the way (Shapiro *et al.* 2014b). Many of these are "swirlers," but even excluding those who leave and come back, the data shows that over a quarter of those who completed degrees within eight years of their first enrollment in 2006 had actually earned them at a different institution from the one they started in (Shapiro *et al.* 2014a). Taken as a whole, it is a safe assumption that the share of students who are on a multi-institution pathway, either transferring in, transferring out, or both, makes up a larger part of the enrollments on the average college campus than many student professionals would think.

Not only are the numbers of mobile students large, but their pathways are also complex. More than one-quarter of students who have enrolled in more than one institution have also crossed state lines in the process (Hossler *et al.* 2012). Nearly 16 percent of new, first-time entrants into postsecondary educa-

tion are now entering as dual-enrollment students while still in high school, meaning that when they enter college as "freshmen" after graduating from high school, they may also expect to bring transfer credits with them (Shapiro *et al.* 2013a). Students starting at four-year institutions are, when they transfer or swirl, equally likely to switch to a two-year college as to another four-year. The same is true of students starting at two-year institutions. Some of them will eventually want to bring their new credits "back home" to their original institution; others, perhaps not. Indeed, most who start at a two-year institution and transfer to a four-year without completing an associate degree may not know that "reverse transfer"—sending four-year credits back to their starting institution in order to receive the associate degree if, by chance, they do not complete their bachelor's—is even possible. Yet, many state policies now encourage it, and there are as many as two million students nationwide who may be eligible (Shapiro *et al.* 2014b).

The growth of non-traditional students, particularly adults, part-time enrollees, or those returning to college after a long stop-out, is often assumed to contribute to trends of increasing student mobility and the growth of transfer students. Surprisingly, however, non-traditional students are often among the least mobile on many campuses. They tend to have less geographic freedom than traditional-age students, largely due to employment and family constraints, and thus find themselves more tied to the specific programs at specific institutions and locations that best meet their needs. They are also considerably less likely than traditional-age students to pursue a bachelor's degree by starting at a two-year institution (Shapiro *et al.* 2013a). Students in the military and student veterans, however, appear to be an exception to this rule. Their frequent stop-outs and geographic dislocations due to service demands and redeployments make them more likely to change institutions than their non-veteran adult peers (Cate 2014). Thus, the growth in the student-veteran population, expected to continue to accelerate, may lead to a reversal in the overall trend for non-traditional students.

Student mobility is important to institutions because of its impact on their efforts to manage enrollments and retain students. For many students, the process of transferring credits among the institutions in their increasingly complex educational pathways is often fraught with unexpected hurdles and barriers that can create frustration and dampen momentum (Monaghan and Attewell 2015). Recent attention to the challenges of credit transfer has led to many policy initiatives, particularly at the state level, to address the perceived inefficiencies of "lost" credits through regulation. Institutions that find ways to further streamline this process may be better positioned to avoid undesirable regulation while also becoming more effective at supporting progress and success for their mobile students.

Student mobility and transfer are also important at the overall system of postsecondary education, and particularly in terms of national and state-level goals for increasing college completion and attainment rates. Unfortunately, the resulting focus on institutional accountability and measures of student success often includes measures of success that do not count students who transfer, such as institution-based retention and graduation rates, and our national attention to these measures thus causes both institutions and the public to greatly underestimate the real rates of postsecondary student success. This leads to a diminished public perception of the effectiveness of higher education, and of the value that it returns to students, families, and society's investment. It also causes students to suffer from a narrowed horizon of opportunity and reduced capacities to plan realistic pathways to goal achievement, because neither they nor their advisors and counselors typically have access to complete or accurate statistics on the availability of multi-institutional pathways and their successful outcomes. By improving their understanding of the transfer pathways of students, enrollment professionals will be better able to counter these trends and support the goals and expectations of their mobile students.

xvii

TRANSFER HANDBOOK

PROMOTING
STUDENT
SUCCESS

Deciphering
the Data

THE

TRANSFER HANDBOOK

PROMOTING
STUDENT
SUCCESS

Understanding the Data and Best Practices for Supporting Transfer Students*

BRUCE CLEMETSON
*Vice-President for Student Affairs,
Linn-Benton Community College*

LEE FURBECK
*Director of Undergraduate
Admissions and Student Transition,
Cleveland State University*

ALICIA MOORE
*Dean of Student and Enrollment Services,
Central Oregon Community College*

* Previously published as "Enabling Student Swirl: Understanding the Data and Best Practices for Supporting Transfer Students,"
Strategic Enrollment Management Quarterly. 2013, October, issue 1:3. Copyright 1999–2015 John Wiley & Sons, Inc.

Understanding the Data and Best Practices
for Supporting Transfer Students

The inspiration for this chapter comes from the growing commitment among those in our profession to improve student success for students who have an end goal in mind, yet attend more than one institution to achieve it. The pathway to a degree is becoming less linear as students have more options for where and when they can access and complete courses. Such enrollment patterns are a trend that has been developing for quite some time. De los Santos and Wright (1990) are credited with coining the description of transfer behavior among institutions as "student swirl" in their study of student enrollment trends at Maricopa Community College. More than two decades later, students continue to swirl. Given the increasing volume of transfer students and multiple patterns of transfer, a recent National Student Clearinghouse (NSC) report (2012a) notes "...a new view may prove useful, one in which students are the unit of analysis and institutions are viewed as stepping stones along a diverse set of educational paths."

Public policy makers at both the state and federal levels are calling for stronger accountability systems. National data on retention and graduation are frequently consulted to provide a basis for accountability reports about institutional performance leading to student success. This data has strengths and weaknesses: it provides information about student enrollment (as measured in credits accumulated) and attrition, but it does not reveal information about actual learning. What it does do well, however, is highlight the growing number of students who take courses from more than one institution. Regardless of their eventual educational outcomes, many of these students currently are counted as institutional failures. Understanding and supporting today's swirling students is critical to assisting them in meeting their educational goals and for meeting state and national goals regarding accountability and completion rates.

This chapter offers perspective and suggestions for SEM professionals to address this

5

student population in order to increase the success of students who transfer between educational opportunities. The authors review transfer student characteristics along with transfer student data and trends, offer a rationale for why adjusting services for swirling students is important, and suggest best practices for improving success of transfer students.

Transfer Student Characteristics

As student affairs practitioners, we often make broad-based assumptions about students. At a breakout session during the 2012 AACRAO Strategic Enrollment Management conference, a group was asked to brainstorm what they knew about transfer student characteristics and some of their responses were:

- "Students who transfer do so because they are doing poorly and want to start over somewhere else."
- "Part-time students transfer more frequently than full-time students."
- "They weren't engaged in support services at their first institution, so left before they really needed to."
- "Transfer students don't know what they want to do for a major...or a career."
- "They are not very committed to their education."

...and multiple other commonly-held assumptions. Recent research by the National Student Clearinghouse (2012a) and Noel-Levitz (2011) both upholds and dispels many of these assumptions. Highlights from these two reports include:

- 40 percent of all transfer students did not complete Algebra II while in high school.
- Transfer students are typically traditional-age.
- 32 percent of all transfer students earned more than 20 credits prior to their first year of transfer.
- Transfer students are less engaged with and experience a lower sense of belonging at their transfer institution than other students.
- 53 percent of all transfer students, regardless of destination of transfer, indicate that financial reasons will interfere with their ability to finish.
- Transfer students typically seek out assistance with academic advising at their transfer institution at a rate higher than other students.

The above characteristics paint a complex picture, but provide reliable data upon which an institution may consider adjusting services to best support this population. Potential ideas are explored later in this paper.

Transfer Students and National Data Trends

It is widely known among the nation's higher education leaders that today's students rarely follow a linear path to certificate or degree completion; more and more frequently, it is uncommon for students to start, continue, and finish at just one institution. It is also widely known that national completion metrics do not take transfer student enrollment

6

patterns into consideration. However, recent in-depth research regarding transfer student enrollment patterns and completion rates provides compelling talking points, especially for policy makers focused on traditional measurements. Highlights from this research follow.

RATE, TIMING AND FREQUENCY OF TRANSFER

The National Student Clearinghouse (NSC) conducted two in-depth examinations of transfer student enrollment patterns. The first of these reports, *Transfer & Mobility: A National View of Pre-Degree Student Movement in Postsecondary Institutions* (NSC 2012a), reviewed data on 2.8 million first-time students whose enrollment information was submitted to the Clearinghouse for fall 2006, following these students through summer 2011. Of the 2.8 million students, 33.1 percent of all students transferred at some point in their academic career, with the largest percentage of students transferring during their second year (37%); surprisingly, 22.2 percent of students transferred in years four and five. Nearly 75 percent of transfer students did so only one time, while approximately 8 percent did so three or more times. Transfer rates of students starting at a two-year or four-year, public or private institutions were relatively similar, with 32.1 percent to 34.4 percent of this population transferring, while an average of only 17.9 percent of those who started at a for-profit institutions did so.

DESTINATION OF TRANSFER

According to the National Student Clearinghouse (2012a), the most common transfer destination was to two-year public institutions, regardless of the student's institution of origin. Of the transfer students who began their academic career at a four-year public institution, more than 85 percent transferred to another public institution, either two-year or four-year. However, the transfer destination for students who began at four-year private institutions is relatively evenly disbursed between public institutions and private institution peers.

In addition to the type of institution to which students transfer, it is important to note that transfer students also frequently cross state boundaries when transferring. According to research by Cliff Adelman and the U.S. Department of Education (1999), 40 percent of students who transferred did so by transferring to an institution in another state, while NSC data indicates that 27 percent of all transfer students do so (2012a). Regardless of the number, this data raises compelling questions regarding the value of in-state course and program partnerships, and demonstrates the limitations of state-specific reporting metrics (NSC 2012).

ENROLLMENT STATUS

One of the most frequently heard assumptions about transfer students at the 2012 SEM Conference is that they attend part-time. However, NSC describes a very different picture of the fall 2006 transfer student cohort in that 32.6 percent of students who started full time transferred at least once, while 33.9 percent of part-timers did so. Despite this similarity in percentages, it is important to recognize that

7

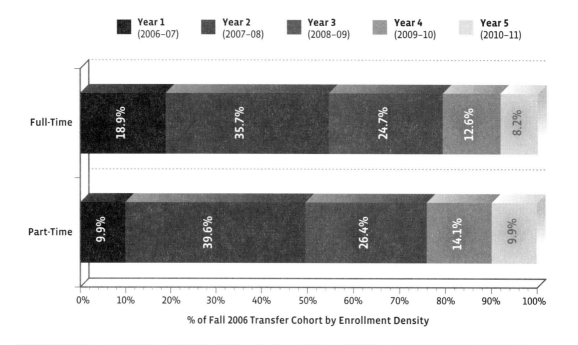

Figure 1. Timing of First Transfer by Initial Enrollment Intensity, Students Who Enrolled Part- or Full-Time in Fall 2006 and Later Transferred at Least Once
SOURCE: NATIONAL STUDENT CLEARINGHOUSE RESEARCH CENTER

"full-time transfer students transferred earlier in their careers than part-time students did" (NSC 2012a, 24; *see* Figure 1).

REVERSE TRANSFER

The second National Student Clearinghouse Research Center report focuses on 'reverse transfer' students, or rather, students who start at a four-year institution and transfer to a two-year institution. Data findings of note:

- While nearly 81 percent of summer-only course takers returned to their original institution, only 16.6 percent of students who took community college classes at other times of the year returned to their original institution.

- Reverse transfer students who took a community college class only during summer term had completion rates of nearly 78 percent at their 'home' institution, as compared to 58.4 percent of students who never enrolled in a summer class at a community college (NSC 2012b).

- More than half (55.1%) of reverse transfer students "did not return to any four-year institution by the end of the study period" (NSC 2012b, 5).

8

For individuals wishing to further explore transfer student characteristics and national data trends, each of the aforementioned resources provides much more extensive and in-depth information; many thanks to the National Student Clearinghouse Research Center and Noel-Levitz for the research in this regard.

Defining and Managing Different Types of Student Swirl

Today more than ever, the drivers that create student swirl are in full force. For adult learners and some traditional student populations, the quickest route to the degree or credential is the winner. Students attend multiple institutions in their pursuit of a degree, and swirling is increasingly a part of students' long-term plans to achieve affordable degree completion via transfer, dual enrollment in high school, or concurrent enrollment. Couponing and "getting the most for less" have gone mainstream, and so has the consumer approach to getting a college degree. With costs skyrocketing and penny-pinching in vogue, attending multiple institutions on the way to a "discount" degree is not the negative that it once was.

In 2003 Alexander McCormick defined multiple types of transfer student enrollment patterns, labeling such students as "swirlers." Each type demands a different approach for those attempting to assist these students in meeting their educational goals, but the actual transfer of credit and what courses or prior learning experiences actually "count" toward a degree is important for all. Clear and accessible information pertaining to transfer equivalencies and transfer policies, timely access to staff well-versed in transfer issues, cooperation and alliances between institutions sending or receiving students from one another, clear transfer pathways, a flexible curriculum, adequate retention initiatives, and an understanding and appreciation of what these students bring to a campus are mechanisms for accommodating all types of swirlers.

TRIAL AND SUPPLEMENTAL ENROLLERS

McCormick's first two types of transfer students are not always thought of as swirlers. McCormick begins by identifying students who take a few courses to explore the possibility of transferring as "trial enrollers." Creating internal mechanisms to identify these students, such as by monitoring credits that are being transferred to the "home" institution, allows for early intervention and can keep the trial enrollers engaged. McCormick continues to define "supplemental enrollers" as those who accelerate their progress by taking courses during break periods. Both the student and the institutions involved can benefit from this enrollment behavior. By providing clear, accessible transfer equivalency information, informed advisors, and a mechanism for pre-approval of outside coursework, the home institution benefits by keeping students on track for graduation; the supplemental institution benefits from additional tuition revenue.

9

CONSOLIDATED AND SPECIAL PROGRAM ENROLLERS

McCormick identifies other groups as "consolidated enrollers," or students who intentionally select courses at a variety of institutions to complete a degree program at a specific institution. Variations include students who alternate enrollment at two institutions or enroll simultaneously at two or more institutions. Those interested in opportunities not offered by their home school may engage in "special program enrollment." These are the students that come to mind most often when one thinks of swirlers. From the student perspective, colleges, community colleges, and universities are all part of the same system of higher education and, increasingly, a commodity purchase. Just as one might furnish a home with pieces from multiple sources, one can piece together a degree using a credit from various sources. These students are intentionally choosing non-traditional enrollment patterns. As with supplemental enrollers, these students can be kept on track for graduation if identified, tracked, and provided with good advising and a clear pathway to a degree.

SERIAL TRANSFERS

Other students who do not find a "fit," McCormick states, may move from institution to institution as a serial transfer. These students may start at either a two- or four-year institution and may move between sectors for a variety of reasons including poor grades, financial constraints, no clear goals or direction, family pressure, or a lack of understanding how to navigate higher education. Identifying these students and providing the necessary support are keys to success for the individuals and the institutions involved.

Populations most likely to begin at a community college with the intent of transferring include students of color, first-generation students, recent immigrants, students who work while attending school, single parents, and non-traditional students. According to the National Student Clearinghouse Research Center, only one in five community college students transfer to a four-year institution—and 60 percent of those who do so earn a bachelor's degree within four years, while 71 percent of those who first complete an associate degree do so. Agreements allowing for reverse transfer of credit from a four-year to a two-year can assist by providing credentials to a student who left a two-year institution before earning a degree while also boosting the community college's completion rate. "Recruit back" programs for students who left without earning a degree open opportunities for collaboration between institutions that can help these individual get back on track. Financial counseling can also assist students with making wise decisions about borrowing and enrolling, putting them back on the path toward graduation.

NON-DEGREE STUDENTS

McCormick (2003) also points out students who may take courses for personal or professional benefits at a variety of institutions, unrelated to a degree program. People who register for massive open online courses

10

(MOOCs) are said to include faculty seeking teaching tips and stay-at-home parents and retirees craving intellectual stimulation (Rivard 2013). Each year, hundreds of colleges and universities offer free or substantially-reduced tuition for senior citizens who enroll in courses on traditional campuses. While some programs are voluntary, state policy exists in many areas of the country guaranteeing senior opportunities to enroll at public institutions on a space-available basis. For example, Texas public colleges, universities, and community colleges offer free tuition for up to six credit hours per semester in an effort to "encourage senior citizens to continue their education and keep involved" in their communities (College for All Texans 2013). In Virginia, residents aged 60+ who have completed at least 75 percent of their degree requirements may be allowed to enroll in courses for credit at the same time as paying students. With the population shifting as Boomers continue to age, the number of students in this category of "swirl" will continue to grow. Managed correctly, institutions and seniors can benefit from such arrangements as older students can inspire younger ones and contribute real-world examples in the classroom while remaining intellectually active and learning new skills. Senior citizens also bring with them a network of business and community contacts that can be tapped into by the institution (Keathley 2012).

STUDENT SUPPORT SERVICES

For those students who are truly academically adrift, support services are critical. Early warning systems and timely intervention may keep these students from leaving in the first place. For those that do transfer, providing information regarding applicability of transfer coursework and managing expectations about admissions to selective programs can help students make the best choices. Once the decision is made, dedicated transition programs for transfers, mentoring programs, and transfer student clubs and organizations can serve as vital initial points of entry into a new campus culture. Academic advisors who are well-versed in transfer credit issues and career exploration and other staff who can help students make good decisions regarding a major and course selection can also help students find a path and stay on it.

TRANSFER CREDIT POLICIES

The types of credits earned by students who swirl challenge transfer policies of credits granted by institutions through various programs that accelerate credit accumulation, such as dual credit high school programs, military credit, and MOOCs. Prior learning assessment is growing in importance for higher education professionals working with both traditional and non-traditional students. Learners can include everyone from high school graduates with enough dual enrollment credit for an associate degree to adults with military or job-training credentials to successful completers of MOOCs.

A Note on MOOCs. The recent rise and rapid expansion of massive open online courses (MOOCs) is testing assumptions about how college credits are awarded. Heralded by many as a harbinger of unprecedented change in higher education, MOOCs and other experiments with online pedagogy are beginning to thrive as students seek cost-effective access and convenient delivery. Coursera already has 11 million users from around the world and courses for free from 116 leading colleges and universities (2015). Users include high school students and college students looking for more ways to study a subject they are learning in a traditional classroom. Most MOOCs are offered as noncredit courses. In early 2013, however, the American Council on Education determined that some MOOCs are similar enough to traditional college courses and have sufficient controls in place that they should be eligible for transfer credit (Kolowich 2013). As the debate gears up, MOOC's are poised to be a big player in transfer swirl. While some American universities award "badges" or certificates of completion, to date only a handful of institutions award credit for successful completion of a MOOC, usually requiring an exam to demonstrate proficiency. For instance, Colorado State University's Global Campus has agreed to provide students full transfer credit toward a CSU bachelor's degree for an introductory computer science MOOC (Rivard 2013).

Institutional Partnerships to Support Swirlers

The movement of students between unique institutions is best supported when there is a focus on the student and the role institutional relationships play in facilitating successful transfer. Institutional responses to improving transfer student success at universities and community colleges are important efforts. However, institutional partnerships that make visible and support the bridge between the community college and university hold promise for supporting degree completion by student swirlers. The two-year/four-year partnership continuum (Clemetsen 2009) provides a model delineating institutional relationships for supporting student transfer (*see* Figure 2, on page 13).

The initial partnership level to support student swirl is grounded in the need for strong academic articulation. Strong articulation gives clarity to students who are compiling courses from a pair of institutions, noting that articulation is a time intensive and ongoing effort on behalf of institutions. Accurate agreements require commitment to an ongoing inter-institutional relationship and trust. As SEM professionals, we are aware of the growing number of states that have developed statewide articulated degrees, common course numbering to support articulation, and transfer student bill of rights to legislate academic arrangements to reduce credit loss by students. Our challenge will be to assess increasingly complex enrollment patterns and establish articulations that support a swirl pattern that is becoming less linear.

Strong articulation supports the next level of the two-year/four-year partnership continuum, the establishment of co-admission programs, albeit with in-state or out-of-state partners. These programs connect the student with the university early in the transfer process, creating the opportunity for stu-

12

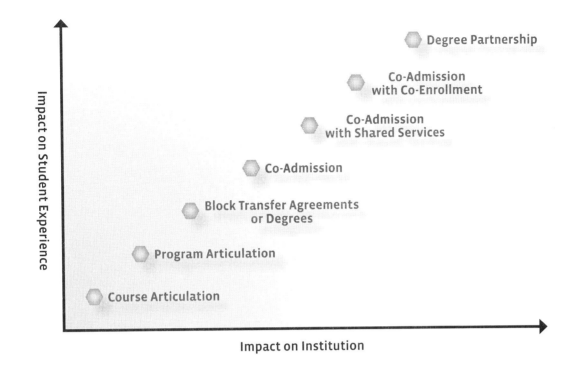

Figure 2. Two-Year/Four-Year Partnership Continuum

The chart shows the following labels plotted against "Impact on Institution" (horizontal axis) and "Impact on Student Experience" (vertical axis):

- Degree Partnership
- Co-Admission with Co-Enrollment
- Co-Admission with Shared Services
- Co-Admission
- Block Transfer Agreements or Degrees
- Program Articulation
- Course Articulation

dents to connect to advising information for improved course planning while attending the community college. Co-admission establishes the criteria for bachelor's degree completion, adding guidance to course selection at other institutions.

The last levels of two-year/four-year partnerships involve co-admission, co-enrollment, and even coordinated financial aid. Institutions that establish partnerships that coordinate academic, enrollment, and student life actually facilitate student swirl. Peter and Carroll (2005) reported that, "Students who began in public two-year institutions who had co-enrolled had higher rates of bachelor's degree attainments and per-

sistence at four-year institutions than their counterparts who did not co-enroll" (19). This level of partnership allows students to create the educational experience they believe best meets their needs, using the resources of more than one institution to accomplish their educational goals.

Swirling students appear to be following unpredictable enrollment patterns. These patterns place them at risk of not completing a degree due to a lack of structure for choosing courses and experiences. Institutional partnerships offer an opportunity to establish structures to guide and support a student in utilizing resources at multiple institutions in a manner that supports completion.

13

Conclusion

Students are increasingly mobile as they pursue their educational goals. By attending multiple institutions, swirling students can reduce cost and improve access to desired courses and experiences. Without analysis of student enrollment patterns and success rates, institutions will not meet the evolving goal of increasing graduates. Students are developing educational pathways that do not necessarily follow institutionally-structured and preferred progression; they are creating new pathways in spite of us.

Swirling students confound our current structures, yet there are actions institutions can take to support these students to better ensure their success; this includes initiatives to support students, changing institutional processes, and building relationships among the institutions students swirl between. These approaches can be informed by data from the NSC Research Center, evolving state and national data sets, and other resources. Our relationship with students and other institutions will require change if we are to effectively support students who are swirling. Seeing these students as "our" students might be a good place to start our conversations.

CHAPTER TWO

Lost Credits:
The Community College Route to the Bachelor's Degree

PAUL ATTEWELL
Distinguished Professor of Sociology,
City University of New York

DAVID MONAGHAN
Candidate and Research Associate,
Center for Advanced Study of Education,
City University of New York

CHAPTER TWO

Lost Credits: The Community College
Route to the Bachelor's Degree

Presently, public two-year colleges educate about 40 percent of undergraduates. Enrollments in this sector are increasing—in part because their tuition is typically much cheaper than at four-year public colleges, and in part because community colleges are often the convenient local college. Most students commute to their community college from home.

Increasingly, students enter community colleges with the ultimate goal of earning a bachelor's degree; that is, they view community college as a stepping stone towards the bachelor's degree, a place where they can inexpensively take courses and earn credits that they will later take with them to an institution that grants a four-year degree (Horn and Skomsvold 2012). However, scholars who track samples of undergraduates and compare those who begin at two-year colleges with otherwise similar students who start at four-year colleges have consistently found a huge gap in completion between the two routes. In national data, the gap in B.A. completion is between 14 and 25 percentage points. Most students who enter community

college do not attain their goal of getting to the B.A.; they stop out or drop out along the way (Monaghan and Attewell 2014).

Researchers have tried to discover why the community college route to the bachelor's degree is not working well. Some answers are obvious. The typical degree-seeking community college student is less academically prepared than the typical student entering a four-year college, in terms of high school GPA and types of coursework taken in high school. Community college entrants also tend to come from lower-income families and are more likely to be the first generation in their families to go to college, compared to four-year college entrants. They are also more likely to work and have family responsibilities. However, those factors have already been adjusted for in the estimates of the large gap reported above. The problem must lie elsewhere.

The authors' research was conducted with the aim of identifying any structural or institutional barriers to success for those pursuing the community college route to the bachelor's degree. This was done by analyzing transcript

17

18

data from a nationally-representative sample of American beginning undergraduates who started at both two-year and four-year colleges (Monaghan and Attewell 2014).

The first possibility examined was that community colleges might be less effective at maintaining their students' interest and academic focus than four-year colleges. This might be indicated by a much lower accumulation of college credits over time by community college students compared to their four-year counterparts. However, the data show that in terms of attendance and number of credits attempted, the gaps between two-year and four-year entrants are not large for the initial years of college, after controlling for students' backgrounds. The gap only becomes statistically significant towards the end of the third year of college and widens rapidly after that. Community college students' rate of failing or withdrawing from classes does increase by the end of the second year.

A second focus of the research looked at the transfer process: How many community college students who say they intend to get a bachelor's degree actually make the jump to a four-year college and, of those who do transfer, how many complete the degree? Here, interesting patterns emerged. Only 42 percent of the community college students who said they intended to transfer actually did so. Of the community college students who had accumulated sixty or more credits while at community college and said they intended to transfer, only 60 percent transferred into a four-year college. Consequently there appears to be a major hurdle in the transfer pro-

cess that is keeping many community college students from realizing their B.A. aspirations.

The available data do not directly explain why so many community college students with credits do not make it to four-year colleges. However, transcript data can be analyzed to examine how the transfer students fared after they entered four-year institutions. The first discovery of note was that transfers from community colleges are just as likely to obtain their bachelor's degree as similar students who started at public four-year colleges. Evidently, the preparation that transfer students received at their community colleges and the skills they developed there left them well able to complete a B.A.

The second discovery of note was that transfer students often lost credits when they transferred. For about 14 percent of the transfers, their new institution accepted fewer than 10 percent of their community college credits. An additional 28 percent of transfers lost between 10 percent and 89 percent of their credits. Only 58 percent were able to transfer 90 percent or more of their community college credits. This loss of credits in the transfer process was consequential: the larger the proportion of credits transferred, the higher the likelihood of graduation with a bachelor's degree. This leads to the assumption that if this credit loss had not occurred, the B.A. graduation rate among community college transfers would be around 54 percent instead of the current 45 percent.

This research demonstrates that that the bridge between community colleges and public four-year colleges is not working as well as one would hope. Many aspiring students who have successfully completed credits at community colleges are not managing to transfer to four-year colleges. Additional studies of why this is the case are needed, as well as efforts to facilitate the advisement of community college students and coordination between four-year and two-year colleges to improve the transfer pipeline.

Some of this attrition may be reasonable: some students may drastically shift major when they transfer, making some of their old credits inapplicable to their new major. But there is also the issue of certain courses not transferring because they are perceived to be of lower academic standards. This repetition of the same course at two institutions exacts a considerable cost from the transfer student as well as from the state.

Many states have promulgated articulation agreements that specify that degree credits earned at public two-year colleges must be counted when a student transfers to a four-year public college. However, research suggests that articulation agreements are not having the impact one might expect (Anderson *et al.* 2006). At the City University of New York (CUNY) a state articulation agreement is in place but has not prevented the substantial loss of credits that has occurred

for transfers from community to four-year colleges. The state articulation mandate can be evaded by granting transfer students "optional credit" for all their community college credits, but only granting a smaller proportion of community college credits towards required courses. In effect those optional credits can be nearly worthless.

In the last two years, CUNY has instituted a program known as Pathways to ensure transfer of lower division credits to four-year colleges. This was met with lawsuits from the faculty union and forceful opposition from faculty governance organizations (CUNY 2014; Wood 2011). Nevertheless, the new policy is in place and is building pathways of course sequences that lead directly from certain community college areas of study into corresponding high-enrollment four-year college majors. Faculty from four-year colleges and two-year colleges collaborate on the curricula to ensure that community college coursework better meets the needs of majors at the four-year level.

Initiatives like these at the college-level, alongside better state regulations and oversight, will be required to improve the effectiveness of the community college route to the bachelor's degree.

19

THE

TRANSFER HANDBOOK

PROMOTING
STUDENT
SUCCESS

Enrollment Management

THE

TRANSFER HANDBOOK

PROMOTING
STUDENT
SUCCESS

Transfer Student Success and Retention

NORA MANZ
*Associate Director of Transfer and Articulation,
Delaware County Community College*

CHAPTER THREE

Transfer Student Success and Retention

Essential to the national college completion agenda is understanding three aspects of student transfer: the pathways of student transfer, how transfer students succeed, and the processes required for retention.

As expounded in the previous chapter, research shows that 45 percent of all bachelor degrees are now awarded to students who have transferred from a community college (Monaghan and Attewell 2014), and community colleges now enroll over eight million students annually (Strempel 2013). Today's transfer student is not always a vertical transfer (transferring from a two-year institution to a four-year institution), but can be a lateral transfer (transferring to the same type of institution), a reverse transfer (transferring from a four-year institution to a two-year institution), or a swirler (a student who moves among multiple institutions). This list is not exhaustive; new populations have emerged such as dual enrollment students (high school students taking college courses) or concurrently-enrolled students (students

taking courses at both a two-year and four-year institution simultaneously) (Poisel and Josephs 2011).

Addressing Different Needs

These diverse types of transfer students create a challenge for educators and policy makers—how can institutions offer robust programs that address these needs and lead to successful transitions and retention? Currently, institutional programming is often geared towards the vertical transfer student and addresses issues such as the academic rigor and classroom attendance requirements of a research institution versus a community college. This type of programming may not be as relevant for the lateral and swirling transfer students.

Elements of Student Success

Defining transfer student success has proven a challenge. Ling writes: "While the literature on transfer students has identified the many problems that transfer students face, relatively

25

little research has examined the variables related to the success of transfer students as a unique population in the university setting" (Ling 2006, 11). Traditional measures of assessing student success include standardized testing, grades, and credit hours earned, but student success can also be measured through the lens of student development—the degree to which students feel comfortable, assimilated, and affirmed in their environment—or even from a scholarly standpoint, such as their proficiency in writing, speaking, critical thinking, and quantitative and qualitative skills. (Kuh *et al.* 2006). From the perspective of a community college, student success can be defined as the rate of transfer to a four-year institution; however, dependent on the students' goals, attaining or upgrading a job upon graduation can be an alternate assessment of success as well.

According to Kuh *et al.* (2006), community college students can pursue a variety of goals. The research found that student goals included:

- To earn an associate degree, 57 percent;
- To transfer to a four-year school, 48 percent;
- To obtain or upgrade job-related skills, 41 percent;
- To seek self-improvement and personal enjoyment, 40 percent;
- To change careers, 30 percent; and
- To complete a certificate program, 29 percent (2006, 5).

In recent years, a greater focus has been placed on transfer students, particularly be-

cause their enrollment affects various divisions such as student affairs, academic affairs, enrollment management, financial aid, and housing (Strempel 2013). With this focus and the national completion agenda, various entities are concentrating on the implications of transfer students on higher education, allowing further research to identify various characteristics of transfer student success.

Ling further suggests that transfer student success can be identified through several academic, psychological, and vocational variables (2006). Vocational awareness, or career identification, is correlated to psychological well-being, which in turn correlates to student success. Providing students with ample access to career information is crucial. Self-esteem and freedom from depression can additionally serve as accurate measures of psychological well-being (Ling 2006). Students with high self-esteem tend to fare well in adverse situations, such as transitioning from one institution to another and demonstrating better academic and social adjustment and social connectedness.

Grade point average (GPA) is both an academic and a psychological variable, and an indicator of student success. GPA correlates to social integration, a student's confidence to succeed academically, and emotional factors such as low self-esteem, depression, and alcohol consumption (Ling 2006). Transfer shock is defined as a drop or decrease in GPA when transferring from a community college to a four-year institution (Glass and Harrington 2002; Hill 1965; Pennington 2006). Transfer shock has also been connected to an increase in the dropout rate in the first semester or first year of enrollment (Glass and Harrington 2002).

Retention and Persistence

In conversations with colleagues, the words "retention" and "persistence" are often used interchangeably, when in fact they are not synonymous. Retention is a student's continued enrollment (or degree completion) within the same institution for the fall semesters of a student's first and second year, whereas persistence is a student's continued enrollment (or degree completion) at any institution (NSC 2014a). These different definitions are important, as the initiatives put in place throughout the nation's institutions and those reviewed later in this chapter place an emphasis on improving both retention and persistence.

Establishing Successful Practices

Transfer students provide four-year institutions with a needed net tuition revenue stream by 'filling in' gaps left by attrition and vacancies created by students studying abroad (Strempel 2013, 2). Transfer students also fill in gaps for students who have left the institution for other reasons, including financial constraints, unsuccessful academics, homesickness, and personal or family loss. The National Student Clearinghouse Research Center reports that 45 percent of all bachelor's degrees are now awarded to students who have transferred from a community college (2012c). This statistic indicates the importance of making transfer student success a central focus of four-year

institutions, from training the admissions staff, counselors, advisors, and even faculty, to be cognizant of transfer students' needs and helping them succeed and retain.

Statewide Initiatives

Although statewide initiatives are not a novel idea when referring to practices that assist transfer students, new initiatives are gaining momentum as more legislative and financial resources are being allocated to them. State legislatures and higher education policymakers in Maryland, Tennessee, Oregon, Pennsylvania, Colorado, and Mississippi are passing bills requiring common course numbering for general education courses or the development of a framework of courses to be completed at the community college which meet the general education requirements at the four-year institution.

Additional initiatives include "reverse transfer" or "transfer back," which grant an associate degree to students who transfer credits completed at the four-year institution back to a community college. This student-centric approach has been noticed by foundations such as the Lumina Foundation, which, in conjunction with the Kresge Foundation, Helios Education Foundation, US Funds, and Bill and Melinda Gates Foundation, have created "Credit When It's Due," a grant awarded to twelve states whose statewide systems promise to use the funds received to scale up any previous renditions of this type of initiative in their state (*see* Chapter Fifteen, "Reverse Transfer: The Newest Pathway to Student Success," on page 197 and Chapter Eighteen, "Implementing Reverse Transfer in Ohio: A Case Study," on page 231). This type of initiative is especially relevant in states like Maryland where 92 percent of community college students who transfer to a public four-year institution do so without an associate degree (Lumina Foundation 2014). Although this percentage was the highest of the states that received the grant, non-completers ranged from 67 percent in Arkansas to 58 percent in Hawaii. The grant ran from October 2012 through September 2014, after which institutions are expected to raise the funding to continue these efforts. During the two-year grant period, the institutions were tasked with utilizing technology to promote and execute the reverse transfer process. For some, this means developing the technology. For others, it means utilizing the software already in place. In addition, institutions commit to collaborating with community colleges on this initiative, as well as educating faculty, administrators, and advisors. This also entails educating the students, which is sometimes the most challenging part as those who leave the community college early often have no intention or desire to earn the associate degree.

The benefits of earning the associate degree—whether it be speedier attainment of the baccalaureate degree, a promotion or pay increase at work, or even the safety net of having earned a degree if it becomes necessary to stop at the baccalaureate level—unfortunately often remain unsuccessfully communicated to students. This grant and the immense amount of work being put forward by the twelve states, which in total claim to

award between 12,000–13,000 associate degrees in the two-year time frame, should draw attention to how a reverse transfer program would or could work at other institutions. As the Credit When It's Due grant comes to a close, all professionals working with transfer students should seek out the results of what are potentially groundbreaking enterprises.

Transfer student success and retention initiatives find support in such bills as Maryland's College and Career Readiness and College Completion Act of 2013. This completion law, enacted July 2013, deals simultaneously with K–12 schools, community colleges, and four-year institutions. On the higher education side, Maryland proposes that 55 percent of adult learners ages 25 to 65 will hold an associate degree by 2025 and that all degree-seeking students enrolled at a community college will earn an associate degree before leaving the community college or transferring. The bill boasts one statewide articulation to include at least 60 credits of general education, elective, and major courses toward an associate of arts or associate of science degree that will transfer to any public senior higher education institution and count towards a bachelor's degree. Also required by July 2016, a statewide reverse transfer articulation is to be developed and implemented ensuring that at least 30 credits earned towards a bachelor's degree at any public, four-year institution in the state be transferrable to a community college in the state for credit towards an associate degree.

To encourage the success and retention of these students, the bill requires that each public institution of higher education develop and implement incentives for students to obtain an associate degree before enrolling in a public senior higher education institution and that a statewide communications campaign will be implemented to identify near completers—students who have earned 45 credits at a community college or at least 90 credits at a four-year institution. Incentives would be offered to this population as well, encouraging them to re-enroll and earn a degree.

In keeping this Act of 2013 student-centric, community college students pursuing an associate degree must have a completion plan when they enter, which requires advisor consultation in a major. This pathway must include benchmarks for academic majors and a general education program for undeclared students and college-level math and English courses taken within the first 24 credits for first time students.

Maryland's College and Career Readiness and College Completion Act also includes a dual enrollment piece that states that a public institution may not charge tuition to a student who is dually-enrolled in a public, K–12 school and a public institution of higher education. Although this initiative may be new to Maryland, many individual institutions throughout the United States have partnered with high schools to offer free or reduced tuition for high school students. Such a program also exists at Delaware County Community College, where students in sponsoring school districts are offered reduced tuition for college-level courses. These students use Delaware County Community College courses to bolster their

college applications or high school academics, but the real benefit of this relationship includes completing an associate degree which guarantees admission to partner institutions, thus allowing students to save money and earn a quality education, while receiving merit-based scholarships. This student-centric approach allows students to meet with advisors to create academic pathways, enroll in partnership agreements, retain, and persist—ultimately, what individuals employed in higher education consider successful.

Pennsylvania, similarly to Maryland, has instituted a new statewide program-to-program articulation that requires the 14 community colleges and 14 public four-year institutions, as well as any private institutions that would like to participate, to articulate course requirements for 25 designated majors. Schools that already offer the identified majors must comply with the new competency-based program requirements. Institutions that do not offer a designated major may opt to implement one, but must meet the competencies set forth by the Oversight Committee. These program-to-program agreements benefit students and promote transfer student success and retention by identifying which major must be completed at the community college to meet the parallel requirements at the four-year institution. The agreements are competency-based, so advisors and students need not worry about taking the "right" course as courses designated in the major are guaranteed to transfer and meet 60 credits of the 120 credit major at the four-year institution.

29

In addition, Pennsylvania has established a 30-credit framework of general education courses to primarily assist undeclared students to complete courses that will transfer and count towards graduation at the four-year institution. The state has also established a "one-stop" web portal that provides information to the public about the transfer system, the participating institutions, and the transfer student process. With these initiatives, the state has set a precedent on their commitment to transfer students and transfer student success.

Institutional Initiatives

Reviewed above are several statewide initiatives that have been implemented or are being implemented to assist transfer students in their college completion. Now it is important to review what several institutions have prioritized for meeting the needs of their transfer students. As Strempel states, "a transfer-friendly culture affects every aspect of the organization, including marketing, admissions, financial aid, housing, orientation, advising, curricular coordination, career services, students services, alumni relations, and—most critically—faculty" (2013, 1). Each of these departments and individuals are essential to transfer student success. The office of admissions is the gatekeeper for the institution and the face of the institution for the transfer student. Transfer students often accept an offer of admission based on the number of credits accepted and applied towards a parallel major, in addition to financial aid and best fit. These decisions reside across multiple

departments, and it is crucial for communication to exist not only between the offices of an institution, but also with students. One common pitfall is the lack of individuals who work solely with transfer students and provide them with guidance and encouragement. Who should a student contact if they have further questions? Should the admissions counselor they have already established a rapport with lead them to the correct individual for answers? This handoff, in turn, educates the student on the process at their new school. Establishing a transfer admissions office can present a fiscal hurdle for certain institutions, but student-centric contact like this is often the deciding factor for many students.

Orientation

Mullendore and Banahan advise that "orientation can be the defining moment in the transition to college for the student—a time in which basic habits are formed, that influence student's academic success and personal growth—and marks the beginning of a new educational experience" (2005, 391). If establishing a transfer admissions office is not a possibility, consider offering a separate transfer student orientation. Data shows students who attend orientation are more likely to persist and graduate; similar data is now surfacing for transfer students.

Those students who attend transfer orientation have been more academically successful, persisting through graduation as well. Although it is important to offer an effective and unique orientation for transfer students, institutions should make sure not to isolate transfer students; therefore schools must incorporate events with those of the larger student body. Providing role models, such as transfer students as leaders during orientation, is essential. This allows transfer students to see firsthand that integration is possible and feel confident of their inclusion in this new community.

During orientation, students should have the opportunity to register for classes with an advisor, buy books, acquire a student ID, meet with faculty, and tie up loose ends such as make payments or meet financial aid requirements. Orientation should accommodate students by being offered for the fall and spring semesters, as well as over several days. Many institutions incorporate an online orientation since transfer students often work or balance a family life in addition to school.

At West Chester University of Pennsylvania, a 2013 assessment of their Transfer Student Orientation identified that 75 percent of the 245 respondents to their survey stated that they agreed or strongly agreed that after attending orientation they felt more prepared to begin their career at the University. Over 80 percent of the respondents agreed or strongly agreed that they have a general understanding of how to use the West Chester University portal and the integrated learning platform. These students stated that the most enjoyed parts of the day were meeting their peers and taking a campus tour. Aside from learning about campus resources and services, students take away a feeling of belonging. This facilitates student success and reduces the stress experienced by students in

transition. Offering and requiring attendance at orientation is an important part of creating a transfer friendly culture on campus.

This sense of belonging is also integral to overcoming transfer shock. When students feel like they belong, they feel less isolated and more motivated to engage with their peers. These interactions allow transfer students to feel comfortable enough to ask for help, with their school work and/or with finding the right resource, such as the tutoring or counseling center. This engagement has also proven to increase persistence and decrease transfer shock.

Articulation Agreements

When reading about the initiatives mandated by many states, it may seem necessary to ask why articulation agreements are still relevant. The response will depend on the person being asked. A community college advisor may say they cannot do their work without them. Articulations are used on a daily basis to advise students on the courses appropriate to their associate and baccalaureate major. The applicability of transfer courses is of primary importance for students as they transfer into a four-year institution.

The act of forging an articulation represents the commitment each institution makes towards their transfer students. In publicly identifying specific majors, degrees, or courses that will transfer, the four-year institution is by virtue saying, "welcome, we want you here, and we want you to know ahead of time how your courses will transfer." The days in which students are unable to receive a transfer audit until after they have given a hefty deposit should be over. For schools that still follow this procedure, they may encounter students who are unwilling to commit without notification of the transferability and applicability of courses. Reflective of the consumer generation, students are becoming much savvier by shopping around in search of the best value, and finding the right "fit" includes knowing the applicability of courses, cost, culture, and inherent debt.

Articulations allow students to safely self-advise, empowering them to make appropriate decisions regarding course selection and providing a sense of accomplishment. Articulations also allow faculty and staff at the community college to be able to assist students considering transfer.

Delaware County Community College has implemented a web-based application that assists prospective and current students in determining the best course of action for a seamless transfer. In real-time, current students are able to see how their courses meet requirements for a specific major at a specific partner institution. This takes the guesswork out of deciding which degree requirements at the College meet the degree requirements at four-year institutions with which the College has articulation agreements. The content in this application comes from the articulation agreements forged with area institutions, and the data gleaned from student usage shows that articulations are still relevant. Transfer students want to see how their courses transfer and apply before they make an application to a four-year institution.

Articulations not only benefit students, but also allow transfer counselors to appropriately advise students. They additionally reduce the time that a four-year admissions counselor or registrar must spend on creating degree audits because the transferability has already been established.

Transfer Shock

Finding an institution that meets all necessary criteria—degree major, affordability, accessibility, and fit—constitutes one component of success. The other component is a transfer friendly institutional culture, one that understands that transfer students exhibit different needs and that these needs cannot be met with a uniform intervention. This is particularly accurate when discussing transfer shock. As noted earlier, transfer shock describes a student's experience of culture shock when transferring, predominantly from a community college to a four-year institution.

Transfer shock manifests in multiple ways, including a decrease in grade point average, lack of interest in friendships or school work, frustration, anger, and feelings of isolation (Davies and Casey 1999; Glass and Harrington 2002; Hill 1965; Pennington 2006; Ling 2006). Students say that they have undesirable experiences such as being unable to finding parking, dealing with larger crowds, longer lines, and not receiving the same individual attention they were given at their community college (Davies and Casey 1999).

Of the multiple barriers transfer students face, overcoming transfer shock is one in which both the community college and four-year institution can play positive roles. Helping students to integrate academically and socially should be shared by both constituents. A workshop given to students transitioning from the community college is one effective offering.

A transfer shock workshop can be provided free of cost to students at the community college to educate them on the expectations at a four-year institution. The most effective way of delivering this workshop is by co-presenting with a colleague from a local four-year institution. This legitimizes the workshop for community college students because the information is also coming from a representative of a four-year institution and not "just" the community college counselor.

The workshop should cover an explanation of transfer shock: what it means and how to overcome it. It should also offer examples of coping mechanisms: familiarizing oneself with new courses and new peers, sitting in the same seat in each class to establish a smaller locus of community, and searching for formal and informal support systems (Flaga 2006). Friends and family should not be the sole source of support; students must seek out advisors, connect with faculty, and, when needed, seek out a tutor, the writing center, or psychological services.

Students may need to be reminded that the academics will be more rigorous because they are studying 300 or 400 (or higher) level courses, and that they must be prepared for more work. Students should also be encouraged to attend orientation and given examples of the benefits proffered (information about registration, advising, parking permits, housing, financial aid, etc.). It is crucial to stress management that orientation is the one-stop shop for finding one's way at the new institution and where the majority of questions will be answered.

Faculty Workshops

Coordinating workshops with faculty from the four-year institution at the community college can also assist in preparing students for transfer shock and teaching them the necessary skills to overcome it, as well as many other benefits. It indicates to students that faculty from their transfer institution are dedicated to their well-being and success; it conveys the message that they are welcomed; and it provides a sense of belonging to the four-year institution (Davies and Casey 1999; Flaga 2006; Ling 2006; Strempel 2013). In addition, connection with faculty has shown to be a positive factor in overcoming transfer shock (Berger and Malaney 2001; Flaga 2006; Laanan 1996; Ling 2006).

Campus Visits

Additional suggestions for overcoming transfer shock include providing students with the opportunity to visit the four-year institution. Too often students who want to transfer have never actually experienced the transfer school's campus first-hand. A campus visit not only allows students to familiarize themselves with the new environment, but by touring the campus, seeing new housing options, trying out the cafeteria, learning about parking and work study options, and other visit experiences, they are better equipped to determine whether the school is a best fit for them. Assessing their comfort level on the campus is paramount to feeling welcomed and assimilated. Students should also be given the opportunity to spend a night at the campus with a student ambassador because the culture of an institution changes, sometimes dramatically, in the evening. While overnight stays are not always ideal for every transfer student, offering events in the evening provides students with another chance to view a different aspect of campus culture. As mentioned, there is not one intervention that meets the needs of every transfer student, therefore a broader perspective when creating programming will help increase the success of transfer students.

Mentor Programs and Transfer Seminars

Additional suggestions include offering a mentor-mentee program in which transfer students at a four-year institution go back to their community college to mentor students looking to transfer. This type of programming is not for everyone, as it requires a great deal of coordination and sometimes funding. By jointly administering the program, the community college and four-year institution can help alleviate the cost impediment.

Transfer students can also benefit from attending first semester seminars or transfer seminars. These courses earn academic credit and are an extension of the transfer student orientation. The seminar should be designed to assist students in the transition, as well as

their academic and career goals. It should focus on practical skills for transitioning and helping students prepare for their careers through co-ops, internships, and campus involvement, in addition to graduate school preparation.

According to Pennington, students should be encouraged to complete much of their coursework, if not the entire degree, at the community college (2006). Results have shown that students who are academically prepared for the four-year institution thrive when compared to their counterparts. So, not only will students be academically successful, but they may also receive additional benefits, such as earning the general education or core requirements while completing the associate degree, earning scholarships, and reducing the amount of time required to complete their bachelor's degree.

Transfer Information Week

An additional example of programming for promoting a successful transition is a Transfer Information Week, such as those offered at Delaware County Community College and Austin Community College. Transfer Information Week is a weeklong immersion program that offers community college students the opportunity to attend workshops covering topics such as transferring for single parents, transfer shock, how to search for scholarships, transferring for LGBTQA students, and success tips for veteran students. Transfer Information Week can provide the opportunity for students to visit with multiple schools during transfer fairs and allow them to tour campuses at local institutions.

Each component of the week is created to maximize the student's interaction with the transfer process and promote the transfer services offered by the institution. It also helps students identify their advocates at the community college and how to receive additional support when needed.

Lastly, providing students with printed takeaways is a critical component of disseminating transfer information. As mentioned earlier, every transfer student and the path they take is unique, therefore, providing students with takeaway pieces that explain the different transfer pathways, partnerships, scholarships, timelines, etc., is an inexpensive way of communicating information to students. This may be their first step to considering transferring to a four-year institution.

Final Thoughts

Berger and Malaney appropriately state that "the adjustment to four-year universities, in terms of satisfaction and academic performance, is most strongly influenced by how well transfer students have prepared for the transfer process" and that "campus leaders at both types of institutions, community colleges and universities, should make sure that community college students interested in transferring to four-year institutions are actively engaging in seeking advice about and learning the requirements of the transfer process and requirements at four-year institutions" (2001, 13). The suggestions given in this chapter will lay the foundation for creating a transfer friendly culture—one that will promote transfer student advocacy, transfer student success, and retention.

Although this chapter provides a general overview of transfer student success initiatives and data reflecting transfer student retention and persistence, the extensive information regarding the impact of various gender, racial, ethnic, and socioeconomic backgrounds to transfer student success, as well as degrees being sought, is also significant as institutions and states make policy changes and implement new initiatives. Individuals looking to enhance their institution's transfer student success initiatives need to incorporate resources that are relevant to all students. Despite the lack of one clear intervention, implementing the suggestions provided in this chapter address the majority of needs and, in doing so, offer transfer students the best opportunity for success.

35

THE

TRANSFER HANDBOOK

PROMOTING
STUDENT
SUCCESS

CHAPTER FOUR

Creating Institutional Teamwork for Transfer Student Success

SUSAN DAVIES
*Associate Vice Chancellor of Enrollment
Management, Appalachian State University*

JANE REX
*Director, Office of Transfer Services,
Appalachian State University*

LORI STEWART GONZALEZ
*Senior Advisor to the Chief Academic Officer,
University of North Carolina*

Creating Institutional Teamwork for Transfer Student Success

Creating a Case for Institution-Wide Transfer Programming and Service Initiatives

The increased focus on baccalaureate attainment at national and state levels requires four-year institutions to increase investment in student success for all students, including transfer students. Although transfer students may make up a significant percentage of the enrollment at a given institution, questions still persist around the need for increased investment in transfer students. Four-year institutions must recognize their responsibility to create supportive campuses ready to welcome community college graduates (Handel 2007; Mullin 2012). To be successful, four-year institutions need to work closely with two-year institutions; a true partnership will allow universities to provide a clear academic pathway for a disproportionate number of students from low-income homes as well as students of color (Bautsch 2013; Handel 2011).

Forty-five percent of all college students were at two-year public institution in 2012

(AACC 2014), and enrollments are expected to continue to increase (Hussar and Bailey 2013). Transfer students also make up more than 40 percent of students graduating from four-year institutions (Baker 2014). Furthermore, of the seven million community college students currently enrolled, 42 percent are the first in their family to attend college, 46 percent are receiving financial aid and 45 percent are from an underrepresented ethnic minority (Handel 2011, 9).

Support for transfer students also addresses a fiscal reality that transfer students offer an important avenue for increasing enrollments. By focusing student success efforts on two-year community college graduates, institutions are likely to improve their success metrics. Nationally, students who transferred to a four-year institution with a credential (*i.e.*, associate degree or certificate) obtained a four-year degree at a higher rate (71.6%) compared to those who transferred with no credential (55.9%) (Shapiro *et al.* 2013, 5).

39

In 2009, President Obama set the goal for college completion at eight million new graduates from community colleges and universities by 2020 (College Board 2011). He also introduced a new rating system "so students and families have the information to select schools that provide the best value" (White House 2013). Among the outcomes, institutions would be "graded" on the graduation rates of transfer students (AACC 2014).

STATE GOALS

At the state level, many higher education authorities have established degree completion goals in their strategic plans. As an example, in its most recent strategic plan, *Our Time, Our Future*, the University of North Carolina (UNC) set the goal of increasing the percentage of North Carolina citizens with bachelor's degrees from 26 percent to 32 percent by 2018 (University of North Carolina 2013). The UNC plan includes strategies for seamless transfer, targeting military students and developing core competencies for general education—all designed to improve the experience of transfer students.

Statewide efforts to develop transfer and articulation policies can assist campuses in creating more seamless transfer. Factors leading to seamless transfer can include common course numbering systems, a general education core, and reverse transfer (Bautch 2013). Currently, 25 states have some performance-based funding metrics in place for a portion of resource allocation to institutions (National Conference of State Legislatures 2014).

An additional five states are in the process of initiating performance-based funding. Inclusion of metrics related to transfer students increases the need for four-year institutions to be more deliberate and focused on services, policies, and activities for transfer students.

INSTITUTIONAL GOALS

Considering the declining number of high school graduates attending college, enrollment goals for many campuses will be met with two-year transfer students (Prescott and Bransberger 2012). Additionally, targeting out-of-state students for attendance at many four-year institutions has limited utility given that this population has grown only slightly since 2000 (Prescott and Bransberger 2012). Four-year institutions must also deal with increasing student mobility, or "swirl." In the 2012–2013 academic year, over nine percent of college students attended more than one institution with 75 percent of those students attending a two-year institution during their college careers (NSC 2014c).

Tackling the transfer issue requires campuses to look closely at their services and policies. Through appreciative inquiry strategies and deep conversation, campuses can identify and optimize their strengths and areas of excellence before considering their barriers to student success (Hanna 2003). Changing campus attitudes regarding transfer students will prove most successful when making evidence-based decisions. Data serve as the best tool for myth busting on campus; when the campus community sees data on completion rates and overall performance for transfers

Table 1. Transfer Talking Points

Transfer Student Demographic and Performance Data	Transfer Students Compared to Freshman (Native) Students	Telling the Transfer Student Story
Establish the growing enrollment trends for transfer students by providing national, state, and institution figures over a five-year period.	Compare a transfer student cohort's four-year graduation rates to native freshmen cohort six-year graduation rates.	Establish opportunities to tell stories of successful transfer students in student newspapers, university magazines, on the home page of your university website, and via other internal communication outlets.
Include the percentage of transfer students enrolling from two-year colleges vs. four-year colleges (e.g., 67 percent of transfers are from two-year colleges at Appalachian State University).	Compare a transfer student cohort's mean GPA after first year of enrollment to native freshmen cohort after second or third year of enrollment (depending upon the percentage of transfer students who are sophomores or juniors when they enroll at your university.)	Tell stories of successful alumni who were transfer students in the university magazine, to prospective transfer students, and other media outlets.
Provide the mean and median cumulative GPA's of transfer students prior to transfer to establish their academic capability related to freshmen students.	Compare a transfer student cohort's mean GPA by major to native freshmen cohort.	Highlight faculty and staff who were transfer students via internal communication outlets. Create a slideshow to showcase these faculty during Transfer Student Orientation.
Include demographic information such as race, age, full-time/part-time status, military, home region, and other characteristics important on your campus to understand the unique transfer student population.	Compare persistence rates of similar cohorts (e.g., native juniors to transfer juniors).	Offer a Transfer Student newsletter to highlight transfer student stories on your campus.
Include the percentage of graduating students who began as transfer students (e.g., about 30% at Appalachian).		
Provide the mean number of years a transfer student is enrolled at your institution before graduating (e.g., 2.6 years at Appalachian) to illustrate the need to immediately impact the transfer student experience upon initial enrollment.		

compared to native students, the negligible difference between the two groups often becomes clear, making it imperative for admissions officers and enrollment managers to tell the story of transfer students. Table 1 outlines potential demographic and data comparisons that describe transfer students.

Strategies to Enhance Collaboration across Campus: Frameworks for Change

Articulating a vision of transfer student success is the first step in creating dialogue to foster a transfer-friendly campus culture. The next step involves convening campus part-

41

ners to build collaborative efforts. The implementation of a culture for transfer student success can originate from either a "planned change" framework or an "emergent change" framework; however, using both approaches simultaneously can result in more immediate change. Planned change flows from an intentional effort informed by institutional research, program reviews, or other knowledge. Emergent change arises from decentralized, grassroots efforts. In this change model, the role of the leaders shifts to facilitating opportunities and resources for creativity and experimentation to occur at the grassroots level. Bess and Dee explain: "Sometimes emergent change can gain the support of top-level administrators who then provide substantial support to expand and institutionalize the grassroots efforts" (2008, 808). Some examples of planned change include strategic plans, articulation agreements, and performance funding metrics, and involve senior leadership staff answering the question of who is responsible for transfer student recruitment, advising, retention, and persistence. At Appalachian State University, this approach of planned change led to the creation of an Office of Transfer Articulation, to meet the immediate need of credit evaluation occurring in a timely manner. This office then expanded into an Office of Transfer Services that now includes recruitment, transition advising, and transfer retention services. Other universities have also developed transfer student centers on campus that serve transfer students with both services and a "home" with common space to meet other transfer students. Ex-

amples of offices like this can be found at the University of Arizona, University of North Texas, and University of Central Florida.

Additional best practices in the planned change, or top-down model, include organizational restructuring and changing the names of offices to better communicate dedication to transfer students, thereby emphasizing the transition and transformation that transfer students experience between their sending and receiving institution. For example, at Syracuse University the Office of Orientation was renamed the Office of First Year and Transfer Programs. Transfer teams can also be established with one transfer student expert in each office on campus. The creation of these offices and identified staff members signals to the campus community and to transfer students that the university has invested resources in transfer student success. While developing a transfer center or office represents one key visible step to indicate the importance of transfer students to the campus community, other steps can be implemented in transfer student success policies and practices in order to achieve a transfer-friendly culture working toward the academic and social integration for transfer students (Jain *et al.* 2011).

A TRANSFER-FRIENDLY CAMPUS CULTURE

Policies, organizational structure and resources, and institutional support by decision makers are important attributes of planned change. Jain and colleagues (2011) offer five elements of a transfer-receptive culture:

■ Establish the transfer of students, especially non-traditional, first-generation, low-income, and underrepresented students, as a high institutional priority that ensures stable accessibility, retention, and graduation;

- Provide outreach and resources that focus on the specific needs of transfer students while complementing the community college mission of transfer;
- Offer financial and academic support through distinct opportunities for non-traditional reentry transfer students where they are stimulated to achieve at high academic levels;
- Acknowledge the lived experiences that students bring and the intersectionality between community and family; and
- Create an appropriate and organic framework from which to assess, evaluate, and enhance transfer-receptive programs and initiatives that can lead to further scholarship on transfer students (258).

Creating a transfer friendly culture must also start at the grassroots level as emergent change, with individual faculty and staff members recognizing the aspects of the culture that need to be improved or enhanced for transfer student success. In a study of recent community college transfer students, Ellis (2013) strongly recommends that universities offer more professional development for their staff regarding transfer student needs. This includes sharing "myth busters" and telling the transfer story, and should lead to a staff-wide understanding of the big picture of the transfer transition. Building relationships among key stakeholders across campus is the cornerstone for establishing a culture for transfer

student success on a college campus. Identifying existing partners on campus, as well as the strength of the relationship with the partners, is a good first step. These relationships start with open, honest, and intentional dialogue and campus conversations based on trust and respect. For example, at Appalachian State University the Associate Deans of academic colleges meet monthly with Enrollment Management staff, including the Office of Transfer Services, to focus on recruitment and retention initiatives. These monthly gatherings allow for a sharing of information and advocacy for transfer students.

Furthermore, five key initiatives were implemented at Appalachian State University to establish relationships, create a dialogue, and move the institution closer to a transfer-friendly culture. These were to build a transfer student mentors program, to name faculty mentors, to create the transfer advisory board, to create a transfer services team, and to host a campus-wide transfer symposium.

- **Transfer Student Mentors**—Transfer Student Mentors (TSMs) are key components of the Jump Start Appalachian transfer transition program. Currently enrolled transfer students were invited to apply for these paid positions. TSMs undergo training and then are able to provide presentations, serve on student panels, and represent transfer students at community colleges, orientation programs, or in other official capacities.
- **Faculty Mentors**—Faculty Mentors are identified for each academic department, and are often former transfer students. They

serve as contacts in the department for any transfer student who may have difficulty with credit evaluation, getting connected, or making the transition to the university. Their presence creates a dialogue within the academic department and provides a point-person that is equipped with the information and knowledge to serve transfer students, and is also in a position to share information with their colleagues.

- **Transfer Advisory Board**—The Transfer Advisory Board (TAB) includes 12 members—three community college representatives from the top three partner institutions, seven key decision-makers and influencers from the faculty and staff, and two students, including one representative from the Student Government Association. The purposes of the TAB are to:
  - ▶ Enable and improve communication about transfer issues between the university and schools from which students transfer;
  - ▶ Provide information and education that will increase the preparedness of students who transfer, especially in the context of curriculum;
  - ▶ Develop specific policy and procedure initiatives that will improve communication, student preparedness, and ease of transition and recommend those initiatives to appropriate policy-making bodies; and
  - ▶ Provide faculty and staff professional development opportunities to both university and primary transfer institutions in areas such as course development,

teaching, and advising that will improve the preparedness and success of transfer students.

- **Transfer Services Team**—The Appalachian State University Transfer Services Team was created in collaboration with the Provost and the Vice Chancellor for Student Development. It is chaired by a senior staff member from the Office of Transfer Services, and is charged with:
  - ▶ Researching national trends related to transfer student success;
  - ▶ Utilizing current data available to identify transfer student needs and where the university is meeting or not meeting those needs;
  - ▶ Reviewing the UNC Strategic Plan to ensure alignment;
  - ▶ Conducting a campus audit of transfer culture (that asks "What do we do? How do transfers fit in?");
  - ▶ Examining first-year programming for transfer students; and
  - ▶ Making recommendations regarding the mission/vision of a Transfer Services Center and best practices in programming and services to adequately address current and future needs.

The Transfer Services Team includes representatives from the following offices or positions:
- ▶ Student Representatives
  - ▷ Student Government Association
  - ▷ Transfer Student Mentors
  - ▷ Tau Sigma National Honor Society
- ▶ Faculty Representatives

▷ Faculty Mentors

▷ Faculty from the top ten
  transfer departments

▷ Faculty who were transfer students

▶ Staff Representatives

▷ Financial Aid

▷ Office of Admissions

▷ University Housing

▷ Orientation

▷ Academic Advising

▷ Student Involvement/Leadership

▷ Parent and Family Services

▷ Learning Assistance Program

● **Transfer Symposium**—A one-day event to create a campus conversation about transfer student success, the inaugural Transfer Student Success Symposium included more than 200 participants from about 70 departments on campus. The objectives were to engage in a campus conversation about creating an institution-wide vision for transfer students, learn about transfer students, understand why transfer students are important to the university, and learn how to best serve transfer students both in and out of the classroom. Agenda items at the symposium have included an introduction from the Provost to explain the importance of transfer students on campus; a data and demographics "myth busters" session; and concurrent sessions on academic integration, social integration, and current services for transfer students. Facilitators worked to capture the ideas and brainstorming in the sessions and produce a proceedings paper to be shared on campus. A

comprehensive website was also developed with a toolkit of pre-conference materials, additional transfer resources, conference presentations, and the proceedings paper.

After the symposium, participants were invited to apply for funding to enhance learning, services, or programming for transfer students; to conduct research regarding transfer students; or to attend a national conference focusing upon transfer students; and to present their findings at the following Transfer Student Success Symposium.

In combination with the articulated case for institution-wide support for transfer students, these five key initiatives have achieved the objective of creating a campus conversation about transfer student success.

Creating Transfer Student Success through the Transfer Transition Process

The challenges of the transfer transition process can be broken down into three phases: the prospective student phase, the admitted student phase, and the enrolled student phase. Transfer-friendly services and resources made available at each of these stages enhance the transfer student experience and impact the likelihood of student success, and are most effective when synchronized.

PROSPECTIVE STUDENT PHASE

The challenges of the prospective student phase include a lack of basic transfer information, opaque credit transfer policies, and dif-

45

ficulties in preparing for transfer to multiple institutions with varying requirements. A key element of this phase involves obtaining information relevant to the admissions process, transferability of credit, and pre-advising. Admissions representatives identified and trained specifically to assist transfer students and to be the welcoming face to the institution are critical in helping the transfer student better understand "institutional fit." One-stop websites allow transfer students to find answers to questions and to identify resources and services that will assist them at any stage in their experience. Additionally, transfer policies and information aimed at special populations such as military and non-traditional students should be accessible to all students.

At Appalachian State University, targeted transfer visit events, called Transfer Track campus visit days, include a presentation with representatives from the offices of Admissions, Transfer Services, and Academic Advising. In addition, all visits include a Q&A with a student panel of TSMs who provide prospective transfer students a glimpse of the transfer student experience.

Students who are attempting to identify "institutional fit" request preliminary credit evaluations prior to an admissions decision and often times, prior to submitting the application. Unfortunately, many institutions are finding it difficult to dedicate resources to pre-admission advising. Whether the institution can provide this information electronically via websites, instructional videos, chat rooms, or webinars, the need for pre-advising remains one of the most sought after

services by prospective students and community college transfer counselors alike. Thorough pre-advising can minimize the number of "empty" credit hours a student transfers, minimize duplication of coursework, and pave the way for satisfactory progress in their intended degree program.

At Appalachian State University, a Transfer Transition Advisor is responsible for working exclusively with prospective students and community college transfer advisors. The Transition Advisor provides information and access to resources that will enable students and community college advisors to select and register for the most appropriate courses prior to transfer. Additional strategies for successful transfer may include individual outreach, informational videos, and online advising. Transfer Four-Year Guides clearly outline course sequencing in each program of study.

These combined resources afford the student the ability to make informed choices as to which institution will allow the student to move seamlessly through the credit acquisition process and shorten the time to degree. It is also at this juncture that prospective transfer students begin to recognize whether or not the institution has a transfer-friendly culture.

Finally, building relationships with community colleges is paramount to seamless transfer for community college students. Team-teaching college transfer readiness courses, collaborating with orientation programs, and maintaining an "on-campus" presence all serve to support the needs of students, faculty, and staff at community colleges.

ADMITTED STUDENT PHASE

Communication, engagement, and intentional orientation programs are key components to transfer student success after admission, as the transfer student begins the transition to their new community. Admitted students are often contacted for administrative reasons regarding the tuition payment schedule, orientation, and registration, but they have unique needs, questions, and concerns that also need to be addressed.

The Jump Start Appalachian program, initially piloted as a grant, provides Appalachian State University with a regular presence on the community college campus, primarily through the Transfer Student Mentors (TSMs). In addition to traveling to the partner community colleges at least once per month, TSMs also answer questions that students post on the Jump Start Facebook account.[1] The TSMs provide support for Transfer Track campus visit days, open house, orientation, and other designated transfer events, making them an integral part of the campus community. The diversity of the TSMs—race, ethnicity, age, gender—afford incoming students an opportunity to establish meaningful connections prior to their arrival on campus.

The admitted student phase serves as a critical time to ensure that coursework has been evaluated and articulated, and that a current student record is available for academic advisors to accurately advise students at orientation. Given that 60 percent of college graduates complete their degrees with credits from multiple institutions (Poisel and Joseph

2011), transparency of course equivalencies and navigational tools, such as websites and equivalency databases is critical in the decision-making process. Often credit evaluation is the responsibility of the admissions or the registrar's office where there are competing priorities that do not allow this level of support. An Office of Transfer Services, or a dedicated unit for transfer credit evaluation, can serve as the "expert" in transfer credit for all constituents internally and externally.

At Appalachian State University, the Office of Transfer Services evaluates, articulates, and advocates for transfer credit. Staff members cultivate relationships with departmental chairs, dean's offices, advising units, and general education so that awarding academic credit becomes a shared enterprise. It is important to create policies and procedures that maintain the academic integrity of the institution while balancing the practicality of how credits transfer into a program of study. Establishing a relationship in the academic community opens the doors for more dialogue and a collective understanding of the student's "body of work" that illustrates his or her academic skills and knowledge. Ideally, upon acceptance to the institution all transcripts are evaluated within two weeks so that students can appropriately plan for any additional coursework at their transfer institution or at the time of orientation. Clear communication should be provided to students regarding the status of courses-in-progress, necessity of final transcripts, and assistance in petitioning for credit to ensure that all relevant

---

[1] See ‹www.facebook.com/Jumpstartappstate›.

coursework becomes a part of the student record prior to orientation if possible.

Orientation programs differ for each institution. The National Academic Advising Association (NACADA) clearly outlines the components of a successful orientation program; however, the delivery method of transfer orientations also needs consideration. As a part of Appalachian's orientation redesign, the Office of Transfer Services and the Office of Orientation and Advising used results from satisfaction surveys and focus group responses to offer several options for transfer students. Appalachian previously offered three one-day orientation sessions that included a general opening session, an opportunity to attend a meeting in his/her academic department, advising, and registration. According to student surveys, this was an exhausting experience and one which provided little of the "nuts and bolts" that transfer students need to get acclimated to a new environment. The orientation redesign consists of the following:

- Transfer Pre-Orientation Program (T-POP) is a day of activities designed to help newly admitted Appalachian transfer students find the answers to all of their questions and prepare for their upcoming orientation session. A typical day involves sessions on financial aid, transfer of credit, advising, and involvement in campus life. It also includes a Transfer Student Mentors Q&A session and a tour of the campus. Students and family members attending T-POP are required to attend the general one-day orientation.

- The traditional One-Day Orientation Program focused on advising and registration. Transfer students reported that there was a great deal of time wasted in the day waiting for individual advising appointments and registration. At the same time, departments across campus (*e.g.*, Career Development, Housing, the Center for Student Involvement and Leadership, and Financial Aid) identified a need to communicate their services with transfer students as soon as they arrived on campus, if not before. This synergy was transformed into a "conference style" approach that included concurrent sessions as well as advising and registration.

- An assumption exists that transfer students do not want, nor will they attend, a two-day orientation program. However, for the first time in the summer of 2014, the Office of Orientation and Advising piloted a Two-Day Transfer Orientation Program. Although the number of transfer students participating were very low, the survey results were positive. This led to the assessment that a variety of orientation options should be available for transfer students.

ENROLLED STUDENT PHASE

Through implementing all the strategies from the previous phases, the transfer student will be well on his or her way to quickly becoming integrated into the campus community. Integration, engagement, and having the knowledge and access to services that will support academic success are vital. Intentionally welcoming transfer students to campus through events such as a welcome weekend

48

and welcome receptions in academic departments promote the transfer culture on campus. Targeted co-curricular and student life programming, dedicated transfer learning communities in residence halls, and transfer specific organizations, such as Tau Sigma National Honor Society show the commitment and value that Appalachian has placed in the persistence and retention of transfer students. MAP Works (Making Achievement Possible) also provides a channel for all faculty and staff who work with a transfer student to connect and collaborate, ensuring the student receives all the support he or she needs to successfully transition to Appalachian. This online resource helps all incoming freshmen and transfer students stay on track, by directing them to resources specific to their individual needs (*e.g.*, financial, health, homesickness, social integration).

These programming successes were made possible through deliberate relationship building, dialogue, and collaboration with student service offices, academic departments, deans offices, and partner community colleges. The success of these partnerships determined the creation of a transfer-friendly culture on campus, as well as supported transfer student success. These services began at Appalachian State University in the summer of 2010 with many initiatives beginning in 2011 and 2012. Meaningful historical data is not yet available; however, preliminary data shows that students from Jump Start community colleges have a higher GPA and persistence rate when compared with students from non-Jump Start community colleges. Satisfaction surveys from events, such as the Transfer Pre-Orientation Program and Transfer Tracks, are consistently rated as good or very good. Each program and many services have an assessment component. Retention, persistence, graduation rates, and overall student satisfaction will be measured as cohorts track students.

Conclusion

Creating a transfer-friendly culture that focuses upon transfer student success can be accomplished through a combination of planned and emergent change. If the right structure exists, with people passionate about transfer student success having access to the data to tell the transfer student story, then institutional teamwork can begin. Four-year institutions will likely recognize the need to partner with two-year institutions as a way to establish an ongoing pipeline for highly qualified students. The payoff for both institutions, and most importantly the students, is worth the time and resources dedicated to transfer students. Higher education is at a critical juncture in terms of access, opportunity, and enrollment. Attention to these students who choose to begin their educational journeys at a two-year institution stands as the only way the states and the nation will meet their college completion goals.

49

THE

TRANSFER HANDBOOK

PROMOTING
STUDENT
SUCCESS

CHAPTER FIVE

Recruiting Transfer Students

SHANEE R. CREWS
Associate Director for Transfer Recruitment,
Office of Admissions,
Virginia Commonwealth University

JOANNE E. JENSEN
Director of Marketing and Communications,
Division of Strategic Enrollment Management,
Virginia Commonwealth University

Recruiting Transfer Students

Changing demographics, diminishing state and federal funding, and a trend toward rising tuition costs are contributing to the growth in the number of students choosing to attend two-year institutions upon high school graduation before transitioning to a four-year institution. In response to the needs and demands of the transfer student population, four-year institutions are seeking ways to attract these students through targeted recruitment campaigns.

According to U. S. Census data, the Current Population Survey (CPS) indicates that the number of students enrolled in college in 2011 was up by 4.5 million students from a decade earlier; 40 percent of this enrollment growth was attributed to an increase in two-year college attendance. In 2011, 6.1 million students were enrolled in two-year colleges, up from 3.9 million in 2000 (Davis and Bauman 2011, 1). According to Stokes and Somers, the cost of education is a strong factor contributing to the likelihood that a student will choose a two-year college; "stu-

dents who are price conscious and have fewer resources available for college are more likely to choose a two-year college" (2009, 10).

Transfer students expect a high level of customer service from their institutions of choice, and in particular look for collaboration between their transfer institution and the university campuses to which they hope to transfer (Ellis 2013, 83). It is essential to these students to find accurate information about transfer requirements and processes through a variety of media. They expect communications between themselves and institutions to be highly responsive (Ellis 2013, 82).

The authors of this chapter represent Virginia Commonwealth University (VCU), a large public research university with an urban campus. Currently VCU enrolls the third largest number of transfer students among public universities in the Commonwealth of Virginia. This chapter discussion will focus on the recruitment, marketing, and communications tactics that have proven successful at VCU. It examines strategies used

53

to engage prospective transfer students who are predominantly transitioning from the community college system, as well as defined methods for developing relationships with the community college system's faculty.

The Big Picture

When seeking a four-year school to transfer into, like their first-time freshman counterparts, transfer students look for a place where they can accomplish their academic goals. For transfer students, important factors for considering a four-year school include the availability of their major, the cost of attendance and opportunities to receive financial aid, the amount of academic and social support offered to transfer students, the university's academic reputation, and its location.

Students transferring to a four-year school are concerned with how the university supports transfer students and want to be assured of an uncomplicated transition from a two-year school to a four-year school. In "Successful Community College Transfer Students Speak Out," Martha Ellis identifies some specific characteristics of transfer students. She notes that they want assurance that their credits will transfer to their desired degree program; and that the university's academic advisors are available to help them understand how courses transfer and how they will count toward degree completion (2013). In addition, at VCU, students have indicated that it is important that support services, resources, and opportunities such as internships, service learning courses, and study abroad are available in order to increase the value of their degree.

When recruiting transfer students it is crucial to have an infrastructure that supports these students' needs and a recruitment plan that promotes the key resources and programming the university has set in place to assist them with achieving their goals.

Understanding the Market

The first step a university must take in the development of a successful recruitment plan is to identify the target market most likely to enroll at the institution. Targeting should be focused on the student type, the region, the feeder institutions, and the most attractive academic majors.

Knowing where students commonly transfer from is one of the key components to developing a thorough understanding of the university's transfer recruitment market. Questions that should be considered include: which feeder schools are known to be a source of transfer students? Is the institution located in an area near military bases where potential transfer students or their family members may be stationed?

In the case of VCU, most transfer applicants are current or previously enrolled community college students within the Virginia Community College System (VCCS). While VCU does enroll a number of students transferring from four-year colleges and out-of-state community colleges, the university does not actively recruit this population of prospective transfer students. VCU's transfer recruitment efforts are focused primarily on in-state community college students. VCU's institutional research data indicates that 58 percent of fall 2013 transfer applicants were VCCS students. Of the 23 VCCS community colleges, six specifically serve as main feeder colleges for VCU. This subgroup of VCCS colleges accounts for the university's largest percentage of its transfer student population. Specifically, the university data indicates that in fall 2013, 57 percent of the total number of newly enrolled transfer students transferred from these six main feeders.

In addition to determining which feeder colleges the institution should focus on, it is imperative to the transfer recruitment effort to have at least a fundamental awareness of the academic programs offered by the university and in particular those which tend to be attractive to transfer students. Transfer recruiters should have knowledge of the programs that are most popular among prospective students, and an effective recruiter should know which of those programs offered by their institution are unique and highly ranked.

Developing a Recruitment Plan

To best utilize the institution's resources, a well-thought-out recruitment plan should be established and agreed upon by the appropriate leaders within the university, including the Office of Admissions. Based on the experience of the transfer recruitment team at VCU, the development of a transfer student recruitment plan should include, but not be limited to:

- determining target markets;
- assigning staff to territories and markets;
- implementing a well-designed plan that outlines the types of communication that will be made with prospective students and transfer counselors at two-year colleges (messaging can be specialized and sent to targeted groups), such as:
  ▷ electronic messages/email/social media/website;
  ▷ written publications distributed via various methods; and
  ▷ telephone blasts;
- developing planned programming designed to focus on the unique needs of transfer students, as well as continuous contact between the transfer admissions staff and the staff of community college transfer advisors.

RECRUITMENT TERRITORIES AND TEAMS

The determination of recruitment territories should be based on data collected by the university, which illustrates over a time continuum where the largest concentration of applicants is located.

Some universities have recruiters or admission counselors who act as generalists, responsible for recruiting both first-year students as well as transfers, while others have formed a special team of recruiters to focus primarily on transfer student recruitment. VCU operates with a team of several admissions counselors who work as generalists along with an additional team whose work focuses on the needs and interests of transfer students. Led by the Associate Director for Transfer Recruitment, this specialized team includes two regional transfer counselors.

The transfer recruitment team determines the strategies for working with and attracting transfer students to the university. Several variables are taken into consideration when assigning recruitment territories to staff. Territories are outlined based on the location of feeder colleges and the data collected showing the trends in the numbers of applications received from those feeders. It is then determined which locations or regions warrant a greater presence of the four-year college on their campuses.

VCU's largest transfer recruitment territories are the local surrounding area of the university (Richmond city and surrounding counties) and Northern Virginia. Because community colleges also benefit from their students being well-prepared for transfer to four-year schools, creating partnerships with a college's primary feeder institutions has proven to be beneficial. Partnerships between the community colleges and VCU have given students the opportunity to make connections with their future university, from the campus of their community college.

PARTNERSHIPS

VCU has partnered with the two community colleges located within its largest feeder regions: Reynolds Community College and Northern Virginia Community College. For the fall 2013 semester, students transferring from Reynolds Community College and Northern Virginia Community College accounted for 358 and 404 of newly enrolled transfer students, respectively (35 percent of the total transfer student population). Through these partnerships, VCU was granted space at those community colleges to create satellite transfer admission offices. The university's presence in these two satellite offices allows VCU to place the regional transfer recruiters within those community college campuses and gives students the opportunity to meet with admissions representatives early and throughout their community college career. These early connections make students aware of admissions requirements and application processes, resulting in potentially better prepared students who complete university graduation requirements at a faster pace.

In addition, having transfer counselors located on these campuses enables the university to provide daily access for community college students and faculty to meet with VCU admissions representatives to receive advisement and information regarding the transfer application process, course recommendations, and the university in general.

The on-site transfer counselors are able to visit all campuses of the feeder community colleges on a regular basis, with most being visited at least once per month. At these partner community colleges, the transfer counselors provide office hours for individual counseling, information tables, information sessions, special program events like "lunch and learn" and coffee breaks, and, on occasion, specially planned on-site decision days. Data is collected, when possible, at all of the events offered, as well as during office visits to help assess the success of these offerings. Community colleges which send fewer transfer students to VCU are visited as well, but on a less frequent basis.

Guaranteed admission agreements (GAA), program articulation agreements, and resources provided by the university that assist with academic advising of prospective transfer students further solidify community college-university partnerships. GAAs are official, signed agreements between a university and specific community colleges, or in the case of VCU, the entire state community college system. In general, GAAs assure that if specific criteria are met, a student is guaranteed admission to the designated university.

Articulation agreements are more specific, officially signed agreements between academic departments at the community college and the respective academic departments at the university. Articulation agreements typically list a curriculum of coursework, approved by the academic faculty of the university, to be completed at the community college prior to transferring. The purpose of these agreements is to keep the student on track towards graduating from the university at the same rate of a native student (Rhine *et al.* 2010). It is the university's responsibility to promote both GAA and articulation agreements. At VCU, these agreements are listed on the Office of Admissions' undergraduate admissions website.[2] (*See* Appendix B, "Sample Articulation Agreement: Colorado Statewide Transfer Articulation Agreement," on page 253.)

To further forge partnerships and assist with transfer student recruitment, VCU uses documents called Transfer Pathways.[3] VCU's Transfer Pathways are documents created by the university's Transfer Center and designed as a resource to recommend the best-suited associate degree programs to complete in preparation for transfer into specific majors at the university. This provides an additional level of advising that assist community college faculty as they discuss major options with transfer students.

Communications, Marketing, and Events

Transfer students want to find the right four-year institution for them. Does the institution offer their major? Will their credits transfer and how will they be applied toward their chosen degree program? Does the institution provide them with resources to determine the best pathway toward graduation?

These questions must be answered throughout the recruitment process—from print publications to online and electronic media. Marketing and communication plans directed to community college students provide a base upon which the recruitment team will promote the institution and answer these questions. The messaging targeting these transfer students needs to address the unique and specific concerns that they have when transitioning to a four-year school.

The methods for reaching out to these students should be comprehensive, meeting them both in the community colleges where they study and in the communities where they live and work. Outreach should

---

[2] *See* ‹http://ugrad.vcu.edu/apply/transfer/agreements.html›.

[3] *See* ‹www.transfer.vcu.edu/VCCS/what-courses-should-i-take.html›.

include personal visits, special events on- and off-campus, and the usage of traditional, electronic, and social media platforms. This means promoting the institution through:

- on-site, in-person visits that focus on the application process;
- on- and off-campus special events focused on the transfer student experience;
- brochures and targeted publications that provide information specific to transfer student interests;
- dedicated sections for transfer students on the admissions website;
- targeted communications through emails and call blasts that provide current and relevant messaging; and
- targeted messages via social media venues such as Facebook and Twitter where students can find up-to-date information about the university and also feel connected to campus life.

In addition to creating publications, it is imperative to have a designated transfer student section on the university's website where potential transfer students can find answers to questions specific to the transfer process. Results of focus group research conducted in spring of 2009 among eight campuses of the University of Texas system indicate that "students rely heavily on websites to find information and to perform processes such as registration, financial aid, tuition payment, and textbook ordering" (Ellis 2013, 82). In addition to a current and accessible website, having a strong social media presence is essential to a university's efforts to connect with this population of students. An electronic and social media presence increases opportunities for the university to connect with and be more responsive to transfer student needs.

Universities should show transfer students that they are welcomed and considered an asset to the overall student population—best demonstrated by including transfer students in recruitment events and attending and planning events especially for transfer students. The outreach to this population of students should not only occur during the recruitment and the enrollment stages, but should continue after the students are enrolled. In all cases, the focus of the communications at these events should reflect on the transfer students' informational needs.

VISITS

VCU offers daily admissions information sessions open to both prospective first-year and transfer students. It should be taken into consideration that while transfer students have "been through college already," they may still require as much hand-holding, if not more, than new freshman students (Townsend and Wilson 2006). Every transfer student starts at a different stage in his or her college career. To accommodate the unique and sometimes very specific questions regarding the transfer process, VCU has begun to offer monthly admissions information sessions specifically for transfers. In addition, transfer students are invited and encouraged to attend one of the three large-scale undergraduate admissions open house events hosted each year by VCU.

Recruitment travel—visiting community colleges in an effort to distribute and communicate information regarding the university, its programs, and the admissions process—is another essential part of the transfer recruitment plan. Traditionally, universities' transfer recruitment efforts include a combination of attending transfer fairs hosted by community colleges, private visits, and special programs. Transfer fairs are events where a group of four-year colleges host tables in a central location at a community college to showcase their college to prospective transfer students. Typically, a number of four-year colleges are invited to participate in these events.

The term "private visit" describes a number of different options. Generally, a private visit refers to a transfer counselor from one specific university visiting the campus of a community college. The visit may consist of one or more of the following: hosting an information table in a high student traffic area, conducting an admissions information session in a classroom or auditorium setting, or meeting with students individually in an office setting to discuss their questions or concerns.

At larger feeder community colleges, private visits can be very successful; however, at the community colleges that typically yield fewer applicants, it is often in the best interest of the university to visit during transfer fair events, as they tend to generate a larger audience of students.

EVENTS

Planning special events that incorporate social interactions, lunch or refreshments, and an admissions information presentation can yield great responses at larger feeder community colleges. These events should always be well-advertised by both the university as well as the community college.

Yield events for accepted students serve as one of the university's final efforts to encourage students to accept their offer of admission and enroll in courses. VCU offers three yield events for transfer students. The first is a preview day that is similar to an open house, but only open to accepted first-year and transfer students. In addition to preview day, two receptions for accepted transfer students are hosted. One is held on the campus of the embedded Northern Virginia regional transfer counselor, and the other on VCU's campus. These events, hosted by the Office of Admissions, are also attended by representatives of the university's Transfer Center and academic programs. These events give students the opportunity to meet other new transfer students, allowing them to form relationships prior to enrolling. Events hosted for fall 2013 and 2014 were successful, with yield averaging between 83 and 88 percent.

Helping Transfer Students Transition from Two-Year to Four-Year Institutions

According to T.J. Rhine *et al.*, "Student academic progress is most likely to be impeded by administrative obstacles to transferring and social concerns" (2010). Taking this into consideration, recruitment of transfer students does not end at the application process, the offer of admission, or at the enrollment of a transfer student. It is crucial that a university also provide services and resources to assist students as they make the transition from their previous college to their transfer institution. These resources can come in many forms, including an office of new student programs, a transfer center, and strong reliable academic advising.

While many assume that transfer students are more knowledgeable and independent than first-year freshmen, this population often has unique concerns and not only feels anxious about the idea of attending a new university where native students may be well established in their social circles, but also understand the expectations and level of rigor of the university's course work. Regardless of age, some students will be apprehensive about transferring to a new college (Townsend and Wilson 2006).

At VCU, the Office of New Student and Family Programs manages new student orientation and offers programming for students that focuses on transitioning to the new university environment. Transfer student orientation is held separately from the freshman student orientation, thus allowing transfer students and the staff working with them the opportunity to focus on the variables that make transfer students unique. VCU has a Transfer Center, staffed by a director and transfer advisors, which is dedicated to providing assistance to transfer students to help them connect to their new campus community. Starting as early as the week prior to the start of the fall semester, during the university's Welcome Week, the Transfer Cen-

ter offers opportunities for social interaction among the new transfer student population. Informational programs are hosted as well; the goals of these programs are to promote student engagement and success while at VCU, and the programming focuses on encouraging students to take advantage of the university's extensive resources and student organizations. The Transfer Center also offers a transitional leadership program which pairs returning students who made a successful transfer transition with new transfer students in need of a little extra help. Additional programming targeted to the interests of transfer students is offered throughout the year by the Transfer Center, including seminars and workshops.

Conclusion

The rapidly changing higher education landscape offers transfer students more choices for achieving their educational goals. In order to be competitive in this environment, four-year institutions must be prepared to respond to the complex needs of transfer students. Collaboration with two-year institutions enhances opportunities for the students who eventually will transfer to the four-year university, and increases potential success for these students. Offering transfer students the chance to engage with university representatives early and often allows these students to take an active role in their success.

In order to ensure that the information and services offered to these students is relevant and helpful, universities should engage in continuous dialogue with these students as they integrate into the university community.

Formal surveys can assist the university with discovering areas for improvement and to understand what has worked in the past. Continuing discourse with transfer students once they have enrolled also provides them a voice and can assist universities in planning for future recruitment and student success activities. Allowing students to become involved in leadership roles while they are enrolled also encourages them to take an active role in the future of the university.

Looking forward, universities must continue to provide transfer students with relevant and important information about the transfer admission process beginning at the recruitment stage. Upon acceptance to the university, these students should be embraced as a part of the university community, and offered resources and transition services that ensure successful assimilation into and matriculation from the university.

61

THE

TRANSFER HANDBOOK

PROMOTING
STUDENT
SUCCESS

CHAPTER SIX

Non-Traditional Students and Transfer:
A Focus on Military and Veteran Students

MARIE-JOSÉ CARO
Registrar,
Embry-Riddle Aeronautical University,
Daytona Beach, Florida

EDWARD F. TROMBLEY III
Registrar,
Embry-Riddle Aeronautical University,
Worldwide

Non-Traditional Students and Transfer: A Focus on Military and Veteran Students

Non-traditional students, particularly military and veteran students, pose challenges for universities to serve efficiently and well. For the purpose of this discussion, the non-traditional student is defined as one with a delayed entry to college after high school completion, who may bring time-management conflicts due to work and family commitments, and who may have a variety of transcripted and non-transcripted credits to consider for transfer or advanced standing.

While it might be assumed that the non-traditional student is easier to work with than the traditional student who is new to post-secondary education and often has little life experience, this is not always the case. Traditional students are closer to their high school education, and therefore bring a "fresher" experience with math and English skills, including composition and research paper writing, as well as test-taking skills, which may prove more valuable in the student experience than the "life skills" and workplace exposure brought by the non-traditional student to the classroom. Traditional transfer students generally have Advanced Placement (AP), International Baccalaureate (IB), and transfer credit from two-year colleges, which is much more standardized for evaluators to equate. Non-traditional students may not remember or disclose the full extent of their education history and may need to be prompted by university admissions staff to review the institutions that they have attended over the past several years. In addition to standard college work, they may also present with possible credits from life experience, military training, certifications, workplace training, and national examinations. This variety of credit, as well as the potential age of the credit poses a challenge to academic evaluators who are more accustomed to standard transfer credit.

Military and Veteran Students

Military and veteran students experience similar obstacles to other non-traditional students, and also tend to be older and facing scheduled or unscheduled military obligations, reassign-

65

ment, and relocation challenges. In addition, they often bring Servicemembers Opportunity College (SOC) guaranteed credits and military-based ACE credit recommendations for assessment. Non-traditional military students often possess specialized military training and education, however, they often have either never developed, or are rusty in, the skills required to successfully convey those experiences in an educational setting.

Assessing the value and academic worth of military credit brought to a postsecondary institution can prove quite complicated and frustrate institutional credit evaluators who may not possess the expertise to interpret the credit values of military experience. As with the other non-traditional students, military students have often attended a variety of educational institutions and must be prompted to review these in order to provide full disclosure. It is important to review their educational history in order to maximize the student's tuition coverage, as military funding will generally not allow duplicated classes.

Despite increased obstacles facing military and veteran students, a review of the postsecondary educational outcomes for nearly one million student veterans who utilized Montgomery and Post-9/11 GI Bill benefits between 2002 and 2010 showed "strong postsecondary outcomes for the current generation of student veterans" (Cate 2014, iv). This study concludes that a slight majority of student veterans earn postsecondary degrees or certificates despite their challenges in doing so. The majority of student veterans enroll in public institutions (79.2%), with private non-

profit (10.7%) and proprietary schools (10.1%) serving the remainder of that population. The majority of veterans who graduate do so from public schools (71.1%), while the remaining graduates emerge from private non-profit (15.5%) and proprietary (12.9%) schools. Of those who graduate, the study concludes that nearly 9 of every 10 (89.7%) student veterans initially earn degrees at the associate level or above, as opposed to a small percentage who earned vocational certificates (2014).

This being the case, it is in the best interests of any university to consider the role of the student-veteran population, regardless of the percentage of their population, and to formulate policy and procedure with ample flexibility to support the needs of this challenged, but dedicated, segment of the student population.

Enrollment Trends of Non-Traditional Students

In both the public and private sectors of colleges and universities, tracking of non-traditional students, specifically in relation to persistence and graduation, has not been as consistent as tracking of traditional students. However, with the numbers of non-traditional students growing at triple the rate of traditional age students, the need for more data collection is even greater. The available data indicates that while their enrollment numbers are increasing, non-traditional students are not as successful as their traditional student counterparts in persistence and graduation (Taniguchi and Kaufman 2005).

According to the National Center for Education Statistics (NCES) 2011 six-year report,

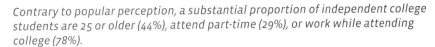

Contrary to popular perception, a substantial proportion of independent college students are 25 or older (44%), attend part-time (29%), or work while attending college (78%).

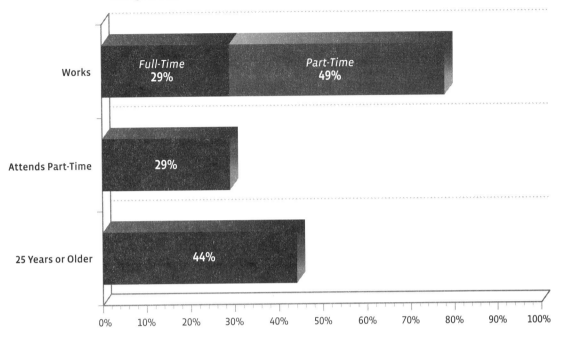

Works — Full-Time 29% | Part-Time 49%

Attends Part-Time — 29%

25 Years or Older — 44%

0% 10% 20% 30% 40% 50% 60% 70% 80% 90% 100%

Figure 3. Enrollment of Non-Traditional Students
SOURCE: NATIONAL ASSOCIATION OF INDEPENDENT COLLEGES AND UNIVERSITIES (2003, 10).

a large percentage of undergraduates were at least minimally non-traditional (based on a combination of factors including marital status, age, and dependency status). These students were much less likely to have earned a degree within five years of beginning their education than traditional students, and they were more than twice as likely to leave school within their first year as their traditional counterparts. According to the 2002 NCES "Findings from the Condition of Education Report," 50 percent of non-traditional students were no longer enrolled after three years (versus 12 percent of traditional students). However, non-traditional students may also have educational goals beyond earning a degree, such as specific job skill improvement or non-degree certification (Choy 2002).

According to the National Association of Independent Colleges and Universities, in 2006 the number of non-traditional students enrolled in private, not-for-profit colleges and universities was 44 percent (*see* Figure 3). The increasing enrollment numbers, differing educational goals, and tendency towards attrition of this type of student points towards the need to provide appropriate services, early interventions, and advising support beyond that which is designed for traditional students.

67

68

Enrollment Trends of Military and Veteran Students

While members of the military currently on active or reserve duty and veterans may have some differing characteristics and needs, for analysis and statistical purposes within postsecondary education, these two categories of individuals are typically measured as one. According to the U.S. Department of Veterans Affairs, "'Student Veterans' include active-duty service members, reservists, members of the National Guard, and veterans" (2014). According to a National Center for Education Statistics (NCES) study of students in the 2007–2008 academic year, about four percent of all undergraduates and about four percent of all graduate students were veterans or military service members. About two-fifths of military undergraduates and one-fifth of military graduate students used GI Bill education benefits. Of these students, a majority of military undergraduates and military graduate students were male, and more likely to be married than nonmilitary students. These students also studied at private nonprofit four-year institutions, pursued bachelor's degrees, took distance education courses, and studied information sciences more often than their non-military peers. Finally, there was a span of seven or more years between completing their bachelor's degree and starting graduate school, and they were more likely to take classes on a part-time basis (Radford 2011, 3).

These key findings point to a number of issues, needs, and trends regarding student veterans. For instance, while only ten percent of service members and veterans are female, a larger percentage of those female veterans are enrolled in postsecondary education (roughly 27%). This might indicate a need for additional recruitment emphasis for male veterans and/or specific support services for female veterans. More veterans than non-veterans are married, and nearly half of student veterans have children, perhaps requiring different housing considerations and flexible scheduling options. More military students than non-military students delay their transition from undergraduate to graduate school, possibly increasing the need for strong academic support services, and veteran students are more likely to take one or more distance education courses, highlighting the need for flexible schedule offerings and delivery modes.

While the overall number of veteran students may still be relatively small, that number is growing dramatically with no sign of lessening American military involvement in international conflict. According to the Department of Veterans Affairs, one million student veterans were enrolled in higher education and receiving benefits in 2013, as compared to 500,000 just four years earlier (VA Campus Toolkit Handout). Knowing this, institutions of higher education would be wise to explore policy and procedure reviews and service analyses to best serve this growing, dedicated, and deserving student population.

Admissions Challenges of Non-Traditional Students

Non-traditional students are generally viewed as relatively stationary, due to their commitments to community, job, and family, and that they typically do not transfer among schools in the way that their traditional counterparts might.

Non-traditional students are often wary of testing. Applicants who have been away from institutions of higher learning for an extended length of time, in some cases for many years, remember the stress of test taking more often than they may remember the feeling of accomplishment at having mastered a new skill or subject area. As a result many applicants balk at the idea of admissions testing to determine eligibility to attend a university. Military and veteran students, feeling that their life experience outweighs traditional classroom instruction, are sometimes reluctant to approach admissions testing positively or with an open mind.

At Embry-Riddle Aeronautical University (ERAU), this issue is approached by making the admission decision based upon static criteria from former institutional attendance (*e.g.*, cumulative GPA, completion of master's program pre-requisites at the undergraduate level, etc.). Entry testing results are used primarily for placement, rather than for admission. Therefore, a student enters into testing assured of their admittance, while the tests determine his or her current aptitude in math and English. Placement exam results are used by academic advisors to assess the student's need to enroll in lower-level remedial classes; these classes are still 100 level or above and count as credit toward degree completion. Students who have transfer credit for basic English and math classes, but score poorly on placement exams, will be counseled by

their academic advisor to consider taking the lower-level classes in order to best assure their success, but are under no obligation to do so with transfer credit available. Giving non-traditional students options, using test scores for support, allows them to participate in their educational plan. This method can also be helpful later if the student is unsuccessful after selecting the higher-level course, as the advisor is on record having recommended participation in a "remedial" course first.

Transferring Military Credits

Due to their military service, deployment schedule, or base assignment, military students are more likely than other non-traditional students to move about frequently, often at irregular intervals, and to collect credits from several different institutions if they continue pursuing their education as they move from one posting to the next. This can present challenges for military and veteran students who have pursued academic credits at multiple institutions, as they may not remember every institution at which they have earned credit when asked to provide a complete set of academic credentials to a university at the point of application. For this reason, it is important to make a concerted effort during the admissions process to obtain a complete list of past institutions for each applicant and to determine if all prior school transcripts have been collected, before to moving the candidate forward for acceptance to the institution. At Embry-Riddle, for example, the institution maintains the right to revoke an offer of admission or dismiss a student for failure to disclose a prior educational experience if an omission is discovered during the admission process, particularly if the student suppresses the information regarding their attendance elsewhere due to poor performance, as this is a deliberate misrepresentation of the academic history and is a student code of conduct violation.

Military and veteran students may, in addition to prior educational experiences that have been transcripted by traditional or military institutions, be eligible for academic credit based upon military experience and/or training. These are listed on the Joint Services Transcript (JST) used by the Army, Navy Marine Corps, Navy, and Coast Guard and can also be assessed by the American Council on Education's (ACE) credit recommendations. ACE, under a contract from the Department of Defense that is administered by the Defense Activity for Non-Traditional Education Support (DANTES), conducts academic reviews of military courses and occupations, utilizing a team of teaching faculty from relevant academic disciplines, representing multiple colleges and universities. This team assesses and validates whether the courses or occupations have the appropriate content, scope, and rigor for credit recommendations. The award of transfer credit remains the discretion of the college or university (ACE 2014).

ACE recommendations can be challenging to understand for the unfamiliar evaluator. They should be reviewed thoroughly as some courses and occupations may be approved if offered at specified locations, during particular time frames, or for specified durations, whereas other training, if not from that time, place, or of that duration, may not be approved. Perhaps ACE has not had a request to review the alternate setting for equivalency, or the time frame allowed by the initial ACE review has elapsed. It is then a challenge to explain to the military or veteran student population why one student who had a particular training may receive credit, while another with essentially the same training, but at another place or time, does not receive credit.

The Air Force provides a more traditional transcript via the Community College of the Air Force (CCAF), a federally-chartered degree-granting institution, offering an Associate in Applied Science and other academic credentials. CCAF partners with 106 affiliated Air Force Schools, 82 Education offices located worldwide, and more than 1500 civilian academic institutions, making CCAF the world's largest community college system. CCAF coursework is pass/fail: any student who successfully completes a course is given a grade of "S" on his transcript, which CCAF equates to a grade of "C" or better. Schools accepting transcripts from CCAF will not be able to use the transcripted coursework to establish an incoming GPA and will not be able to expect letter grades to assist them with admissions eligibility determination (Community College of the Air Force 2014, 7). Still, the CCAF transcript represents a facet of the applicant's prior education.

Other sources of military credit are FAA flight ratings and military occupation codes, which can be evaluated and approved by appropriate academic officials.

Embry-Riddle accepts the minimum scores recommended by ACE on all exams offered by the College Level Examination Program (CLEP), Defense Activity for Non-Traditional Education Support (DANTES), and Excelsior College Examinations (ECE, formerly REC or ACT-PEP) for the award of undergraduate academic credit. In addition, the amount of academic credit and the academic level (upper- or lower-level) designation recommended by ACE for a passing score on each of the exams will be accepted by the University. The number of credits accepted via exam is limited by ERAU to 15 credit hours. As per University policy, credit earned by examination must be completed prior to the time the student reaches the last 30 credits of a bachelor's degree or the last 15 credits of an associate degree, although active-duty undergraduate military students may complete national exams (CLEP, DANTES, etc.) at any time while pursuing their undergraduate degree, and are not restricted to applying exam credits within their last 15 credits for associate degrees or 30 credits for bachelor's degrees.

Advanced placement may be granted on a limited basis, based upon the existence of earned credit at a postsecondary institution determined by the University to demonstrate a higher level of competency, only in the areas of English, math, or accounting course requirements. Under the advanced placement ruling, a course may be waived and considered for the purpose of student advisement to be met; however, the student must make up the credit deficit. The deficit may be made up in electives unless otherwise specified by the department chair.

Social and Cultural Challenges for Student Veterans

While student veterans come to higher education with greater life experience than the traditional age student, as well as the possibility of academic credits, the veteran transfer student faces a variety of challenges in adapting to not only the academic rigor of higher education, but also to the social life and culture of a residential campus. Universities and colleges have placed great emphasis in creating a full education experience that goes beyond the classroom and includes experiential learning and social education. Today's students are expected to excel in the classroom while also participating in campus activities, contributing to their community, working on academic projects in groups, and representing their campus community well.

Student veterans sit in classrooms side-by-side with traditional students who often cannot understand or appreciate the veterans' life experiences, maturity, and challenges. While traditional students concentrate on their academic studies and social engagements, veteran students often concentrate on their studies in conjunction with family obligations, work obligations, financial concerns, and sometimes service-related stress issues. While traditional students can work on projects together after classes, during campus events, or in residence halls at night, veteran students often have to immediately leave cam-

71

pus to fulfill other obligations. Consequently these students face difficulties integrating with a residential campus culture.

According to a focus group conducted by the non-profit RAND Corporation, with support from Lumina Foundation for Education, for ACE, only about 10 percent of student veterans surveyed felt the transition to civilian academic life had been relatively smooth. The group found that 90 percent "reported encountering substantial transition challenges. Among focus group participants, the most frequently discussed challenges were meeting academic expectations, balancing academic and other responsibilities, relating to fellow students, and coping with service-related disabilities and post-traumatic stress disorder (PTSD)" (Steele, Salcedo, and Coley 2010, 36).

These students often feel alienated from their younger, more relaxed classmates, as well as administrators and faculty who may not have been trained to recognize or deal with issues specific to veterans and active-duty military members. These students often report a desire to—and difficulty with—integrating into the campus community, as well as a desire to retreat to a social space specifically restricted to other students with similar backgrounds. Researchers found: "Still, the most common reaction among participants was a sense of difference and frustration with what was seen as younger students' immaturity and sense of entitlement'" (Steele, Salcedo, and Coley 2010, 38). Further, the authors state: "When asked for their views on how higher education institutions might more effectively

recruit and support student veterans, participants suggested providing study skills support groups for veterans, building a veterans' lounge on campus, and coordinating opportunities for student veterans to volunteer in their communities" (44).

Universities and colleges enrolling student veterans would do well to create programs and processes that speak to both of these somewhat conflicting needs: integration and specialization. While non-traditional students, particularly military and veteran students, may have legitimate challenges facing them in pursuit and completion of their degrees, nonetheless they must be made aware that obstacles for successful course completion in their lives are not sufficient to excuse them from the expectations of their courses or the rules of the university. Retaining these students may prove especially challenging as more varied issues compete for their time and attention and have real-world implications for them and for their families.

ACE's Center for Policy Research and Strategy (CPRS) analyzed U.S. Department of Education (ED) data from the 2011–12 academic year to better understand the factors that place undergraduate student veterans at risk for not staying in school to complete their academic goals. ED identifies several risk factors which may impede student persistence and completion rates:

- Delayed enrollment
- No high school diploma
- Part-time enrollment
- Financial independence

- Having dependents
- Single-parent status
- Full-time employment

Among student veterans, 44 percent were found to display four or more of these risk factors (Ang and Molina 2014, 2–3).

Universities should tackle these possibilities with the students through initial counseling. Military and veteran applicants should be encouraged during the admissions process and through ongoing academic advising to anticipate potential problems during their degree work (deployment/reassignment, childcare/eldercare, family illness, etc.). Further, they should be encouraged to consider creating back-up plans for each of these circumstances, as this will prove a valuable retention tool. Failure to fully address these concerns usually manifests as an applicant who does not follow through to registration, a student who disappears mid-semester from a course, or a student who fails to re-register for subsequent terms.

The needs of non-traditional, military, and veteran applicants who complete the admissions process and become students of an institution continue to differ in many ways from the traditional student. While staff members hope that the age and experience of this population will result in a responsible, practical, and worldlier student, academic advisors, faculty members, and registrar's office personnel may also face questions and objections involving bargaining with these students for exceptions to curriculum and policy based upon their history, experience, and circumstances. Em-

bry-Riddle advising staff faces the following exceptions to policy and procedure requests: student age ("I am an adult..."); the age of the instructor ("My teacher is just a kid..."); a customer attitude ("I paid for this course..."); ignorance of the law ("Nobody told me that..."); and treatment of the university schedule as a personal calendar ("I was on vacation/travelling for work, so I should be excused from...").

A sense of entitlement to exceptions can characterize the non-traditional student. This tendency is documented in a study of perceptions of non-traditional students, including those with military background, toward the requirement of a community college in west Texas for all students to take an effective learning/student success course (Gordan 2014). The responses to the study, though limited in number, coalesce around several key themes, including the belief that traditional students need a student success course, while non–traditional students do not. One respondent, a military veteran and a former police officer, notes that he "felt he knew exactly what it would take to be a successful student," and states, 'I felt like [this class] was a waste of my time. I could use this time more effectively for something else that [my field of study] requires. It just ticked me off that I had to take it'" (Gordon 2014, 167).

The university should communicate expectations clearly and peremptorily. Objections will be best avoided via student participation in robust orientation programs, admissions counseling, and ongoing academic advisement. Efforts to alert and remind this student population to the requirements of their cur-

74

riculum of study, courses, and of the university in general should be ongoing. It is necessary to remind students that university policy is in place to guarantee academic outcomes and to provide educational equity, and that fair and consistent application of policy allows for the highest quality graduates. Additionally, it is generally helpful to appeal to the student's sense of fairness and equality among the entire student population: a reminder that all students, regardless of their life circumstances, are subject to the same rules.

Additional challenges facing universities working with non-traditional student populations include applicant fears and phobias surrounding a return to school, testing and failure, distance of time since last participating in educational pursuits (and the fading of knowledge that goes with it), and loss of student study skills. While military and veteran students will return to school boasting a range of new knowledge and skills from their military training and experience, they may lack the student skills required to exploit that background in an academic setting.

ERAU has been concentrating recent efforts toward creating a more robust orientation experience for military and veteran students. From the onset, universities should stress to non-traditional students the importance of following a set process and not just skipping to an end-goal. Key factors, such as writing skills, using the APA citation format, citing sources and plagiarism, and study and test-taking skills, must be addressed to help students to reach their goals. Waiting until students have been cited for plagiarism or

failed classes due to poor writing or test-taking skills is often too late to successfully address the problem. Once students confront this failure in their educational pursuit, they are more likely to become "failed to re-register" statistics.

Tools to Serve the Non-Traditional Student

ERAU WORLDWIDE

As a university that serves a diverse population including a large population of non-traditional, military, and veteran students, ERAU has developed many policies and procedures to assist this population with the challenges of returning to school and remaining in school should life circumstances change.

Embry-Riddle's Worldwide division is a network of more than 150 campuses, military bases, and learning centers throughout the United States, Europe, and Singapore, as well as an online division. Staffing for these locations varies depending upon the student population and number of classrooms; however, all Worldwide students expect upon enrollment that some of their coursework must be taken online. Offering degree programs in this manner affords flexibility for students coping with work or family conflicts, or military scheduling difficulties.

Many universities enforce a customary "active student" policy stating that if a student does not take classes in any given term, they must formally withdraw and then reapply or go through a "re-admit" process to return to the university in the future. To accommodate its non-traditional students, Embry-Riddle offers a two-year continuing student status policy, allowing students to take a class any time within two years of completing their last class and maintain continuing student status with the University in their initial catalog year curriculum. Embry-Riddle's two-year continuing student status "window" permits students to move in and out of enrollment, without penalty, as their military/professional careers and personal circumstances dictate. ERAU's advisors do not encourage students to leave the University for intervals of nearly two years at a time; however, because they may do so when necessary allows them the flexibility to accommodate changes in job, work schedule, or military assignment, and often prevents the complete loss of the student.

ERAU's Worldwide division offers shorter term lengths, standardized at nine weeks, allowing students to complete classes more quickly and balance educational goals with their work and home schedules. Contact hour requirements are met through additional reading, research, and group work assignments outside of the classroom setting. Online classes have participation requirements as set by their instructors and offer discussion thread postings to facilitate group interaction for geographically dispersed students. The University offers online classes via synchronous and asynchronous platforms. The Worldwide division offers 12 terms per year at the undergraduate level and five terms per year at the graduate level, and full- and part-time status is redefined to accommodate the shorter terms. Students generally take one or two classes per term in the nine-week sessions.

Staff at the campus locations provide advising for Worldwide students, with students of the online division advised by staff centered at Worldwide headquarters in Daytona Beach. Faculty access and support is required of all teaching staff, both full-time and adjunct, and their responsibilities in these areas are presented to faculty via an academic credentialing program which all teaching staff members must successfully complete.

Embry-Riddle's academic programs are primarily non-cohort, letting students move in and out of programs beginning at varied intervals, without fear of the loss of an established peer group. The University also offers courses in multiple learning modalities, permitting students enrolled at one of the residential campuses to move, via an intra-university transfer process, to a Worldwide campus location or online, should their physical location or availability to participate in classroom classes change.

The primary Worldwide graduation ceremony is held on the Daytona Beach, Florida residential campus, the headquarters of ERAU Worldwide. This allows any Worldwide graduate that had completed a degree program during the previous year and prefers a "traditional" college graduation ceremony to share in that experience. Multiple ceremonies are also held at venues throughout the country and in Europe, as well as at military base locations, who host "recognition ceremonies." This program of multiple ceremony offerings permits as many graduates as possible to participate in a graduation ceremony in their area, while still allowing the University

75

to control the setting and the experience of the graduation and provide the proper support of academic presence at the ceremony, caps/gowns, and graduation programs, etc.

Processing of Worldwide graduates is centralized at the Daytona Beach headquarters, with degrees conferred monthly and diplomas printed weekly, made possible by a concentrated term structure. As non-traditional students often seek degrees to assist with new employment, promotion, or military advancement, diplomas are printed in-house to facilitate quick distribution after conferral. Worldwide students may then begin to benefit from their status as degree-holders. Embry-Riddle's residential campus locations confer degrees three times a year in May, August, and December at the conclusion of their traditional terms.

ERAU DAYTONA BEACH

ERAU Daytona Beach is a traditional residential campus designed to maintain the advantages and feel of university campus life, while offering some of the flexibility of the Worldwide campus, such as short-term offerings and all-online degree work. Campus administrators regularly meet to review policies and procedures with an eye toward removing barriers for non-traditional students, while maintaining the standards and commonalities of campus life. Examples of adjusted policies include requiring first-year students or students with minimal transfer credits to maintain residence on campus: this requirement is waived for non-traditional students who meet certain requirements, such as marital

or family status, age, or veteran status. First-year and low-credit transfer students are also required to take a "University 101" course to integrate them to campus life. Veterans can be exempted from this requirement if it causes a hardship, however, they are strongly advised to participate, and special veteran-only sections of this class are offered to encourage participation. These classes help students adjust to campus life, while also creating connections between fellow veterans and addressing military-specific student issues.

Services provided for non-traditional students include 24-hour commuter lounges and study spaces, extended hours in service departments, and opportunities to mentor traditional age students. These students often thrive on discussing their life experiences, presenting in conferences and at poster sessions, and translating classroom work to their current work experiences and career experience into their classroom work. Non-traditional students—especially military and veteran students—benefit from the ability to share their leadership skills, self-discipline, and strength of camaraderie to their younger counterparts, and traditional students, of course, benefit from this as well.

At ERAU Daytona Beach, a team of individuals known as MyVets, short for "Military and Veterans Enrollment and Transition Services," works together to meet the specialized needs of current military and veteran students. The specialized veterans program administrators who staff the MyVets office foster peer connections, coordinate university and community support, provide information about benefits available to current and past service members and their dependents, and offer other advisory and counseling services. The MyVets office is located within a separate but centralized building, which also provides tutoring and study space, access to professional advisors, and opportunities for socializing with fellow student veterans. This space is also associated with the University's ROTC programs, allowing student veterans the opportunity to be mentors and role models for future service members.

While MyVets consists of a dedicated, specially trained group of experts, the Veterans Response Team (VRT) is made up of cross-campus representatives of administration and faculty. These individuals, under the guidance of MyVets, meet regularly to ensure the dissemination of information about student veteran needs across campus and the appropriate provision of services to these students at every level and location around campus. The VRT includes not only on-campus resources, but also representatives from community resources such as county and state Veterans Administration offices and medical centers. VRT members attend training and seminars on current military and veteran student needs and pass this information along to their respective offices and college departments in order to adequately serve this special, deserving category of students.

Conclusion

While non-traditional students bring life experience, work and career knowledge, self-discipline, and a strong work ethic to their academic endeavors, they also possess special needs and challenges. These non-traditional students can be a rich addition to a campus culture and come away from their educational experience with additional skills, tools, and knowledge to help them with their future goals, as long as these needs are met and challenges addressed.

As this nation's current and former military members and their dependents, as well as other non-traditional adult students, continue to enroll in institutions of higher education in ever-increasing numbers, colleges and universities will need to continue providing creative programming, career-specific education, support, transition, and integration services, and both integrated and specialized academic and support services. In doing so, they will ensure that both these students and the campuses they attend will benefit.

77

THE

TRANSFER HANDBOOK

PROMOTING
STUDENT
SUCCESS

CHAPTER SEVEN

Transfer and Technology

NANCY KROGH

*Senior Consultant, Higher Education Project
Management Team at Sierra-Cedar*

Transfer and Technology

The growth in the number of transfer students has led to an increase in the demand for technology to meet the needs of these students as well as to handle the increased workload for institutions. Alongside this demand, the technology has become more sophisticated, complex, and costly in order to meet the multiple requirements of many constituencies. Admissions and registrar's offices already use systems to communicate, to streamline approval processes, and to reduce staffing workloads. Faculty and academic departments want solutions that help them process the approval of courses for articulation and provide information quickly. State boards of education, legislators, granting foundations, and consortiums look to technology to meet the public's requests for easy access to information about transfer; and governing boards and administrators are looking for data to make programmatic and budget decisions to encourage transfer success. Students and their families want accessible tools to understand how their courses will transfer to meet program require-

ments, and they want to know how long it will take them to complete their goals. The pace of development of technological solutions for all of these needs has grown dramatically over the last several years and promises to continue to offer new solutions; however, these advancements usually come with a cost.

The challenge is made greater by the diversity of transfer types. Students earn transfer credit in very different ways that span from earning dual credit in high school to taking the last class from another institution and transferring it back to earn a degree. There are two-year to four-year transfers, reverse transfers, summer school transfers, service members coming with multiple transcripts, and returning adults with older coursework, just to name a few.

This chapter examines the history of the tools used for transfer, the common systems now in use, and possible trends for the future. It is not intended to give an in-depth description of all the technologies utilized for transfer student support, but rather to outline the tools being applied today so that institutions

81

can think in new ways about the technology they are using or may want to investigate further. In addition, this chapter will discuss emerging trends, as well as the situations that we do not yet have effective tools to address, in an effort to stimulate discussion about developing technology for future needs.

Historical Tools and Technology

Fifty years ago student transfer was the exception, and the technology used to handle it was straightforward. Paper and pencils were used to record the courses and do the evaluations, and bringing credit in from another institution was a manual and time-consuming process. Fifty years ago, transfer was not the norm, nor was it expected or encouraged.

Deciphering information from old transcripts can be challenging. Many administrators have experience with elderly World War II veterans who left college when called to service and later regretted not completing their degree. Finding a path to completion for these veterans was a lengthy process. The first step was usually to evaluate the transcript to understand how close the student was to a degree when they left and then conferring with the appropriate academic officer to decide on options for completion. Of the few who had transfer credit, interpreting what the courses were and how they were transferred and articulated could also present a challenge. The process had the potential to take months as the transcript clerk would first ask the student to bring in a catalog from the transfer institution, as there was no online catalog service or website to check and there

was no copy machine or fax to duplicate the syllabus or catalog description. Additionally, the student may have also needed to bring the textbook used for the professor (at the receiving institution) for evaluation. The professor would then write a memo and send it through campus mail or drop it by the registrar's office; a note would be put in the student's file explaining how it was evaluated towards the degree. Another memo would be sent to the faculty advisor who would put the information in the student's file and do the evaluation again when it was time to meet with the student. Notifying the student would occur by mail or in person. Of course, this information was created and stored for only one student, making it difficult to establish any articulation patterns or transfer agreements.

In time, a creative staff member would begin a spreadsheet of articulated courses for reference, but this record was not typically archived for future transfer staff reference. The next development was student information systems (SISs) to store transfer information—but the early versions rarely had robust transfer functionality, and this information still had to be entered manually and was not accessible to those who did not have direct access to the transfer module.

The past few decades have seen dramatic changes in transfer trends. The growth of community colleges, articulation agreements, and partnerships among colleges and universities have encouraged students to consider transfer as a viable option for continuing their education. Students who began taking courses from their hometown campus during the summer or who were enrolled through dual credit or concurrent enrollment were given the means to transfer their credits and get a head start in pursuing their degrees.

Today, some university offices still use a version of the paper and pencil process for evaluating transfer credits. While email may have replaced the pencil, and manual entry of the credit in the SIS, the paper, the manual evaluation and recording of credit can still present a time-consuming and expensive problem. Fortunately, better technology is available to support transfer students, faculty, and advisors.

Technology Today

Higher education professionals employ a variety of technological tools to manage the work of transfer. Many of the tools are not specifically for transfer students, but are applied in creative ways for efficient processing and information-sharing. Today, technology is used as a solution for four primary functions dealing with transfer. First, it is used to provide information to students and to their support networks to make their decisions about college choice. Many states have taken additional steps to require campuses to participate in statewide websites and databases containing both course equivalencies as well as transfer information so as to inform the public about all transfer options. Second, institutions also use technology to recruit transfer students and to inform students of the benefits of transfer. The third use of technology is to reduce the workload required by manual processing and to reduce the cost of increased staff time to evaluate and post transfer credit. And finally,

technology is implemented to meet external requirements, from boards, legislatures, financial aid providers, and public expectations for data, service and transparency.

A scan of higher education offices provides a look at the tools commonly used today.

STUDENT INFORMATION SYSTEMS

All major systems used by admissions and registrar offices have functionality for entering and storing transfer credit for incoming students. For many offices this entry is one course at a time, but most systems now also have an articulation function which stores previous evaluations of courses and allows for quick entry of the record of the next student who transfers in the same course. Unfortunately, this work load must often be prioritized with other work, and institutions may only be able to evaluate and enter transfer work for admitted or enrolled students. Therefore, some manage the workload by providing an evaluation only upon student request. Some student systems also offer functionality to provide the equivalencies to a website, although many institutions have had to design their own Web interface to present this information to the public.

WEBSITES AND WEB SERVICES

Both individual institutions and statewide consortiums now provide transfer policies, articulations, and information to help students understand the transfer processes and to make informed choices on the web. Some allow additional tools and support by using web services technology.

83

SELF-SERVICE WEBSITES

Institutions often provide the official transfer evaluation by giving access to the self-service module of the SIS. This provides notification of the evaluation to the student immediately after processing and includes individual detail.

EMAIL

Electronic notification is still the tool of choice for communicating with students about an update in the self-service module, answering their individual questions, or notifying them of missing required documents. The primary limitation of email is that it may not be read or may be deleted by students.

IMAGING SOFTWARE

Many institutions use imaging software to convert paper or electronic transcripts and evaluations into a single electronic record. These systems also often have a workflow function that supports communication and approval of evaluations from various sources across campus. In addition, many imaging systems include optical character recognition, thus saving time by allowing the image to be converted into text.

ELECTRONIC TRANSFER OF TEST RECORDS

Many offices electronically upload test records from the College Board, ACT, or other providers of test scores that are articulated into college credit. Some institutions electronically evaluate and apply the test scores to the student transfer record and automatically notify the student.

EQUIVALENCY DATABASES

Most campuses have some form of an equivalency database to store decisions of transfer course evaluations. The databases used range from spreadsheets, to functions contained within the SIS, to commercial software that provides an interface to the SIS and allows equivalency research from national catalog and syllabi databases, as well as online search access for students. Often the commercial systems offer integration support into the institution's SIS.

ARTICULATION AGREEMENTS

These agreements are often static documents, updated with each new catalog edition, precisely outlining how courses from partner institutions will be applied to the student record. Some institutions have developed complex systems to record, store, and track these agreements, as well as interactive web pages to provide information about the agreements to students.

PATHWAYS PROGRAMS

These programs go one step beyond articulation agreements by providing information and advising tools to help students choose the best path to a degree. Many states are providing interactive tools on the web to help students choose among degree programs.

DEGREE AUDITS

Systems for tracking requirements towards degree are in use by many higher education institutions, and almost all include posted transfer credit in the evaluations. Degree audits are utilized for recruiting, by admitted students, by enrolled students who plan to take courses elsewhere to transfer back, and to provide information to advisors. The limitation of most degree audits is that they include only posted and officially evaluated credit in the results, although some allow students to enter a course and process a "what-if" evaluation. In addition, most degree audits are not available to prospective students as a tool to decide on the college or program, but only available after a student has been admitted or enrolled.

TRANSFER EQUIVALENCY SIMULATORS

Transfer simulators allow students to enter their self-reported transfer work to see an evaluation of how the courses will transfer into the institution. Some of these simulators allow students to create a login to return and continue to track additional work, and also interface with the degree audit to provide degree requirement evaluations, in addition to course equivalencies.

WORKFLOW

Numerous institutions have adopted electronic processes that allow documents and approvals to move through a defined set of business steps. Workflow systems may be purchased as a standalone product which integrates with other institutional systems and processes, or they may be included as a feature in the SIS or other systems used for transfer. Workflow allows faster approval time for transfer evaluation decisions, as well as a way to track a particular request along the approval chain to completion. And, of course, it eliminates paper and associated issues.

EDI (ELECTRONIC DATA EXCHANGE) AND XML (EXTENSIBLE MARKUP LANGUAGE)

The use of electronic exchange of transcripts among institutions in a format that is both human and machine-readable is well established in admissions and registrar offices. The Postsecondary Electronic Standards Council (PESC) has spent years developing standards for exchange of records and provides resources for understanding the use of both EDI and XML in exchanging student records. AACRAO has provided multiple sessions, conferences, and publications about implementation of these tools for transcript exchange. AACRAO's SPEEDE Committee has been tireless in evangelizing the benefits of electronic exchange and has provided extensive information for institutions to get started. Some individuals who use EDI and XML believe that use should be mandated in order to best capture the value of this electronic exchange for both K–12 and postsecondary institutions. However, the cost of deploying XML and EDI, which includes acquiring the technical and functional knowledge needed to implement and maintain these systems, is still prohibitive for many campuses. For some small offices, the time required to understand the technology and apply it to their business processes seems out of reach. But for those who are already using this technology, this presents a convenient opportunity for saving money and providing faster service for students.

Transfer students come in with expectations different from those of a new high school freshman. They have experienced some college and expect to understand some of what it will be like at the transfer institution. They have different needs from different offices, and the system may not be set up to meet all needs in one place. Many institutions leverage their constituent relationship management systems to individually communicate with transfer students and to tie the disparate services across campus together in unified communications to students. CRMs allow campuses to track exchanges with transfer students and to plan a sequence of service based on prior interactions. CRMs also allow the institutions to research and evaluate the most effective methods of communication and improve those services in the future, based on data collected from the CRM. And of course, every campus reports that over-communication can be a problem for students. As already noted, unread emails and those deleted by students present a challenge. CRMs can help manage the messages and content, but only if intelligently coordinated among the many offices communicating with students.

Public Expectations

What do constituencies expect or want that they cannot currently do? Many of the demands for higher education to improve transfer do not have to do with the technology, but more to do with public understanding of how the transfer process works. For example,

colleagues note that common course numbering projects are still proposed as a technical project by states and legislatures, although the equivalency databases used at most campuses can easily present like courses without a common number. In addition, the public does not always understand the value or the pre-planning services available for transfer students. It is also important to note that courses that are different but are similar in name/appearance may have different content and apply differently to different degree requirements. And of course, the public often does not understand that there are differences in degree requirements among colleges and universities: this affects how courses from other institutions will be accepted in to fulfill those requirements.

Foundations and organizations that award grants are looking for innovative ways to provide transfer information in an effort to shorten the time to degree for students. A degree audit across multiple institutions is often proposed as a solution. However, the practical application of this solution, given the complexity of degree audit software and the specialized nature of individual degree requirements at each institution, is likely far off.

One of the biggest challenges is the expectation that concurrent enrollment should be an easy way to combine resources and share courses across institutions. While the technology is in place to post and articulate completed credit (which has been moved into history and the academic record of the SIS), the ability to record and track courses in progress across multiple institutions remains a significant challenge, and some of the more sophisticated technology to do so may be cost prohibitive for many institutions. The method often used is manual entry of a "place-holder" registration to simulate the enrollment of the course(s) at another institution. When the course is completed the "place-holder" is replaced with the transfer credit. Another method is to duplicate the course across institutions and record a course from a partner institution as if it has been offered at the home campus. However, both methods have drawbacks and problems. Being able to read records across different campus databases is a complex endeavor, even among institutions running like systems, as the entire scheme of higher education recordkeeping is designed for registration and degree requirement completion at a single institution.

Often overlooked in the transfer technology discussion is how many services needed by students require verification of current enrollment, including enrollment across multiple institutions. Financial aid requirements have been built upon the foundation of enrollment status and of courses counting towards the degree. If a student is taking four courses across four institutions, the student may be full-time for financial aid purposes, but verifying that his or her enrollment is current and that the courses all apply toward the degree at any point in time is usually a manual process. In addition, keeping track of students who drop or add during the term across institutions is usually not feasible.

Some state systems or consortia have developed programs to read across institutional databases to track and report concurrent en-

rollments. Unfortunately the solutions are sometimes clunky, have limitations, and are almost always homegrown and expensive, resulting in necessary modifications to other systems in place.

Future Trends

As much as transfer technology has changed over the last 20 years, certain trends could revolutionize transfer service and increase options for students. First, new technology that allows for an increase in the speed of evaluations while decreasing the workload on staff should be expected: this can happen through the ubiquitous use of EDI and XML to transfer coursework and upload data into systems. A tipping point may be reached in the near future where every institution will see these tools as necessary as having an SIS.

It is also important to consider how to use technology to transfer outcomes and competencies, in addition to courses. How will technology evolve to support this? This may include tools to move from analyzing course-to-course equivalencies into processes which break down academic program learning outcomes into transfer equivalencies. These evaluations could equate *outcomes* with programs, not necessarily specific coursework. Another trend treats any courses/outcome as home-based credit; tracking the residency requirement in place in most degree programs is challenging, and the technology to track divergent content across institutions will be demanded if alternative solutions are not discovered.

Transfer students, their families, and advisors are also asking for greater mobile connectivity to transfer resources. Few systems today offer true mobile support for transfer equivalency or advising information, but this feature should be expected soon. Increased access to this equivalency information would aid the student in their research about their own educational options.

And certainly, any technology that supports student success will be in demand. There is much to unpack in the term "student success," and there is of yet no single agreement about how it should be measured. One thing all parties can agree on is that using transfer strategies to support students' options to further their education and reach their goals is a hot topic in higher education reform. The relevant institutional enrollment offices will certainly be at the center of implementing technology that supports these efforts.

Another trend is for increased demand for data and associated analysis: the details stored and generated about students in institutional systems in order to make decisions can border on overwhelming. Many times we see this data presented out of context or in ways that do not correspond to the underlying circumstances, thus it is crucial to examine and determine how the technology leads to valid research and reliable conclusions, while simultaneously protecting students' rights to privacy and their own information.

Finally, financial aid requirements and the struggle to comply with their increasing complexity is not new. Different technology will be required that allows for the track-

ing of complex situations like course repeats across various institutions and at different times in an academic career. Financial aid can be a confusing and complex component of a transfer student's experience.

Final Thoughts and Summary

Transfer initiatives and tools are often considered in terms of software to enroll new transfers or as the means to give students "consumer" information about transferability, but perhaps the conversation should center around transfer success. How is the technology for student success geared towards serving transfer students after they are enrolled? And what can be done to develop the necessary tools to support transfer students in reaching their goals? What is the role of technology in each phase of the transfer of credit?

The policies and definitions that promote conclusive research of transfer outcomes do not yet exist across higher education institutions. However, the demand will continue to increase in higher education policy reform to work together to find solutions that support multiple facets of transfer: access, affordability, and student success, just to name a few.

And of course, the end result of any technological solution is student service. Administration, legislatures, and other policymakers need to remember that the human touch is still important to students. While technology is a significant tool to meet student needs, it is still the individual contact and personal attention that can make all the difference.

THE

TRANSFER HANDBOOK

PROMOTING
STUDENT
SUCCESS

Writing a Transfer Policy:
Principles and Practices

KELLY BROOKS
Registrar,
Capella University

CHAPTER EIGHT

Writing a Transfer Policy: Principles and Practices

As an undergraduate, I attended one of the branch campuses of a large state university. From the day I matriculated as a pre-journalism freshman, I knew that after two years I would transfer to the university's main campus, which was the only campus that allowed students to complete the journalism degree. What I did not anticipate, however, was that I would, by design, end up losing credit in the transfer process. In fact, at least one of these losses was in a required pre-journalism course, but it was not due to a poor grade or because it was from a different institution, exactly. It was simply because the set of four pre-journalism core courses varied in credits between campuses. Needless to say I was both perplexed, disappointed, and frustrated by this apparent "discrepancy by design," not to mention that it resulted in an extra quarter of courses—and tuition—to complete my degree. Today I recognize that my experience was far from unique.

With the nation focused on reducing college costs and fostering degree completion, the ability for students to transfer their cred-

its between institutions is, unsurprisingly, a tenable aim. Depending on which studies one reads and how one defines a transfer student, it is reasonable to estimate that somewhere between 30 and 50 percent of students seeking an undergraduate degree will transfer at some point in their academic career. Combine this with the increasing number of adult students returning to complete their degrees, and the importance of transferability both at the individual and national level is clear.

In 2001 AACRAO joined the American Council on Education (ACE) and the Council for Higher Education and signed the "Joint Statement on the Transfer and Award of Credit," a set of guidelines for institutions developing or reviewing policies dealing with transfer, acceptance, and award of credit (*see* Appendix E, "Joint Statement on the Transfer and Award of Credit," on page 269). Among the many recommendations and considerations outlined in the Joint Statement is a reference to accountability and public communication, which calls upon institutions and their accrediting bodies to ensure that the "public are fully and accurately informed about their respective transfer policies and practices. The public has a significant interest in higher education's effective management of transfer, especially in an environment of expanding access and mobility." The document goes on to especially note that "public funding increases expectations that the transfer process is built on a strong commitment to fairness and efficiency." These facets of political priority, public accountability and demographic change affirm the necessity of crafting a transfer policy that is clear to prospects, current students, and staff alike. Ideally, such a policy would be one that ensures equity for students and integrity for the institution while providing transparency about the transfer credit process.

Lessons from Journalism School

KNOW YOUR AUDIENCE

Years after my own experience with transfer credit loss, I now find myself at a large university, overseeing the policy team and making decisions about transfer credit for our adult population of students, many of whom bring with them many previous college credits as well as significant professional knowledge and experience. The first step in any policy creation or any article a journalist writes is: *know your audience.*

It is important to reflect on the audience when starting to craft any policy. Who will be reading and using this policy? Will they be applicants? Will they be current students? If so, do they typically come from certain schools

or a variety of places? Will parents read this? High school counselors? Staff? Faculty? The answers to these questions should help in the framing of a policy and determining what needs to be included. In addition to the general public, groups across the institution that are responsible for developing, implementing, maintaining, and complying with approved policies, procedures, and practices should be considered as well. Such stakeholders might include staff in the admissions office, registrar's office, transfer credit evaluators, college or departmental administrators, academic advisors, student leadership and/or the faculty senate, depending on the breadth and specifics of the policy.

DEVELOP A LEAD

The second step in developing an institutional transfer policy is: *writing the lead.*

In print journalism, a 'lead' is the most vital, overarching message the audience needs to know, something that draws in the reader and summarizes the story. In writing both a policy or a newspaper story, it is important to first organize the flow of ideas. Consider using titles and even visual aids that might be helpful. In general, policies should answer the users' questions. They should promote effectiveness, efficiency, and consistency; provide clarity of purpose in concise language; and avoid internal contradictions as well as conflicts or contradictions with other policies.

DETERMINE WHAT MUST BE INCLUDED

Of course, when writing a newspaper story, the journalist must review notes and determine which pieces are relevant or necessary

92

to include and which are extraneous. Thus, the third, and perhaps most important step in this process is: *determining and organizing content elements*. In some measure, transfer policy content can be guided by law and the input of professional organizations, although much of the main content of any transfer policy will outline the institution-specific requirements and practices. In accordance with the Higher Education Act of 1965 as amended by the Higher Education Opportunity Act of 2008, higher education institutions must publicly disclose their transfer credit policies and articulation agreements to prospective and enrolled students. At a minimum, this disclosure must include the following:

- any established criteria the institution uses regarding the transfer of credit earned at another institution; and
- a list of institutions with which the institution has established an articulation agreement (National Postsecondary Education Cooperative 2009).

In addition, the law expressly requires that institutions have transfer policies and follow them. Thus, it is important to avoid creating policy that cannot, in actuality, be executed.

SET THE QUALITY STANDARD
Recognition of previous academic credit ultimately rests with the accepting institution. The institutional policy statement should, therefore, specify the conditions under which the receiving institution will accept credit, and identify the line of authority in determining the application of transfer of credit.

Institutions often have a transfer criteria based on quality, which generally equates to the accreditation of the previous institution. An institutional policy should spell out whether accreditation of a previous institution is required for transfer work to be accepted. The policy should also note whether the accreditation must be regional or if coursework from nationally-accredited institutions also may be recognized. If not expressly written in the policy, the institution should consider, under this requirement, how it will manage credits earned by someone who was enrolled when their previous school either lost or gained accreditation. This may extend to particular majors in which transfer credit is subject to some type of specialized accreditation status from the previous institution.

Almost equally common is a quality measure in terms of grades. This kind of transfer policy statement outlines the minimum grade requirements for incoming transfer work at the graduate and undergraduate levels. Some policies also explain whether or not plus/minus grades are included or provide a grade point equivalent. Also, a good policy will also spell out how grades of "pass" are considered in the transfer evaluation.

PROVIDE STATEMENT OF AUTHORITY
It is generally understood and often stated that transfer decisions ultimately rest with the institution, college, or department. It is not uncommon for a transfer policy to include a statement regarding the body or bodies of authority within the institution that make transfer decisions (*i.e.*, admissions of-

93

fice, registrar's office, dean) as well as the process for any appeal of transfer decisions. This speaks to the assessment of comparability of coursework and its applicability to the degree requirements. Along this line, one might also cite any specific transfer policies related to a student's major or college/school of enrollment, such as any limitations on the age of credit accepted for transfer.

INCORPORATE OTHER ELEMENTS

In addition to those mentioned above, other commonly seen transfer policy elements include references to:

- how credits are calculated or converted between quarter and semester systems;
- how physical education, vocational, or technical coursework will (or will not) be recognized for transfer;
- the maximum total number of transfer credits allowed and any other limits such as from a community college, CLEP, credits of "pass," and so on;
- specific coursework deemed unacceptable for transfer. Examples might include remedial courses, English as a Second Language (ESL) courses, practicum, internships, clinical experiences, and orientation courses;
- whether/when courses will be directly matched to an institutional course versus given elective credit;
- any charges or fees assessed for the transfer credit evaluation;
- whether/how grades in the transfer courses will factor in to the institution's GPA and show up on a transcript;

- whether the institution offers "unofficial" reviews for transfer credit estimation;
- what happens to the transfer credit if the student changes their major or degree program;
- what is required for international applicants/students and/or international coursework to be evaluated;
- any institutional "residency" requirement that could impact transfer (*e.g.*, "thirty of the final 60 undergraduate degree credits must be done at our school");
- whether all transfer occurs only at the time of admission or any time throughout the student's academic career at the institution;
- the application of previous coursework taken at the graduate level toward an undergraduate degree or how a graduate program might consider previous graduate coursework taken within an undergraduate degree program;
- the acceptance (or rejection) of American Council on Education (ACE) recommendations on CLEP, DSST, and military credit among other items;
- the opportunity to "test out" of courses or to receive credit for prior learning;
- a list of institutions with which the school has established articulation agreements and any specific alignments or exclusions within those agreements; and
- recognition and application of state transfer pacts or affiliation transfer arrangements such as the Interstate Passport Initiative out of the Western

Interstate Commission for Higher Education (WICHE).

While often not part of the transfer policy itself, links to self-service tools and transfer guides are commonly found on public web pages about transfer policies. The University of Texas at Austin is a good example of incorporating this information.[4] Schools might also, like Ithaca College, provide a general overview of the institution's transfer evaluation process.[5] This explains how and when the transfer process should begin, what documents are necessary for the evaluation, the length of processing time, and how students are notified. It may also cover appeals processes and should clearly provide a specific individual or office (along with appropriate contact information) that may be contacted for questions on the transfer policy.

Conclusion

Some of the most helpful and effective strategies in writing good transfer policy include browsing the web, locating the transfer policies for various institutions, and evaluating them only as written policy, making sure not to make a judgment on whether or not one agrees with the practices being outlined.

This process usually provides an immediate sense of a policy's clarity and usability. It can also illuminate areas that may have been overlooked in an institution's transfer policy, aspects which may be helpful to include in future drafts. Some institutions which I con-

sider to have clear and well-written transfer policies include: Ithaca College,[6] Mount Ida College,[7] and Capella University.[8]

It is also important to maintain a revision history detailing what was changed with possibly some explanation of why it was changed in addition to the date of implementation of each change to the policy. This can be done either within the policy itself or as an internal document accompanying the policy. This policy history can be immensely helpful in advising students and applicants, as well as in training staff and being able to determine when something was changed. Ultimately, as noted earlier, a school must be able to not only *state* the transfer policy but also to *follow* it. Thus, transfer policy needs to be clear and easy enough to implement that staff and faculty can support what has been written.

Finally, one last journalism tenet seems appropriate: *tell them what you're going to tell them.* Tell them. Then tell them what you told them. Reinforcement never hurts whether it comes to academic policy or newspaper stories.

---

[4] See ‹http://bealonghorn.utexas.edu/transfer/admission/factors/transfer-resources›.

[5] See ‹www.ithaca.edu/admission/faqs/faq/310/›.

[6] See ‹www.ithaca.edu/catalogs/ug0910/hshp/policies_and_procedures.php›.

[7] See ‹http://catalog.mountida.edu/content.php?catoid=16&navoid=265#Transfer_Credit_Policies_and_Procedures›.

[8] See ‹www.capella.edu/assets/pdf/policies/Transfer_Credit_Assessment.pdf›.

95

THE

TRANSFER HANDBOOK

PROMOTING
STUDENT
SUCCESS

Transfer *of* Credit

THE

TRANSFER HANDBOOK

PROMOTING
STUDENT
SUCCESS

CHAPTER NINE

Military Transcripts and Transfer Credit

CHRISTINE CARTER

Senior Evaluator,
Thomas Edison State College

Military Transcripts and Transfer Credit

As discussed in Chapter 7, American institutions in higher education continue to respond to the challenge of providing adequate academic resources for the special population of military and veteran students. The U.S. Department of Education (Radford 2009) found that in 2007–2008, about four percent of all undergraduates and four percent of all graduate students were veterans or military service members. The American Council on Education (ACE) conducted two surveys, in 2009 and again in 2012, and found that the average enrollment of service members and veterans had increased "significantly" according to responding institutions (McBain 2012). In order to meet the needs of this special population, some schools have devoted time and resources to determine how best to evaluate military experience for academic credit.

In a 2010 *Service Members in School* study conducted by the Rand Corporation and ACE (Steele 2010), military and veteran students' perceptions regarding the ability and usefulness of transferring their military credit re-

flected their cautiousness about basing their college choices on the potential for credit transfer. According to the 2010 study, 57 percent of survey respondents reported that they had attempted to transfer military credits to academic credits, and only 47 percent of the subgroup were satisfied with the result. The average number of credits students reported they were able to transfer was 18 military credits.

Balancing the institutional need to follow specific transfer credit policies and maintain academic rigor with the recognition of military and veteran students' unique and intensive training and occupations has led to a wide array of military transfer credit options. These options have become increasingly important with the 2010 changes in to the Post-9/11 GI Bill, which have allowed for an unprecedented and ever-growing number of active military, reservists and veterans to pursue undergraduate and graduate degrees.

One institution that is working closely with this unique student population and military transfer credit is Thomas Edison State College.

101

Thomas Edison State College

Chartered in 1972, Thomas Edison State College (TESC) is one of New Jersey's 11 senior public institutions of higher education and one of the oldest schools in the country designed specifically for adults. TESC has been regionally accredited continually by the Middle States Commission on Higher Education for the past 35 years and currently enrolls more than 21,000 students, 38 percent of whom are active military, veterans and reservists. The institution offers associate, bachelor's and master's degree programs in more than 100 areas of study. The average student age is 36. The student body represents residents from all 50 states and approximately 60 countries throughout the world. Most courses offered by TESC are not classroom-based, but are in various online or independent forms.

Thomas Edison State College is a long-standing member of the Servicemembers Opportunity Colleges (SOC). More than 1,900 colleges and universities hold membership in SOC, an organization that actively promotes articulation between members to assure service members and their dependents of transferability of credits between institutions. Thomas Edison State College is also one of approximately 160 member institutions that comprise the SOC Degree System Network. This network works closely with the military to map military training to degree programs through a SOC agreement.

When service members and their dependents from the Army, Navy, Marines, National Guard or Coast Guard apply to Thomas Edison State College, the College provides both the student and SOC an agreement form and a copy of the Academic Program Evaluation, which shows the credits applied toward and those needed to complete the degree.

The Joint Services Transcript

The main source of credit that TESC awards for military training and occupation is based on credit recommendations made by ACE on the Joint Services Transcript (JST).

TESC stores credit for the trainings and occupations listed on the JST by the ACE Identifier in the TESC student systems database. This ever-growing database is searchable by ACE Identifier and is capable of listing the multiple versions that a training or occupation may have, including the dates that these versions are applicable. Each version is broken down by the ACE credit recommendations and assigned a series of compatible TESC course equivalencies as well as the corresponding number of semester hours that ACE has recommended. TESC awards all JST transfer credit(s) a grade of "CR," which does not calculate into a student's GPA.

Each student's JST is reviewed and all ACE-reviewed credit is added to a student's record, regardless of degree type or applicability. For new versions or courses that may not yet exist in the institutional database, the transcript evaluator researches the correct equivalencies and adds them to the database for future use and consistency, using the ACE Military Guidelines website to establish correct equivalencies and set the version dates.

TESC awards credit for passing examination grades listed in the College Examinations section directly from a student's JST, including the College Level Examination Program (CLEP), DSST and Defense Language Institute. As with all non-traditional credit, these examinations are awarded the ACE-recommended credit, with a grade of CR.

The establishment of TESC equivalency credit determines what courses a student receives credit for and where those courses will fall in the student's academic evaluation (degree audit), thus giving the student the tools to determine what courses to take to fulfill degree requirements. The student may also ultimately decide to change degree programs in order to maximize credit usage.

TESC Transfer Equivalencies

All transfer course work, both traditional (from other regionally accredited institutions) and non-traditional (including testing and ACE-reviewed credit) are assigned TESC transfer equivalencies, including a prefix and number. Standardization of equivalencies is the key to ensuring that duplicative credit is not awarded and that consistent credit is awarded for all students. For example, if an ACE recommendation lists First Aid as a course equivalency, the TESC course equivalency HEA-195 First Aid is used. This way, if a student receives First Aid credit as a recommendation multiple times on the JST or on an additional transcript from a traditional institution, the multiple HEA-195 equivalencies will duplicate out, leaving only one on the transcript and student academic evaluation.

TESC houses a course equivalency database with more than 13,000 course equivalencies.

This database includes TESC-offered courses, but these equivalencies were primarily created for use in establishing equivalencies for both traditional and non-traditional transfer credit. Equivalencies are assigned multiple department codes (for example, BIOL for biology courses), which correspond to different degree requirements and include course descriptions. The credit amount is modified to meet the credit recommendation on the JST.

For those courses that have SOC category codes assigned to them, the equivalencies that have been verified in the SOC guide are used consistently for the corresponding ACE recommendation. For example, for the ACE recommendation of "Computer Applications," which also has been given the SOC category code of CS101A/CS101B, CS102A, the approved TESC course equivalency is CIS-107, "Computer Concepts and Applications." This is listed for students to view in the Defense Activity for Non-Traditional Education Support (DANTES) catalog of approved SOC codes listed by institution. Here, students can also see a list of courses from other institutions that have been approved to fulfill a similar requirement, leading to ease in credit transfer amongst institutions.

For students who left the military before 1986, or for whom the JST does not list all ACE-recommended credit, TESC will award credit based on information included on a notarized copy of the student's DD214, DD295 or Enlisted Record Brief (ERB). The additional documentation must list dates in order for credit based on the ACE Military Guidelines to be awarded.

103

Supplemental information is sometimes needed in order to award students correct credit. For instance, when a student has Maintenance Training Management and Evaluation Program (MATMEP) credit listed on their JST. To determine the level of training completed (I-IV), TESC requires that service members provide an official copy of their Individual Duty Area Qualification Summary extract from the MATMEP. The Qualification Summary indicates the level of training completed and the date of completion, which correspond to specific ACE credit recommendations.

Regionally-Accredited Institutions

TESC awards traditional transfer credit for service members and veterans who attended the Community College of the Air Force or Air University, as these are both regionally accredited institutions. Community College of the Air Force transcripts only list institutional credit with a "Satisfactory" grade, thus TESC awards "CR" credit. Official transcripts are needed in order for credit to be awarded. Students who bring credit from the Community College of the Air Force are subject to TESC academic policy that limits transfer credit from junior and community colleges to 80 semester hours towards a bachelor's degree. Credit from junior and community colleges is also considered lower-level credit and assigned 100- and 200-level course equivalencies, in keeping with TESC's community college transfer policy. TESC also awards traditional transfer credit for service members and veterans who attended the Defense

Language Institute, as this is a regionally accredited institution. An official transcript is needed in order for credit to be awarded.

TESC Academic Program Review Credit

Thomas Edison State College also conducts multiple Academic Program Reviews of specific military training, for which students can receive additional credit. An Academic Program Review (APR) is a service that TESC offers to organizations to determine whether the organization's training and education programs provide college-level learning and can be applied as credit to an academic program at the College. An Academic Review Team, comprised of experts in specific subject areas, evaluates training and education programs to determine whether they translate to college-level work. This team also recommends how many credits to award for the training and whether the credits transfer at the undergraduate or graduate level

Military-specific TESC APRs include a review of the Navy's Basic Nuclear Power School. While ACE has also reviewed this training for credit, students who provide a JST with this training listed receive the TESC APR credit, which is equivalent to 41 credits, in lieu of the approximately 25 credits reviewed by ACE. This credit is added to a student's academic evaluation using in-house codes (*e.g.*, NUCL.SCH), which automatically populate the credit for the APR based on the date taken; just as ACE credit is handled.

TESC has created degree programs whose areas of study are designed around the APR credit a student can receive for a specific license or certification. For example, TESC has conducted APRs for many Federal Aviation Administration licenses, which often supplement a military or veteran student's JST aviation-based trainings and occupations. The TESC Bachelor of Science in Applied Science and Technology (BSAST) degree in Aviation Maintenance Technology is designed for students who hold a current FAA Mechanic License. The APR for the Mechanic License comprises 67 credits, which fulfill all of the requirements of the area of study within the BSAST degree in Aviation Maintenance Technology except for the required Capstone course.

Fort Sam Houston Program

Since August 2010, Thomas Edison State College has worked with the Medical Education and Training Campus (METC) at Fort Sam Houston in San Antonio, Texas, to provide a degree completion program for the Interservice Respiratory Therapy Program (IRTP). Upon completion of this program, students earn an Associate in Applied Science (AAS) degree in Respiratory Therapy.

This program combines a classroom experience of specific TESC general education courses (including English Composition II) with the application of APR credit for the Respiratory Therapy Specialists Program, which students receive upon completion of the IRTP. Remaining credits come from transfer credit and credits awarded from the JST or through courses completed successfully at TESC.

Examination Programs

In addition to granting credit for the examinations listed on a student's JST, TESC has developed its own credit-by-examination program, known as the TECEP exam. TECEP exams are developed by TESC mentors who have taught comparable courses and include multiple-choice questions and short answer or essay questions that are graded by subject matter experts.

Other examinations are also accepted for transfer credit, including the New York University Foreign Language Proficiency Testing Program, the College Board's Advanced Placement Program and ACE-reviewed American Council on the Teaching of Foreign Languages Inc. (ACTFL) exams.

Military Transfer Policies

MAINTAINING ACTIVE STATUS

Military students and their dependents enrolled in Thomas Edison State College through contractual and military agreements must demonstrate academic activity by attempting a minimum of three semester hour credits over the course of the 12-month period for which they are enrolled. For example, a student whose course or other credit earning option began on September 1, 2013, must register for another three-credit course before September 1, 2014, to be considered an enrolled Thomas Edison State College student for the following year. Students who do not attempt three credits in an academic year will be deemed "inactive."

Inactive military students are still able to register for classes, view grades and financial aid information, and receive academic advising for their current or potential degree programs. However, their transcript will not reflect any transfer credit that was received and added to their record after the date they went inactive. Inactive students can reactivate their enrollment by registering for a minimum of three semester hours in a course or other credit-earning option, such as a TECEP. These students will continue to be governed by the academic policies in place at the time they began their program.

Military students who remain inactive for five consecutive years must reapply for admission to return to the College and will be governed by the academic policies and degree programs in place at the time of their readmission.

RESIDENCY REQUIREMENT

Although Thomas Edison State College has certain academic residency requirements, it does not have physical residency requirements. All military programs currently have academic residency requirements of 12 credits for an associate degree and 24 credits for a bachelor's degree. This residency has changed over the years, so students who have maintained an active status with TESC are subject to the residency requirement at the time of their initial enrollment. All types of institutional Thomas Edison State College (TESC) credit (including the TECEP examination program and TESC's portfolio assessment program) satisfy the residency.

Degree Requirements

All credit from a student's military transcripts as well as any additional traditional institutional transcripts, APR or examination credit will be added to a student's record once the necessary documentation has been received. However, generally not all of this credit will apply to the student's degree program. TESC provides an online academic evaluation to all applicants to the college that shows them where the transfer credit that they have submitted for review will fall in their chosen degree program and what requirements will still remain.

The academic evaluation also accounts for additional TESC academic policies, including different types of transfer credit limitations (including a current limitation of 80 credits from community college/junior colleges), degree-specific currency issues and GPA requirements. Student-specific notes are shared at the bottom of the evaluation regarding these policies as well as a section of the academic evaluation that lists all of the courses that did not apply to the degree.

As courses are completed through TESC, or additional transfer credit arrives, the academic evaluation is updated. All active military and veteran students are encouraged to set up a phone or online appointment with a TESC academic advisor to review their degree and to discuss other potential degree programs where their transfer credit may be used more effectively.

Resources for Military Students and Veterans

In order to assist military and veteran students navigate the myriad choices of degree programs and degree requirements, TESC's Office of Military and Veteran Education (OMVE) offers different methods of support, including branch-specific information, military and financial forms and detailed information regarding different enrollment programs. Prospective students, applicants and enrolled students are encouraged to contact TESC staff via email or phone. Upon application, military students can also make a phone appointment with an academic advisor or contact TESC's Learner Support Center, a one-stop-shop for student issues.

For active military students, TESC provides an online form that allows them to have a commissioned officer serve in lieu of a Notary Public. This way, even if they are stationed abroad, students can send relevant documentation, such as a copy of a license or supplemental military documentation for credit review. By providing different methods of support and flexibility, including an online student portal for accessing courses and their academic evaluation, TESC ensures that military students, regardless of where they are located, have the ability to access the information necessary to work toward degree completion.

Summary

As part of its mission to offer flexible, high-quality, collegiate learning opportunities for self-directed adults, TESC has been providing over 40 years of specialized educational op-

portunities for members of the United States military that optimize military training and experience. TESC addresses the balance between the institutional need to maintain academic rigor and clear transfer credit policies with military and veteran students' unique and intensive training experience and their need for a variety of flexible means to earn college-level credit. Through the creation and maintenance of a transfer credit database, TESC awards credit for college-level courses completed at other regionally accredited institutions, ACE-recommended credit for all military training and occupations, and multiple examination programs. In addition, TESC has conducted in-house academic program reviews on military training and occupations as well as other licenses and certifications that military students, veterans and their dependents may hold. Many of these academic program reviews are additionally aligned with specific degree programs that benefit specific military populations.

Suggestions

In order to best serve military and veteran students, American institutions of higher education may first consider the applicability of their transfer credit policies to the needs of this special population. Are there methods for military students to apply their military training and experience for transfer credit, and is this credit likely to be degree applicable? Is traditional transfer credit handled consistently? Does the institution allow for non-traditional venues of credit including ACE-reviewed entities and examination pro-

107

grams? Can a student demonstrate knowledge acquired outside the classroom through portfolio assessment or testing?

Second, depending on the mobility of military students, an institution may choose to consider flexibility in the time allotted for degree completion, and methods of courses offered. Are online courses available? How does a military student establish residency and maintain active status with the institution?

Lastly, it is recommended that institutions review their resources that specifically address military student transfer credit options and procedures. These resources should be clear, current and available electronically to allow for ease in student access. Staff responsible for addressing military student concerns should be well-trained in the policies and procedures, and their availability should be made clear so that students can contact them. By providing military-specific resources, an institution demonstrates to these students its commitment to providing them the tools needed for a meaningful and positive academic experience.

108

CHAPTER TEN

International Transfer Credit Evaluation and Methodology

CHRISTY FRY

*Associate Director of International and Diversity Recruitment,
Colby-Sawyer College*

International Transfer Credit Evaluation and Methodology

This chapter discusses the theory and practice of international transfer credit, including evaluation methodology. It is often referred to as an "art and science" because of the need to determine the common denominator (science) of diversified education systems (art).

U.S. postsecondary institutions are increasingly recognizing the value that international transfer students can add to their institutions. Understanding the variables involved in the international transfer credit evaluation process is imperative to ensuring that transfer credit is awarded consistently across a vast number of differing education systems. The essence of the evaluation process is in identifying the "art" of an education system, or what makes it unique, and then using the "science" to formulaically calculate the number of hours in a course and the typical number of credits in a semester or academic year. How to consistently apply these results to one's institutional profile is the culmination of this process. The process begins with defining the evaluation methodology.

Reacquaintance with the U.S. Education System

At the core of evaluation methodology is the comparison of international education systems to the U.S. system. Therefore, one must begin with an understanding of the U.S. education structure and its unique aspects. U.S. postsecondary education begins after 12 years of primary and secondary education, and follows either the semester or quarter calendar. Typically, a postsecondary institution's academic year consists of two semesters, fall and spring, with an optional summer semester. These semesters are 15 weeks in length with a shorter summer semester of 12 weeks; sometimes the summer semester is broken into two or three shorter periods, ranging in length, but commonly six weeks if running two summer semesters. The two 15 week periods amount to 30 weeks of instruction.

The quarter-based system is divided into four quarters and defines three quarters as an academic year (whereby the fourth quarter is optional). The average length of the quarter

111

is ten weeks, making the total number of instructional weeks 30. Quarters are identified as fall, winter, spring, and the optional summer. When comparing the instructional weeks between the two calendar approaches, it is clear that three quarters equals two semesters. As a result, three quarter hours equal two semester hours (or a quarter hour is 2/3 or 0.67 less than a semester hour). This will prove useful to recall later in the chapter when the concept of credit conversion is discussed in detail.

The U.S. unit of learning time or credit originates from the Carnegie Foundation for the Advancement of Teaching.[9] Here the Carnegie Unit, more commonly referred to as the credit hour, was developed and adopted across the country at the K–12 (primary and secondary) and postsecondary levels of education. The application of the credit hour consists of a defined number of hours of seat time equal to a credit, and a defined number of credits to equal a credential (*i.e.*, bachelor's degree). Over the past few years an industry conversation has emerged regarding this concept of seat time as the only accurate and equitable means of measurement. For now, the seat time definition remains the majority measurement tool, as instructed by the International Affairs Office of the U.S. Department of Education.[10]

Seat time must be defined across the various types of courses to provide a clear understanding of the credit hour. For a lecture course, approximately one hour per week in class for 15 weeks equals one credit hour, so the traditional three-credit-hour course

would be equivalent to 45 hours of coursework over a semester. The U.S. postsecondary system also distinguishes lab, practice, and independent study courses. These different course types have varying credit hour expectations. One lab hour a week in class for 15 weeks equals one credit hour, so the three-credit-hour course would be equivalent to 45 hours of coursework and between 45 to 90 laboratory hours over a semester. It is similar in value to the lecture course; however, the practice and independent study hour equals three to four hours per week. This totals between 135 to 180 hours for three credit hours during the course of a semester.

Within the U.S. system, 15 credit hours is considered a full-time semester course load. This would be the same for the quarter credit hour. One academic year consists of 30 semester credit hours and 45 quarter credit hours. It will be important to recall these definitions of credit hours within specific lengths of study later in the chapter. By applying the logical reasoning that the human capacity to learn does not differ greatly from one educational system to another, it can be assumed that students absorb similar amounts of content within similar lengths of study.

Institutional Profile

Considering these key features of the U.S. postsecondary education system is a first step in assessing one's institutional profile and determining how a foreign credential translates to the institution. Additional questions can also help to further assess one's institutional profile, such as:

---

[9] *See* ‹www.carnegiefoundation.org›.

[10] *See* ‹www2.ed.gov/about/offices/list/oU.S./international/U.S. nei/U.S./credits.doc›.

- Does the institution place value on vocational track education?
- Is community service, a language component, internships, or study abroad required?
- Is the institution's transfer credit policy more conservative or more liberal?
- What are the minimum seat hours required compared to your various institutional course types (lab, practice, independent study)?
- Is the institution highly selective, with stringent admissions criteria?
- What type of academic calendar is employed, and what is the definition of full-time credit?

Each of these attributes of the institutional profile must be thoroughly understood when evaluating international credentials for comparability and best fit to the institution.

Evaluation Methodology

Some commonly accepted international transfer of credit practices include:

- Use professionally accepted resources and reference materials;
- Verify accreditation/recognition status of institution prior to conducting evaluation;
- Consider admissions requirements, length of program, program type, and credential/qualification requirements;
- Recognize there are no credential equivalencies, only comparable credentials; and
- Maintain evaluation policies and practices to encompass for inclusion the vast

variety of education systems, including periodic reviews.

Some guiding questions for new or unknown credentials include:
- What do you know about the foreign educational framework?
- Does this credential fit in the educational framework? If so, where?
- What is the language of instruction? What is the official national language?
- What is the level and type of program?
- What are the entrance requirements to the program?

There are two rudimentary methodological approaches to degree or credential assessment. The first method, year counting, requires the evaluator to compare the number of years to complete the foreign degree to the number of years to complete the U.S. degree. Typically, benchmark credentials are used; for example, high school diploma, first university degree, postgraduate degree, and terminal degree. The ultimate admissions decision results from this comparison. A popular example regarding year counting is the foreign three-year first university degree following the standard 12-year secondary education system. Using the year counting method, this first university degree does not meet graduate admissions requirements when compared to the U.S. system, which shares a similar 12-year secondary education system.

The second method used in comparing foreign degrees to the U.S. system is benchmarking academic credentials. In this method, a

113

high school diploma that leads to a bachelor's or first university degree would be comparable to the U.S. high school diploma regardless of years. This method would also recognize the foreign three-year diploma since the three-year degree is the foreign country's benchmarked credential for a bachelor's or first university degree and leads to graduate studies. This method bases the comparability upon the acceptance of a perception. It is the perception that completion of a credential in a foreign country provides a similar knowledge achievement as would be expected with the comparable U.S. credential.

Of the two methods highlighted, neither takes into consideration the actual accumulation of knowledge compared to the similar U.S. credential, which often creates a dilemma for admissions officers. As a result, many institutions (and private evaluation companies) apply a combination of the two methods in an attempt to balance the questions of equity. When a three-year bachelor's or first university degree is awarded, U.S. institutions do not equally accept it as comparable, though an 11-year secondary credential from the British system is typically accepted. This combination of methods usually begins by applying the year counting method. Sometimes, though, admissions officers discover logical questions or information discrepancies about the credential; in these cases, the benchmarking method is applied since it is likely unclear the number of years actually required for the undefined foreign credential.

For example, a foreign credential that indicates two years of study but does not clearly in-

dicate the credential name will require logical questioning to assist in determining the actual value of the credential. Applying the concept of logical questioning to a foreign credential begins by identifying what is the preceding credential in the education system and then identifying the credential following the foreign credential in question. Is this following credential a first university degree? Are entrance requirements defined? Is the curriculum from an external awarding body? These inquiries help define the foreign credential in question. Once it is clear where it resides within the education system, one may apply the evaluation methodology as outlined previously in this chapter. It is always a best practice to follow inquiries about a credential as far as deemed necessary. The more one learns about a credential, and the more this acquired knowledge is compared to other resources available, the more informed the admissions placement will be.

Admissions Placement

While central government bodies provide admissions placement recommendations in most countries, the U.S. government does not provide this service. The absence of this central body in the U.S. means the responsibility rests squarely on the admissions officer of each institution. That being said, institutions tend to follow common standards and practices when it comes to foreign credentials, but defining common standards remains one of the more basic challenges of foreign credential evaluation. This is exemplified in the theoretical situation of Alaska State University Alpha and Alaska State University Bravo below:

114

Alaska State University Alpha offers vocational and technical degree programs. Alaska State University Bravo offers teacher education degree programs. If a student with a German Apprenticeship credential applies to both universities, the common standard for Alpha may very well differ from Bravo. Alpha may define an apprenticeship program as a good fit, but Bravo may not, along with the majority of U.S. institutions that do not accept the German Apprenticeship credential.

In the past, professional bodies within the U.S. such as AACRAO, NAFSA, International Qualifications Assessment Service (IQAS), and American Council on Education (ACE) have made attempts to provide common standard recommendations. More recently some of these same bodies are moving away from defining common standards, allowing for the individual institution to draw its own evaluation conclusions that best match the institutional profile. Evaluation conclusions are judgments of the evaluator and therefore any definition of a foreign credential is an individual conclusion or recommendation, as emphasized by the National Association of Credential Evaluation Services (NACES) and the Association of International Credential Evaluators (AICE). Instead they are focusing on providing the best resources to assist the admissions officers in evaluating credentials consistently, thus placing the responsibility back upon the autonomous institutions.

Institutions, therefore, collect experiences, collegial discourse, and examples over time

and create their own definition of common standards. In doing so, it is important to utilize a few basic guiding inquiries: what is the type of credential, what credential precedes and follows the credential in question, and what are the admissions requirements for the credential? If possible, it may help to include data analysis of how students with this credential have fared academically in the U.S. system. Collecting and assessing this information leads to the establishment of sufficiently researched and supported institution-specific standards.

Accreditation

ACCREDITATION IN THE UNITED STATES

A critical component of due diligence is institutional accreditation or government recognition. U.S. tertiary institutions may obtain four types of accreditation through accrediting bodies recognized by either the U.S. Department of Education (USDE) or the Council for Higher Education Accreditation (CHEA). The types of accreditation available are regional, faith-based, private career, and programmatic. Though international institutions may seek U.S. accreditation, they do not receive oversight from any federal or state body.

CHEA and USDE recognize many of the same accrediting organizations, but not all. Accreditors seek CHEA or USDE recognition for different reasons. CHEA recognition confers an academic legitimacy on accrediting organizations, helping to solidify the place of these organizations and their institutions and programs in the national higher education community. USDE recognition is required for accreditors whose institutions or

115

programs seek eligibility for U.S. federal student aid funds.

Accreditation is an important indicator of quality for receiving institutions, especially in enabling transfer of credit. Other important attributes of accreditation include assuring quality, access to federal and state funds, and creating private sector confidence. International institutions require similar assurances of quality when receiving institutions consider credit transfer. They determine their recognition similarly to the U.S. process.

ACCREDITATION ABROAD

Determining institutional recognition outside the United States may occur in three primary ways: a government agency (*e.g.*, Ministry of Education, Ministry of Higher Education, University Grants Commission), an external authorizing body of the curriculum (*e.g.*, Scottish Qualification Authority, Credit Bank System Korea), or U.S. accreditation.

Government recognition is most easily determined by visiting the official government website. Many websites maintain a directory of recognized institutions, and some also maintain a list of fraudulent institutions. These can be listed via different categories: federal, state, polytechnic, private, or public institutions. Some further distinguish by type of college: independent, branch, or junior college.

The government recognition differs slightly in that the recognition is based upon the curriculum, not the institution. Institutions, conversely, are required to be identified as authorized centers to deliver the curriculum. The final assessment of grade results is conducted by the authorizing body. Typically the authorizing body provides a directory of approved centers on their website.

U.S. accreditation of a foreign institution is possible; however, only CHEA includes these institutions within their directory. USDE does not maintain a directory since it has no governance over these institutions. If a U.S. accreditation agency is identified as the accrediting body, it is important to ensure the accreditation is current. In addition, simply obtaining U.S. accreditation does not automatically indicate that an institution teaches exclusively in English, warranting any English language requirement exemptions. Each institution must carefully assess the official government language and language of instruction separately from accreditation.

IDENTIFYING UNRECOGNIZED PROGRAMS

Without this official recognition to confer degrees, students become at risk for the same challenges as those of a non-accredited U.S. institution. Of further consequence for any student carrying the U.S. degree achieved in combination with transfer credit awarded from non-accredited or unrecognized coursework is the greater risk of the degree not passing an audit by the receiving government. If transfer credit is awarded by your institution from a non-recognized institution, the receiving government is not required to recognize your institution's degree, even if your institution is fully accredited. For this reason it is vital to learn how to identify programs that do not carry any acceptable form of recognition or accreditation.

116

Programs without recognition of credential or qualification tend to have some common indicators, including:

- Lack of standard admissions criteria;
- Program completion does not grant eligibility for higher education;
- Do not identify education level;
- Large number of English courses included within the curriculum for non-English majors (*i.e.,* IELTS or TOEFL prep course, Business English, multiple reading, speaking, and writing courses);
- Do not show degree or graduation completion; may only be one semester to one year of coursework listed on a transcript; may offer a certificate instead of a diploma.

Without full disclosure of any of these standards, additional steps should be taken for verification (*see* Chapter Eleven, "Fighting Fraud: Verifying Credentials," on page 133).

Another vital aspect of any international admissions office involves establishing an institutional practice for verification of institutions or curricula beyond the scope of your institutional resources. The most effective manner of verification is to submit the transcript and degree credentials to the identified government body (*e.g.,* the Ministry of Education (MOE), Ministry of Higher Education, or Ministry of Research and Training). To determine the appropriate verification body, utilize country-specific government contacts, UNESCO IBE Country Education Profiles, or the U.S. State Department's EducationUSA. Official directories of recognized institutions are found within the MOE website, and the U.S. State Department's EducationUSA contacts are also an effective means of determining a good point of contact within the government for verifying credentials and/or programs. Other resources, such as AACRAO EDGE, include lists of institutions. Using more than one resource is advisable in the event of non-exhaustive and/or out-of-date lists.

Examples of recognized institutions include:

- An institute or college of a university found on either the MOE directory of independent colleges or the university's official directory of affiliated colleges/institutes; or
- An institution found on the approved center list of any recognized authorizing body or qualification; the approved curriculum is also listed within each approved center.

Examples of unrecognized institutions include:

- A college or institute that is not listed on the official MOE directory; or
- An affiliated college or institute that is identified as owner of curriculum, yet is not listed on the affiliate's official website.

Institutional Type

After gaining a better understanding of accredited/recognized versus unaccredited/unrecognized institutions, and how to verify institutions, it is essential to consider transfer credit implications. The ideal educational bodies to work with are accredited or government recognized institutions. Unaccred-

117

ited or unrecognized institutions may still provide opportunity for transfer credit (or articulation partnership) through external qualifications such as an industry standard or government vocational curriculum.

Institutions still in the candidacy stage of seeking accreditation constitute a gray area when evaluating transfer credit. This is an important scenario to have defined within institutional policy. Another gray area is loss of accreditation, which requires the evaluator to verify when the accreditation was lost and compare it to the student's attendance period. Options for credit include awarding credit for only those years of valid accreditation, or awarding the entire body of coursework regardless of the timing of lost accreditation as long as the student was continuously enrolled. The institution should also work with the accrediting body to better define its practice.

Evaluating Grades

The mechanism used to assess knowledge represents another critical aspect of the evaluation methodology process and how it relates to awarding transfer credit. Grades, as they are commonly referred to within the U.S. system, are as varied as educational systems. Grades display the level of proficiency in a subject or overall program by employing letters (A–F or H), numbers (0 to 4, and up), percentage (0–100%), or word descriptors (Excellent to Fail or Distinction to Pass Class). How to interpret these various grades is at the crux of credential evaluation. To establish a foundation of consistency, certain questions can be asked by an institution:

- Are foreign grades converted to the system of the receiving institution?
- Are grades weighted based upon coursework rigor or ranking of institution?
- Are individual institutional grade scales accepted or is only the government's approved grade model accepted?

Every country and institution chooses to handle the topic of grades differently. It is often stated that there is no incorrect way to handle grades as long as the method is consistent and meets one's institutional profile. However, certain known factors regarding grades should function as guidelines regardless of method chosen. Some countries have very forthright and specific grading scales, while the lack of oversight exercised by other countries, despite the existence of Ministry of Education-approved grading scales, sometimes results in the modification of grading scales by individual institutions. Grading systems may also be based upon institution or degree program, while others vary according to education level. Ultimately, though, the comparison is made to the U.S. four-point scale.

The U.S. four-point scale equates a pass with a grade of C or above; as a result, foreign grading systems using the concept of pass must not be automatically equated to the U.S. grade of D. A condoned pass within the U.S. four-point scale equates to a grade of C minus or below. The condoned pass indicates a passing grade but a grade not high enough to qualify for graduation. The concept of a D grade is very rare in foreign grading systems. The French 20-point system (where ten is

118

the pass grade, and eight or nine constitute a condoned pass as long as the overall semester average is ten or above) and the Indian system (where a predetermined percentage, usually less than 1 percent below the passable percentage, is a condoned pass) are two such rare examples. When converting to the U.S. four-point system, however, it is possible for a satisfactory pass within a foreign grading scale to equate to a condoned pass grade. For example, a 2.0 out of a 5.0 scale is a pass; however, if you compare it to the U.S. four-point scale, it does not equate to a 2.0 out of a 4.0 scale. It is worth repeating that pass is not automatically comparable to the U.S. grade of D.

Some systems require a higher passing percentage (*e.g.*, 70%) and others, a lower (*e.g.*, 50%). Seventy percent would be satisfactory within the U.S. four-point system because satisfactory signifies a grade eligible for graduation. Fifty would not be considered a condoned pass (ineligible for graduation) within the U.S. four-point system since this grade is comparable to below a 2.0 out of a four-point scale system. This, as a result, is not considered a satisfactory pass. If a system uses a three-tier level of grading, it easily fits within the U.S. system using the A, B, C model. Employing the U.S. system as a consistent guide along the way keeps the interpretation of foreign grading systems from proving too difficult or daunting.

Transfer Credit Evaluation

Armed with an understanding of the U.S. education system and the respective institution's profile, policies, and practices, awarding

transfer credit can begin. The three avenues transfer credit may derive from—foreign institutions, study abroad, and advanced standing—share four basic components of consideration: content and level of course, credit or course value, length of study, and credential type. Questions to ask when considering a credential for possible transfer credit include:

- How is the coursework reported?
- How are the subjects reported, as theory, practice, or both?
- What is the average course load in an academic year?
- What is the typical fulltime duration of the program?
- How many hours/units/subjects are required to complete the program?

Applicability Versus Transferability

The application of transfer credit involves a question of applicability versus transferability. Transferability is understood as meeting the minimum hour requirement (and any other transfer requirements set by the institution) for the course to be awarded in transfer. Applicability involves these same minimum requirements, in addition to course content matching that of another course required within the degree of study at the institution.

Some institutions confirm coursework as transferable but not applicable, meaning that the minimum requirements are met but the course (and content) just does not match any course requirement within the major. Some institutions will award elective credit for transferable courses but it does not apply to

119

the degree requirements. The coursework is reported on the transcript as transfer credit but remains unused.

Credential Type

Next, it is necessary to understand whether the credential is for a three-year diploma program, gap year, or exam-based coursework. This will help determine the length of study to deduce a comparable value to the U.S. system. Specifics such as how the coursework is reported (hours or units; semester or quarter credits) or not reported must be identified. It is crucial to recognize the various units of course measurement before proceeding with the conversion process to U.S. equivalency.

CONVERTING QUARTER AND SEMESTER CREDITS

Many foreign countries use credit systems of a higher value than the U.S., while others do not employ credits at all. The semester credit is the most common with 15 semester credits equaling the average number of credits carried in one U.S. semester, thus totaling 30 semester credits per academic year and 120 credits per U.S. four-year undergraduate program. To convert semester credits to quarter credits, multiply the number of semester credits by 1.5. Conversely, to convert from quarter credits to semester credits, divide the quarter credits by 1.5.

THE EUROPEAN CREDIT TRANSFER SYSTEM

Another popular form of credit reporting is the European Credit Transfer System (ECTS). This system arose upon establishment of the European Union and writing of the Bologna Process. The Bologna Process intends to create a common framework for all European Union countries, thus enabling ease of accessibility and mobility across borders. Having a common credit hour is of particular importance; however, it still requires conversion to U.S. credit. To do so, ECTS credits must be divided by 2 to provide the semester credit equivalent or multiplied by 0.75 to determine the quarter credit equivalency. Generally speaking, one ECTS credit is equal to 25–30 hours of work, and a U.S. semester credit is equal to 15 hours. As a result, it is valid to count the concept of the ECTS credit value as twice that of U.S. credit value. For example, 3 ECTS credits are equivalent to 1.5 semester credits or 2.25 quarter credits; 6 ECTS credits are equivalent to 3 semester credits or 4.5 quarter credits; and 180 ECTS credits are equal to 90 U.S. credits.

Course Content and Level

The course content and level constitutes another very important element in determining transfer credit. Whereas U.S. course descriptions may be easily accessible online and entirely in English, foreign institutions do not always provide course descriptions or syllabi. Even fewer offer the course descriptions in English. Requesting official course descriptions from the student as soon as possible is critical. Institutions are rarely unable to provide course descriptions, and in those cases an institutional policy must be established. Of specific consequence is determining if the receiving institution will allow the student to self-report content.

120

Course content is not only important in determining comparability of content, but it also may provide clues to defining another unique trait of the U.S. higher education system: course level, a descriptor not widely utilized in foreign education systems. Undergraduate U.S. courses are generally identified as lower or upper level, which typically applies to first- and second-year courses versus third- and fourth-year courses. It may also refer to the introductory courses in the program sequence leading to the capstone courses at the end of the program sequence.

Attempting to identify course level within foreign education systems may prove difficult; foreign systems do not always place emphasis on strict sequencing, making determining a level almost impossible. If, however, the institution requires some indication of level, ascertaining the length of the program and identifying any coursework from the first half of the program as lower level and the second half of the program as upper level is a possible solution. Institutions must be aware that this practice may not prove as accurate as it is simple and should use their best judgment. For a more foolproof practice, course descriptions or syllabi should be requested for faculty to assess competency queues and provide comparability to competencies required throughout the institution's program.

In addition to reporting course level, foreign institutions do not always assign course codes, so identifying a course based upon a course code number sequence may not be an option. Requesting a curriculum plan serves as another alternative to determining level in the absence of course codes; many times this will indicate Level One, Level Two, etc., for the length of the program.

Defining the expectation of course content and level within the institutional transfer policy guide will provide the foundation with which to work confidently in these unique cases.

Reporting Formats and U.S. Conversion

The final aspect of the transfer credit evaluation process involves determining the credential reporting type and then converting it to its U.S. institutional equivalent. Academic credentials come in various forms: transcripts, mark sheets, grade notes, exam results, or statement of results. Each one reports the proficiency of subjects attempted within a course of study. How this proficiency is demonstrated varies but the following forms are the most common: credit-based, hour-based, marks/grade-based, and subject/course-based. Below is a step-by-step approach to each of these forms to ensure the most accurate conversion technique.

It is of significance to the conversion process to remember a simple guideline: never award more transfer credit from a foreign institution within an equivalent length of study to the receiving institution. For example, if a foreign transcript reports 50 semester credits for one academic year of study and a typical U.S. institution does not require more than 30 semester credits, then the 50 semester credits must be converted accordingly so as not to award more than a matriculated student at

Table 2. U.S. Credit Hour Table

Length of Study	Semester Credit Value	Quarter Credit Value
Bachelor's Degree	120	180.0
One Year	30	45.0
One Semester	15	22.5
One Quarter	10	15.0
15 Lecture/Theory Hours	1	1.5
45–90 Lab Hours	1 semester	1.5 quarters
135–180 Practice/Independent Study Hours	1 semester	1.5 quarters

Table 3. Converting One Semester of Credits

Course	Credits	Conversion Factor	U.S. Credits
Math	6	0.63	3.78
Science	6	0.63	3.78
English	12	0.63	7.56
Total	**24**		**15**

the receiving institution would earn in an academic year. Ultimately, the goal of awarding transfer credit is to provide students an opportunity to progress in their studies, while also ensuring they are meeting the learning outcomes identified within the degree program. Table 2 illustrates the U.S. credit hour equivalencies and serves as a useful tool in the conversion process.

CREDIT-BASED CONVERSION

Converting foreign credits to the U.S. credit system requires dividing the equivalent study period of U.S. credits by the total foreign credits in the study period. This is the conversion factor, which is then multiplied with each individual foreign credit to equal the U.S. credit. For example, if the study period is defined as one semester, the equivalent U.S. credits are 15. The conversion factor is deter-

mined by dividing 15 by the total number of foreign credits. For example, if the total number of foreign credits is 24 it will result in a conversion factor of 0.63. Each individual foreign subject credit must then be multiplied by the conversion factor of 0.63, as demonstrated in Table 3.

HOUR-BASED CONVERSION

To convert foreign hours to U.S. credits, first add the total number of foreign hours per study period and then divide this into the equivalent total number of hours per study period at the receiving institution. This is the conversion rate. To determine the U.S. credits per course, multiply each foreign subject's course hours by the conversion rate. For the example in Table 4 (on page 123), the total foreign course hours are 115. Because the study period is determined in one semester, we know the U.S. equivalent study period is 15 credits. The 15 credits is divided by 115 to equal the conversion factor of 0.13, and then this conversion factor of 0.13 is multiplied by each individual foreign subject.

MARKS-BASED CONVERSION

To convert grade or marks-based credentials to U.S. credits, the conversion factor is determined by dividing the equivalent study period of U.S. credits by the total marks earned. Each

122

individual subject's mark is then multiplied by the conversion factor to equal the U.S. credits. In Table 5 the study period is identified as one year; since 30 credits are the U.S. equivalent in this study period, they are divided by the total marks earned, in this case 700. The resulting conversion factor of 0.043 is then multiplied with each subject grade to determine the U.S. credits.

Subject-Based Conversion

Converting subject-based credentials to U.S. credit requires determining the conversion factor. This is completed by dividing the equivalent study period of U.S. credits by the total number of subjects in the study period. The conversion factor determines the U.S. credits for each subject. In Table 6, the study period indicates one semester, so 15 U.S. credits are the equivalent. The total number of subjects in the same study period of one semester is three. The 15 U.S. credits are then divided by the three total subjects completed in the semester. The resulting conversion factor is five, and this indicates the number of U.S. credits for each subject.

In some cases, determining the study period is nearly impossible. Sometimes search-

Table 4. Converting One Semester of Hours

Course	Hours	Conversion Factor	U.S. Credits
Math	55	0.13	7.15
Science	60	0.13	7.80
Total	115	—	15

Table 5. Converting One Year of Grades

Course	Maximum	Conversion Factor	U.S. Credits
Math	100	0.043	4.30
Science	150	0.043	6.45
Hindi	200	0.043	8.60
English	100	0.043	4.30
History	150	0.043	6.45
Total	700	—	30

Table 6. Converting One Semester of Subjects

Course	Grade	Credits
Math	65	5
Science	70	5
History	84	5
Total	—	15

ing the institution's website will reveal the total program credits, units, and/or subjects. Other times, the study period should be defined as one subject and the conversion method applied subject by subject.

Understanding the conversion process for the various academic credential forms is a vital component of the transfer credit evaluation process. Once greater familiarity with these conversion techniques is obtained and used with foreign institutions, it will be easier to apply them with more confidence to study abroad, advanced standing, and English language coursework.

123

Study Abroad

For those study abroad experiences approved through an individual's own institution, the coursework is not considered transfer credit in nature. Some institutions choose to only offer experiences approved institutionally, therefore cutting out the need to take into account study abroad transfer credit. Others, though, allow students the opportunity to consider additional experiences beyond their home institutional offerings. It is in these cases that transfer credit would be evaluated using the same practice as that used for transfer credit coming from a foreign institution.

The study abroad provider may utilize a Home of Record (HOR), a common practice within the study abroad industry to facilitate unique programs outside of tertiary institutions to gain recognition and allow matriculated students the opportunity to obtain transfer credit for the experience. Often the HOR is a U.S. accredited institution providing faculty oversight of curriculum, teaching, or actual coursework. If this is the case, the transfer evaluation process immediately becomes more familiar and easier; however, for those study abroad programs where the HOR identified is not within the U.S. accreditation system, the evaluation methodology guidelines in determining institution and/or curriculum recognition as instructed earlier in this chapter should be followed.

Advanced Standing

Coursework completed beyond the secondary school benchmark credential, yet not while enrolled in a tertiary education institution or program, is referred to as Advanced Standing. Only a few recognized scenarios exist for secondary study to earn transfer credit: secondary school and college agreements, advanced curriculum, and coursework beyond the secondary school benchmark credential. Examples of this sort of coursework are the International Baccalaureate (IB), Caribbean Advanced Placement Exam (CAPE), Abitur (German 13th high school year, though you must verify when some German States changed to 12 year credential), three-year Indian Diploma in Engineering or GCE A Level (*see* Table 7, on page 125). A comparable U.S. example is Advanced Placement (AP) coursework developed by The College Board. Many of these examples require an additional year of study beyond the final required year of secondary education completion. Course rigor and length of study play a role in determining how much transfer credit is awarded. Of course institutions must assess and define the parameters of transfer credit awarded individually.

English as a Second Language (ESL) Courses

ESL courses are defined as developmental in nature, since often these courses are not taught at a level of comprehension required of curricular expectations within a U.S. English composition course. Various ways exist to handle ESL coursework in terms of potential transfer credit. Some institutions do not award any transfer credit, while others will award a limited number based upon level of course content. Still others will award any ESL coursework as either free or arts

Table 7. Advanced Standing Credentials

Country	Secondary Benchmark Credential	Number of Years to Complete	Advanced Standing Credential	Number of Years to Complete
Internationally Recognized	Various[1]	Various	IB	2
Caribbean Countries	CSEC-CXC, GCSE, BGCSE	2 (+ 3 years of lower secondary)	CAPE-CXC	1–2
Germany	Certificate of Maturity	6	Abitur[2]	1
India	SSC	2–3	Diploma in Engineering	3
Internationally Recognized	GCSE or previously GCE O Level	5	GCE A/AS Level	1–2

[1] Often, IB curriculum satisfies secondary school completion requirements in conjunction with one to two previous years of coursework
[2] Must verify when German States changed to 12 year credential, from 13 year, to consider transfer credit

and science electives or to fulfill language requirements. Again, a rule of thumb when considering awarding ESL coursework as comparable to a language requirement is to make sure it meets a similar level of content as any other language course offered at the receiving institution. English courses offered at foreign institutions located within countries where English is the official governmental language, as well as language of instruction, would not be considered ESL in nature. Every institution, however, must research and arrive at their conclusions regarding this topic.

Though industry standards do exist regarding each of these transfer credit possibilities, institutions reserve the right to set their individual standards.

Articulation Agreements

Once institutional standards in the form of transfer policy and practice have been established, it will be easier to approach articula-

tion agreements. It is necessary to ensure that these standards are applicable to both domestic and international articulation agreements. Increasingly the articulation agreement is becoming a more popular method to facilitate transfer credit. This method relies heavily upon the cultivation of relationships, thus demonstrating a correlation between strong relationships and successful agreements.

A first step in the creation of articulation agreements is recognizing each of the necessary components. It will become evident during the agreement process with a potential partner just how important it is to have a clear understanding of the make-up of an agreement. Requesting information and documentation correctly from the start not only saves time but also presents the institution in a favorable light; it demonstrates organization and motivation to find a quality partner. This will attract other well-positioned institutions. Conversely, if potential partner

125

institutions are slow or unwilling to provide necessary documentation, they are likely unprepared or unqualified for partnership.

The goal of requesting information and documentation is to acquire enough information to address the main components of an articulation agreement. The Statement of Agreement between institutions and degree programs identifies the potential programs for partnership. A clear degree pathway between the programs should be visible.

The program entrance requirements must include the English language requirements. Depending on the institution and the institutional English language policy, English language exemptions can function as a powerful marketing tool. It is also important to identify whether the partner institution's admissions requirements are similar to those of the receiving institution. If their admissions requirements are less stringent, it is advisable to address any concerns immediately to avoid surprises later. It will also be critical for the partner institution to communicate this effectively with any prospective students.

A clear statement of transfer policy requirements is a crucial component of any agreement. This includes the use of any external curriculum by the partner institution. It is not always clear to prospective students that coursework outside of the approved external curriculum may not be applicable for transfer credit. When conducting the initial evaluation of the partner institution and their curriculum, pay particular attention to the ownership of the curriculum. If the institution uses an external authorizing body's

curriculum, then it must be stated within the agreement. The institution must also be verified as an authorized center to administer the curriculum. This verification may be completed online in some cases or by contacting the authorizing body directly.

The essence of the agreement is the actual course-for-course equivalencies (or block statement of transfer). This should be presented in clean and clear tables demonstrating the correspondences between the coursework from each institution. If an institution will utilize block transfer, then the transfer credit will vary slightly in presentation. A table will be necessary to list the coursework of the partner institution the receiving institution is willing to accept towards a finite amount of study time (*i.e.,* one year or two years). Block transfer is seen as a cleaner approach to articulation agreements as it lacks the tedious work of matching individual courses; however, it requires that the receiving institution conduct thorough research of the partner institution's curriculum to ensure the coursework and objectives meet the compulsory learning outcomes of your institution. Accreditation requirements must always be at the forefront in terms of learning outcome deliverables.

A table listing the remaining coursework towards the degree to be completed at the receiving institution is useful. Often, the partner institution will request a general estimation of amount of time to complete the program. Be sure to state this estimation in such a manner that allows flexibility of student performance and course offerings, as well as indicating whether the estimation includes or excludes any English language requirements. This separate table is also necessary to include if using the block transfer credit model.

Even though the curriculum evaluation is the body of the agreement, a statement of degree completion and inclusion of the academic good standing policy is invaluable because of the different requirements and expectations of degree completion and academic good standing in each educational system. An online link may be provided or the policy spelled out within the body of the agreement to ensure it is read and understood. When choosing to simply provide a link to the online catalog or location of the policy, it should be specifically discussed with the partner institution to highlight any significant differences. This will decrease the chance of any surprises or difficult situations with prospective students.

How does an institution both seek out and attract quality partners? Many institutions debate which model is more effective: signing many agreements in an effort to create many avenues of approach or being more selective to theoretically be more active and productive. This discussion will need to be had within your institution, and it ideally would happen before committing to any major scale articulation initiative. Some things to consider when determining quality articulation partners include:

- Targeted geographical area for recruiting purposes
- Seek a specific curriculum (*e.g.*, Edexcel/SQA)
- Seek specific degree programs (*i.e.*, to match your institutional offerings)

- History of strong faculty collaboration (*e.g.*, research, faculty exchange)
- Similar institutional scope, brand, and size

Having identified the model, the next step is to begin creating an ideal institutional profile. Three possible profiles follow; ultimately, there is no right or wrong method.

- Placing emphasis on degree areas (*e.g.*, STEM) to increase enrollment in key areas or supplement declining areas
- Focusing on diversity within the institutions' international population by targeting partner institutions in specific geographical areas or countries
- Increasing institutional brand by seeking partnerships with institutions recognized in key areas

Each of the above models is self-explanatory in nature; however, key variables within these models require greater attention. Even when deciding to emphasize a specific degree area, the quality of institution for collaboration or the nature of the institution (*e.g.*, a research or teaching institution) must be determined. Whether the size and scope of institution is important, or if these are negotiable is another important aspect to consider. Though not always possible, finding a partner institution which speaks to all or as many of the key components of these three models is the best solution.

It is essential to identify a clear degree pathway with the partner institution. An associate degree or a comparable diploma program

127

Table 8. When to Use an Articulation Agreement vs. an MOU

Articulation	MOU
Handshake agreement that has grown over time	Handshake agreement, on paper
Focused statement of collaboration, with specifics	General statement of collaboration, no specifics
Course-for-course equivalencies, block transfer	General statement of program interests and admission preferences

that would lead into the receiving institution's bachelor's degree, or another bachelor's degree program that shares a common curriculum are examples of how to ensure a degree pathway. Partner institutions wish to see their curriculum valued, while simultaneously assisting their students to progress reasonably in the degree at the transfer institution.

Occasionally, after completing the curriculum evaluation and partner institution review, it becomes clear that the institution is not the best fit for the needs of the receiving institution; however, maintaining the partnership in some degree remains valuable. In this case, a less binding agreement, such as the standard and universally recognized Memorandum of Understanding (MOU) may be something to consider. This option allows for mutual support and dialogue between institutions over a period of time. The look of a MOU may vary; for example, students being accepted to the transfer institution with the application fee waived or the partner institution inviting the receiving institution's faculty to their campus for a workshop or co-teaching opportunity. The MOU exists as a vehicle to cultivate new relationships and potentially lead to articulation agreements (*See* Table 8).

These variables and options take time to research and prioritize, and they may look different from one department or college to another within an institution. Formulating articulation agreements is time-consuming, but this time is critical to the effectiveness of any agreement. It is important to minimize unnecessary delays or misdirection.

Conclusion

International transfer credit evaluation and methodology is an exciting and ever-evolving field within international education. Success will be found by remembering throughout the entire process that transfer credit evaluation and methodology is a fluid, subjective art and science. In applying the theories, techniques and models shared within this chapter, trends in methodology will emerge which may be applied to similar credentials. For those new to the field, it is advisable to create a system to save unique and challenging credential examples. This will establish a working resource within the institution. Consistency and due diligence are the constants in a field of constant change.

The importance of a robust resource collection cannot be understated. Many professional associations offer some sort of resource center; some are free to access, but the majority have a fee. *See* Table 9 for examples. The AACRAO Electronic Database for Global Education (EDGE) is a comprehensive fee-

Table 9. Professional Resources for the International Transfer Credit Evaluator

Resource	Website
AACRAO EDGE	http://edge.aacrao.org/info.php
Association of International Credential Evaluators, Inc (AICE)	www.aice-eval.org
Council for Higher Education Accreditation	www.chea.org
The College Board Advanced Placement	http://apcentral.collegeboard.com
International Qualifications Assessment Service (IQAS)	http://work.alberta.ca/Immigration/international-education-guides.html
National Association of Credential Evaluation Services (NACES)	http://naces.org/faq.htm
NAFSA : Association of International Educators *(Search Online Guide to Educational Systems Around the World)*	www.nafsa.org
National Center for Education Statistics	http://nces.ed.gov
UK NARIC	www.ecctis.co.uk/NARIC/
UNESCO IBE Country Education Profile	www.ibe.unesco.org/en/worldwide/unesco-regions.html
U.S. Department of Education, International Affairs Office	www2.ed.gov/about/offices/list/ous/international/usnei/us/credits.doc
U.S.NEI, International Affairs Office-UDE	www2.ed.gov/about/offices/list/ous/international/usnei/edlite-index.html
U.S. State Department, EducationUSA Advising	www.educationusa.info/help/research.php

based online database, though there are others as well. More than one resource should be utilized for an industry perspective. It is also useful to gauge the industry continuum for any given credential. This will allow determination of an institution-specific definition with confidence.

129

CHAPTER ELEVEN

Fighting Fraud:
Verifying Credentials

ANN M. KOENIG

Associate Director,
AACRAO International Education Services

ED DEVLIN

Evaluator,
AACRAO International Education Services

Fighting Fraud: Verifying Credentials

The education sector is no stranger to fraud. Although professionals in the field of education prefer to think that our environment is safe from fraud and misrepresentation, the reality is that fraud involving our institutions has occurred, is about to occur, or is in progress. Fraud in education can take many forms among students, instructors, administrators, and other members of the institutional community, including cheating, plagiarism, academic and professional misconduct, misuse of the institution's name, misrepresentation of the institution, and credential fraud. AACRAO has published several resources on fraud as it relates to the admissions and enrollment management environment (*see* "Resources on Fraud" at the end of this chapter).

Common Types of Document Fraud

The most common types of document-related fraud seen by the admissions and registrar's offices are incomplete or misleading applications for admissions, altered or fabricated academic documentation, intentionally-mis-

leading English translations of documents from foreign institutions, counterfeit transcripts and documents from real educational institutions, documentation from fictitious or bogus universities or colleges that sell "degrees" (so-called diploma or degree mills), and documents from bogus accreditation bodies that often operate in tandem with degree mills. Transfer credit evaluators should be especially vigilant when reviewing transcripts for prior education. If the documentation is from an institution in the United States, it is imperative to confirm the accreditation status of the institution, and require that the documentation be received directly from the institution, without having passed through the applicant's hands. When reviewing documentation from institutions outside of the United States, evaluators need to verify the recognition status of each institution in the context of the country's educational system, confirm the level and type of education completed, and ensure that the documents presented are authentic.

133

Document Fraud in Transfer Admissions

The value of any product reflects the demand for that product. In an environment in which education is seen as a product, the market value of education increases as demand grows. When access to education is limited or removed, or when authentic academic documentation is not available, an opportunity for fraud is created.

Certain conditions can limit access to education or authentic academic documentation. Globally we usually think of such things as natural disasters, war, political crises, economic disasters, and social upheaval. We must keep abreast of current events so that we can give informed and careful consideration to applications from individuals who have been affected by such conditions. We need to be familiar with resources that can confirm information about these types of conditions and give suggestions as to how to handle these cases.

But another significant factor related to transfer admissions is an individual's educational history, such as an applicant with outstanding debt at a previous institution who cannot get official transcripts; an applicant who never received a high school diploma; an applicant who may have an insufficient grade average for admission or lack prerequisite courses for a particular program at the receiving institution; an executive who has advanced professionally without commensurate formal education. All of these situations might lead an individual to resort to presenting fraudulent credentials in the transfer process.

The thread that connects all of these scenarios is the desire to gain access to education. Academic credentials have become a commodity in the world market. The proliferation of fraudulent documents has, of course, been fueled by the development of the Internet and e-commerce. Be it counterfeit transcripts from real institutions, replacement transcripts and diplomas from replica services, or novelty degrees from degree mills "accredited" by bogus accreditors, it is the *commerce* in e-commerce that is driving the growth of this industry. In short: Degrees = dollars. What sells in this milieu is the name recognition and reputation of your institution and every other school whose name or logo appears on fraudulent documentation, or that becomes a victim of this type of fraud.

Degree Mills, Accreditation Mills, and Bogus Foreign Credential Evaluation Services

A diploma mill or degree mill is an entity that produces and sells documents that appear to be academic credentials (diplomas, degrees, transcripts) from what appear to be universities or colleges, but in reality are academically worthless documents from fictitious educational institutions that represent inappropriately little academic work or none at all. These documents are meant to give the impression of academic achievement, but in reality they are purchased papers that have no academic value.

Many of these bogus entities purport to be foreign universities. An applicant from the United States with no other foreign educational background might present a degree and

134

transcript that appear to have been issued by a "university" in London, an obscure island, a small Swiss town, or other unusual location. The evaluator must review and research these documents carefully. A typical mode of operation for these entities is to claim to be a university in a country outside of the United States, while the operators themselves may be located in the United States, in another country, or even have different parts of the process located in several different countries.

In *Degree Mills: The Billion-Dollar Industry That Has Sold Over a Million Fake Diplomas, Updated Edition* (2012), John Bear and Allen Ezell outline a well-known diploma mill ring called the University Degree Program (UDP), an operation masterminded by a rabbi from New York, with sales pitches in the U.S. for "British degrees" made by telephone from a boiler room in Bucharest, Romania, and using mail-forwarding services in Ireland, diplomas printed in Israel, and banking in Cyprus. The book lists three dozen known fictitious university names used by the UDP. If one takes a comparative look at the documents from these "universities," one can see that they all have the same format, and essentially the same content, including signatures of the same administrators, except for differences in the purchaser's name, the name and date of the degree, and course titles on the transcript, depending on the field of study. They are based on a template used by UPD for the university name it uses. There have been many spin-offs of this operation as former employees have started their own diploma mill businesses. (*See* Figure 4, on page 136.)

Accreditation mills represent a related area of fraud. Some diploma mills use claims of accreditation to sell their "degrees." It used to be more common for diploma mills to speak disparagingly of accreditation and state in their descriptive materials that they did not need accreditation, did not "agree with the philosophy" of accreditors, or otherwise were somehow exempt from or above the notion of accreditation. It appears that in the last decade or so, diploma mills have found that embracing the concept of accreditation can pay off. Some not only create their own bogus accreditors to try to add to the appearance of legitimacy of the "university," but also sell this bogus accreditation to other bogus entities. Instead of decrying accreditation, they have created ways to make it more lucrative.

Some diploma mill operations are large fraud rings that also produce other types of fraudulent documents, such as driver's licenses, Social Security cards, and other identification documents. Many offer associated "student services," including transcript verification, foreign credential evaluation, and even alumnae associations. By calling a toll-free telephone number, the bogus documents can be "verified," the accreditation of the "university" can be confirmed, and the "graduate" can receive an "evaluation" of the foreign transcript showing that the degree is equivalent to a U.S. degree. These services are offered by the same people who set up the fraudulent diploma operation.

This was the case with the St. Regis University diploma mill operation. The masterminds and agents behind this organization,

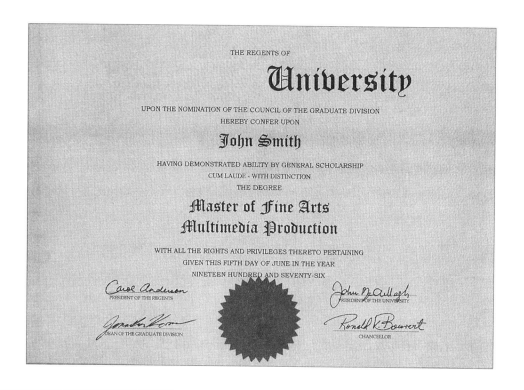

Figure 4. Diploma Mill Degree Template

who operated in Washington State, Idaho, and Arizona, created virtual universities and even high schools claiming to offer distance education from Liberia and recognition by the Liberian Ministry of Education. They created a bogus Liberian embassy website that showed that these schools were recognized and accredited by an equally-fictitious Liberian National Board of Education. This was accomplished by bribing a Liberian embassy official in Washington, DC. In addition, they offered many student services and also provided a foreign credential evaluation service to give the degrees U.S. degree equivalencies. It was the tenacity of researchers such as Professor George Gollin of the University of Illinois and federal law enforcement agen-

cies, combined with the hubris of the operators, that brought this operation down.

A copy of a Bachelor of Science in Nursing issued by St. Regis University, shown in Figure 9 (on page 141), was presented to a major state university in the United States by a freshman applicant to its undergraduate nursing program. The same applicant also presented documents showing a Master of Business Administration in Healthcare Management, Doctor of Education in Healthcare Business Administration, and a Full Professorship in Healthcare Business Administration, all issued by St. Regis University. The U.S. university's admissions office contacted AACRAO International Education Services for assistance and rightly wondered why an

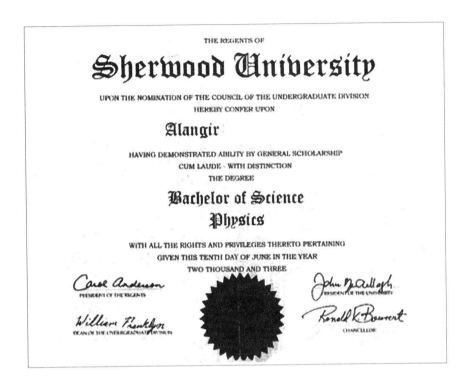

THE REGENTS OF

Sherwood University

UPON THE NOMINATION OF THE COUNCIL OF THE UNDERGRADUATE DIVISION
HEREBY CONFER UPON

Alangir

HAVING DEMONSTRATED ABILITY BY GENERAL SCHOLARSHIP
CUM LAUDE · WITH DISTINCTION
THE DEGREE

Bachelor of Science
Physics

WITH ALL THE RIGHTS AND PRIVILEGES THERETO PERTAINING
GIVEN THIS TENTH DAY OF JUNE IN THE YEAR
TWO THOUSAND AND THREE

Figure 5. Diploma Mill Degree, Sample 1

individual with such qualifications would apply to an undergraduate nursing program as a freshman. Also presented by the applicant was a copy of the fictitious Accreditation Certificate for Saint Regis University from the fictitious Liberian National Board of Education, shown in Figure 10 (on page 142).

Assessing Transcript Legitimacy

How can the transcript evaluator determine whether an institution is a real, recognized, and legitimately-accredited educational institution that really teaches and awards recognized educational credentials? A key aspect of evaluating degrees and transcripts is understanding the way in which diploma mills work; namely, by imitating legitimate activity. The following are potential signs of a diploma mill:

- **Name:** The institution has a distinguished or traditional name, or a name similar to a well-known or legitimate institution;
- **Location:** The university has a website but no physical address, or there is conflicting information about a physical location;
- **Foreign:** It gives the impression of being a foreign university, but may be operating from a different location (*see* "Location");
- **Internet Address:** It may use "edu," "ac," or "uk" in its URL, giving the impression of being a U.S. or British educational institution;
- **Contact:** No contact information is given. The only way to contact the university is via the website;

137

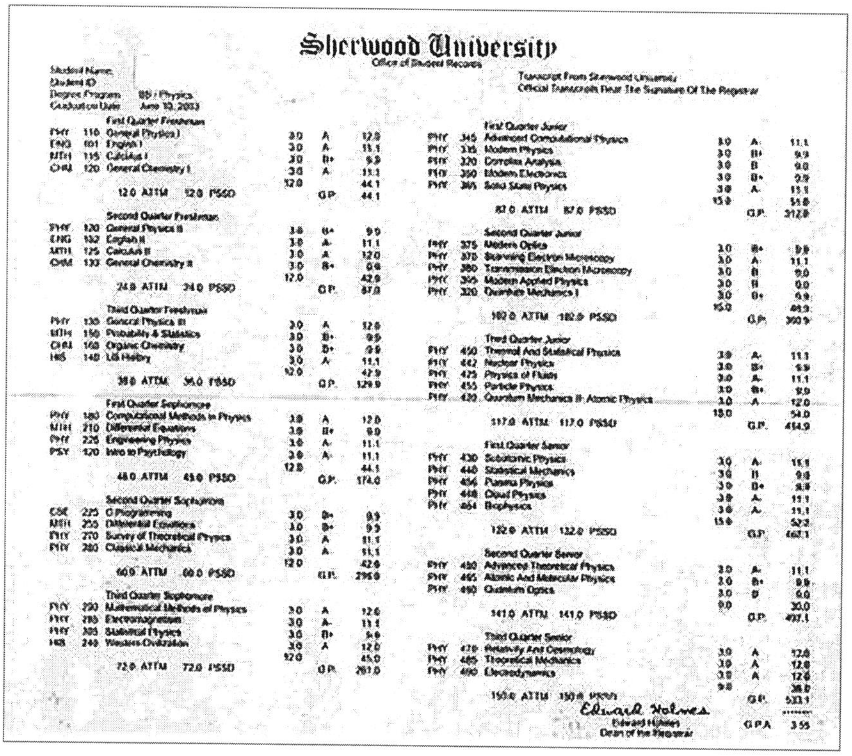

Sherwood University
Office of Student Records

Student Name:
Student ID:
Degree Program: BS / Physics
Graduation Date: June 10, 2013

Transcript From Sherwood University
Official Transcripts Bear The Signature Of The Registrar

		First Quarter Freshman			
PHY	110	General Physics I	3.0	A	12.0
ENG	101	English I	3.0	A-	11.1
MTH	115	Calculus I	3.0	B+	9.9
CHM	120	General Chemistry I	3.0	A-	11.1
			12.0		44.1
		12.0 ATTM 12.0 PSSD		G.P.	44.1
		Second Quarter Freshman			
PHY	120	General Physics II	3.0	B+	9.9
ENG	102	English II	3.0	A-	11.1
MTH	125	Calculus II	3.0	A	12.0
CHM	130	General Chemistry II	3.0	B+	9.9
			12.0		42.9
		24.0 ATTM 24.0 PSSD		G.P.	87.0
		Third Quarter Freshman			
PHY	130	General Physics III	3.0	A	12.0
MTH	150	Probability & Statistics	3.0	B+	9.9
CHM	160	Organic Chemistry	3.0	B+	9.9
HIS	140	US History	3.0	A-	11.1
			12.0		42.9
		36.0 ATTM 36.0 PSSD		G.P.	129.9
		First Quarter Sophomore			
PHY	180	Computational Methods in Physics	3.0	A	12.0
MTH	210	Differential Equations	3.0	B+	9.9
PHY	225	Engineering Physics	3.0	A-	11.1
PSY	120	Intro to Psychology	3.0	A-	11.1
			12.0		44.1
		48.0 ATTM 48.0 PSSD		G.P.	174.0
		Second Quarter Sophomore			
CSE	225	C Programming	3.0	B+	9.9
MTH	255	Differential Equations	3.0	B+	9.9
PHY	270	Survey of Theoretical Physics	3.0	A-	11.1
PHY	280	Classical Mechanics	3.0	A-	11.1
			12.0		42.0
		60.0 ATTM 60.0 PSSD		G.P.	216.0
		Third Quarter Sophomore			
PHY	290	Mathematical Methods of Physics	3.0	A	12.0
PHY	285	Electromagnetism	3.0	A-	11.1
PHY	305	Statistical Physics	3.0	B+	9.9
HIS	240	Western Civilization	3.0	A	12.0
			12.0		45.0
		72.0 ATTM 72.0 PSSD		G.P.	261.0
		First Quarter Junior			
PHY	345	Advanced Computational Physics	3.0	A-	11.1
PHY	335	Modern Physics	3.0	B+	9.9
PHY	320	Complex Analysis	3.0	B	9.0
PHY	350	Modern Electronics	3.0	B+	9.9
PHY	365	Solid State Physics	3.0	A-	11.1
			15.0		51.0
		87.0 ATTM 87.0 PSSD		G.P.	312.0
		Second Quarter Junior			
PHY	375	Modern Optics	3.0	B+	9.9
PHY	370	Scanning Electron Microscopy	3.0	A-	11.1
PHY	380	Transmission Electron Microscopy	3.0	B	9.0
PHY	395	Modern Applied Physics	3.0	B	9.0
PHY	320	Quantum Mechanics I	3.0	B+	9.9
			15.0		48.9
		102.0 ATTM 102.0 PSSD		G.P.	360.9
		Third Quarter Junior			
PHY	450	Thermal And Statistical Physics	3.0	A-	11.1
PHY	442	Nuclear Physics	3.0	B+	9.9
PHY	425	Physics of Fluids	3.0	A-	11.1
PHY	455	Particle Physics	3.0	B+	9.9
PHY	420	Quantum Mechanics II: Atomic Physics	3.0	A	12.0
			15.0		54.0
		117.0 ATTM 117.0 PSSD		G.P.	414.9
		First Quarter Senior			
PHY	430	Subatomic Physics	3.0	A-	11.1
PHY	440	Statistical Mechanics	3.0	B	9.0
PHY	456	Plasma Physics	3.0	B+	9.9
PHY	448	Cloud Physics	3.0	A-	11.1
PHY	464	Biophysics	3.0	A-	11.1
			15.0		52.2
		132.0 ATTM 132.0 PSSD		G.P.	467.1
		Second Quarter Senior			
PHY	450	Advanced Theoretical Physics	3.0	A-	11.1
PHY	465	Atomic And Molecular Physics	3.0	B+	9.9
PHY	490	Quantum Optics	3.0	D	6.0
			9.0		30.0
		141.0 ATTM 141.0 PSSD		G.P.	497.1
		Third Quarter Senior			
PHY	470	Relativity And Cosmology	3.0	A	12.0
PHY	485	Theoretical Mechanics	3.0	A	12.0
PHY	490	Electrodynamics	3.0	A	12.0
			9.0		36.0
		150.0 ATTM 150.0 PSSD		G.P.	533.1
				GPA	3.55

Edward Holmes
Edward Holmes
Dean of the Registrar

Figure 6. Diploma Mill Transcript, Sample 1

- **Accreditation or Recognition:** The website includes false, misleading, or meaningless claims of accreditation, recognition, affiliation, membership, or other types of status that are meant to give the impression of legitimacy, but really mean nothing in the legitimate higher education community;
- **Speedy Degrees:** The amount of time required to obtain the degree is suspiciously fast. A large number of credits, or the entire "degree," might be given based on "life experience" only, with the option to "send your résumé and receive a degree";
- **Costs:** The website shows a price list, or "lump sum" prices for the various degrees and transcripts. Different rates might be charged for including specific courses, grades, or majors on the transcript;
- **Sample Documents:** The website shows samples of diplomas and transcripts;
- **Network of Diploma Mills:** Several bogus universities may operate from the same computer or network. Researching the IP addresses behind domain names may yield valuable results in investigating a university's true identity;
- **Support Services:** Diploma mills often set up their own verification services available through a toll-free telephone number; the people answering the phone to verify are

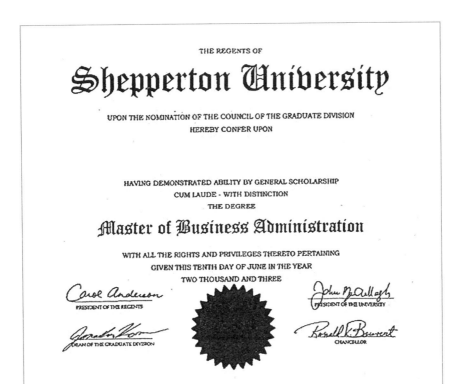

THE REGENTS OF

Shepperton University

UPON THE NOMINATION OF THE COUNCIL OF THE GRADUATE DIVISION
HEREBY CONFER UPON

HAVING DEMONSTRATED ABILITY BY GENERAL SCHOLARSHIP
CUM LAUDE - WITH DISTINCTION
THE DEGREE

Master of Business Administration

WITH ALL THE RIGHTS AND PRIVILEGES THERETO PERTAINING
GIVEN THIS TENTH DAY OF JUNE IN THE YEAR
TWO THOUSAND AND THREE

PRESIDENT OF THE REGENTS

PRESIDENT OF THE UNIVERSITY

DEAN OF THE GRADUATE DIVISION

CHANCELLOR

Figure 7. Diploma Mill Degree, Sample 2

the same ones who sold the degree. The entity might offer foreign credential evaluation and apostille services if the institution purports to be foreign; and

- **Advertising:** Diploma mills have included advertisements in well-respected publications, popular tabloids, comic books, and electronic media.

Counterfeit Academic Documents from Real Institutions

Applicants might also present documents from a real institution, in the United States or abroad, that were not actually issued by that institution. Counterfeit academic documents

are produced and sold for the same reasons that counterfeit money exists: educational credentials are currency. In his book *Counterfeit Diplomas and Transcripts* (AACRAO 2008), fraud expert Allen Ezell presents information on at least three dozen online vendors that sell counterfeit transcripts from real educational institutions in the United States and around the world. The book also includes a list of over 80 websites selling counterfeit Russian and Ukrainian educational credentials, and describes the large-scale counterfeit document industry in China. A table in the book shows a comparison of the characteristics of a genuine University of Florida

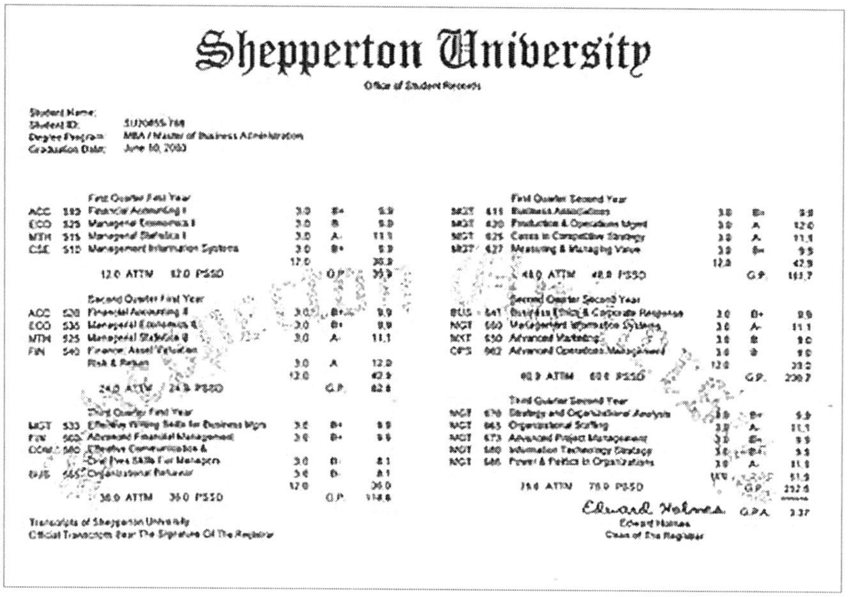

Shepperton University

Office of Student Records

Student Name:
Student ID: 5120855-788
Degree Program: MBA / Master of Business Administration
Graduation Date: June 10, 2003

First Quarter First Year

ACC	503	Financial Accounting I	3.0	B+	9.9
ECO	525	Managerial Economics I	3.0	B	9.0
MTH	515	Managerial Statistics I	3.0	A-	11.1
CSE	510	Management Information Systems	3.0	B+	9.9
			12.0		39.9
		12.0 ATTM 12.0 PSSD		G.P.	39.9

Second Quarter First Year

ACC	520	Financial Accounting II	3.0	B+	9.9
ECO	535	Managerial Economics II	3.0	B+	9.9
MTH	525	Managerial Statistics II	3.0	A-	11.1
FIN	540	Finance: Asset Valuation Risk & Return	3.0	A	12.0
			12.0		42.9
		24.0 ATTM 24.0 PSSD		G.P.	82.8

Third Quarter First Year

MGT	533	Effective Writing Skills for Business Mgrs	3.0	B+	9.9
FIN	560	Advanced Financial Management	3.0	B+	9.9
COM	580	Effective Communication & One Two Skills For Managers	3.0	B-	8.1
BUS	565	Organizational Behavior	3.0	B-	8.1
			12.0		36.0
		36.0 ATTM 36.0 PSSD		G.P.	118.8

First Quarter Second Year

MGT	611	Business Associations	3.0	B-	8.1
MGT	620	Production & Operations Mgmt	3.0	A	12.0
MGT	625	Cases in Competitive Strategy	3.0	A-	11.1
MGT	627	Measuring & Managing Value	3.0	B+	9.9
			12.0		42.9
		48.0 ATTM 48.0 PSSD		G.P.	161.7

Second Quarter Second Year

BUS	641	Business Ethics & Corporate Response	3.0	B+	9.9
MGT	660	Management Information Systems	3.0	A-	11.1
MKT	650	Advanced Marketing	3.0	B	9.0
OPS	662	Advanced Operations Management	3.0	B	9.0
			12.0		39.0
		60.0 ATTM 60.0 PSSD		G.P.	200.7

Third Quarter Second Year

MGT	670	Strategy and Organizational Analysis	3.0	B+	9.9
MGT	665	Organizational Staffing	3.0	A-	11.1
MGT	673	Advanced Project Management	3.0	B+	9.9
MGT	680	Information Technology Strategy	3.0	B+	9.9
MGT	686	Power & Politics in Organizations	3.0	A-	11.1
			15.0		51.9
		75.0 ATTM 75.0 PSSD		G.P.	252.6

Edward Holmes
Edward Holmes
Dean of the Registrar

G.P.A. 3.37

Transcripts of Shepperton University
Official Transcripts Bear The Signature Of The Registrar

Figure 8. Diploma Mill Transcript, Sample 2

transcript with the features of counterfeit University of Florida transcripts produced by three vendors of fake transcripts.

Vendors of counterfeit transcripts, diplomas, and recommendation letters may advertise the documents as replacements, replicas, or novelty items, and issue disclaimers that they are not responsible for the consequences of attempts by customers to present the documents as real. Some use the wording "fake transcript" and "fake diploma" throughout the text of their websites. Often the websites include samples of the documents available, testimonials about the quality and usefulness of the documents, and special offers. Some indicate which institutions' transcripts are *not* available; often they are schools who have taken some level of legal action against the supplier, such as a "cease and desist" warning.

High School Documents and Fraud

Fraud in education is not limited to the higher education sector. The answer to the frequently asked question of whether fraud in education also applies to the high school level is, unfortunately, a resounding "yes." This means that admissions officers and transfer evaluators at higher education institutions must also be vigilant about potentially fraudulent high school or secondary school documents.

Although it appears that there is less fraud connected with high school level documenta-

Figure 9. Diploma Mill Degree, Sample 3

tion, when it comes to the benefits that one can gain from presenting fraudulent high school transcripts, "diplomas = dollars" is still the standard. Consider the case of any individual who has not actually completed high school or secondary school in the United States or abroad, and thus is shut out from many types of jobs or education/training programs. Or the person who has completed secondary school in a different country, but is constantly asked for a high school diploma or GED by people in the United States and is not aware of the existence of qualified foreign credential evaluators. Or the high school athlete who is talented in his/her sport but does not have the academic ability for college admission. Or the

high school coach whose star athlete cannot pass the state's high school graduation examination. Imagine the possible results of one of these scenarios when the individual discovers that it is possible to buy a high school diploma or GED online. It may seem far-fetched or desperate to those of us who work at the level of higher education, but high school documentation has a market value, too.

Protecting Your Institution: Best Practice in Document Review and Verification

Many of the transcripts and documents seen by most admissions offices and transfer credit evaluators come from institutions that are fa-

Figure 10. Diploma Mill Accreditation Certificate

miliar to them, either institutions in the local area, institutions with which there are admissions or articulation agreements in place, or an institution with history as a feeder institution to a particular program at the receiving institution. But what is the best approach when a transcript or document from an unfamiliar institution lands on your desk or computer screen? How can you confirm whether an unfamiliar institution is legitimate? How can you determine whether the documentation is authentic and really reflects actual bona fide work done by the applicant? And how can you protect your institution's documents from becoming a victim of this type of academic credential fraud?

A proactive posture is paramount. Awareness of the problem is crucial, as well as vigilance in following a methodical approach to document review that includes a spectrum of verification processes, from the use of standard procedures and resources to confirm information on transcripts, to written requests for document authentication if questions arise. Professional development and collegial support are also key elements: a solid knowledge base among admissions and transcript evaluation staff, continuing development of that knowledge base, and a strong network of information sharing about document fraud and verification successes.

In reviewing academic documentation, it is essential to take a methodical, consistent approach, and apply it in every case. The following outline presents step-by-step guidance to best practice in assembling, reviewing, researching, and seeking verification of documents. Following these practical guidelines will help safeguard your institution against fraud.

Document Review: A Step-by-Step Approach

STEP 1: ASSEMBLE THE DOCUMENTATION RECEIVED FOR THE FILE. IS IT COMPLETE? IF NOT, WHAT IS MISSING AND NEEDS TO BE REQUESTED?

The keys to actually *receiving* complete application files that include all the necessary documentation are to *know what you need to receive* and then *communicate to applicants what is required* in a precise, clear manner that is upfront and as early as possible in the application process. For international applicants, using indigenous terminology for the foreign academic documentation is very helpful. In all applicant information, clearly define the consequences to the applicant if incomplete, untrue, or falsified information or documentation is submitted, and require applicants to confirm by signature that they understand this policy.

STEP 2: IDENTIFY AND LOCATE RELIABLE RESOURCES TO HELP YOU REVIEW THE DOCUMENTATION.

AACRAO and other professional associations provide excellent opportunities to learn about and develop admissions and transcript evalu-ation resources. To research U.S. institutions, the regional accrediting associations' institutional directories and the AACRAO's *Transfer Credit Practices*[11] are good starting points. To research institutions outside of the United States and the educational systems and documentation practices of other countries, one can use AACRAO EDGE[12] and other resources compiled and developed by AACRAO International Education Services[13] and the international education community.

STEP 3: READ AND REVIEW EACH DOCUMENT CAREFULLY.

- Arrange the documents in chronological order and reconstruct the applicant's "life story" using biographical data, the educational history and the academic documents.
  - ▶ Does the person's educational history appear sequential?
  - ▶ Does it appear that the applicant met the admission requirements for each program? If not, on what basis might the applicant have been admitted to the program, or completed the credential?
  - ▶ Where are the educational institutions attended by the applicant located? Do the locations match the student's life story?
  - ▶ Does the applicant's employment history or current employment situation seem logical or consistent in comparison to the academic history?

---

[11] *See* ‹http://tcp.aacrao.org›.

[12] *See* ‹http://edge.aacrao.org›.

[13] *See* ‹http://ies.aacrao.org›.

143

- Inspect the documents themselves. Pay careful attention to:
  - ▸ Your first impression: Is this an institution you have heard of? Is this a U.S. institution? Is it a foreign institution?
  - ▸ Origin of the documents: How did your institution receive the documents? Where did they come from? Are there a return address and postage stamps/seals on the envelope? (For foreign institutions, always save the envelopes!)
  - ▸ The look and feel of the documents: Easily reproducible fonts? Consistency of typeface? Alignment of lettering? Quality of paper? Appropriate stamps/seals?
  - ▸ Format and wording: Do they match other documents from the same institution? Or do they match *some other institution's* documents in format and wording? Have you seen this document before, from another institution?
  - ▸ Content details: Examine dates of attendance, dates of award of degree, name of degree, course codes, course titles, grades, credits. Do they seem to make sense for the institution issuing the documents and the applicant's biographical and academic background?
- Confirm the accreditation or recognition status of every institution the applicant claims to have attended, and know which types of accreditation are acceptable to your institution.
  - Is the institution regionally accredited by one of the six U.S. regional accrediting associations?

144

- Is the institution accredited by a recognized national accrediting association?
- If the institution is not in the U.S., is it recognized by the appropriate *legitimate* educational authority in its own location, according to its legal and quality assessment systems for institutions offering *bona fide* academic awards?

STEP 4: ADDRESS ANY DISCREPANCIES, PROBLEMS, OMISSIONS, INCONSISTENCIES, ETC.

- Use colleagues as another set of eyes to review the document and your resource materials with you. Ask those who are knowledgeable about the institution, field of study, or foreign country to review the documentation with you.
- If the problem cannot be resolved by checking resources and with input from colleagues, request verification of the documents.

STEP 5: REQUEST VERIFICATION

Verification Process for Documents from U.S. Institutions

To request verification of documentation purportedly issued by a U.S. institution, contact the office of the registrar of the institution. The Family Educational Rights and Privacy Act (FERPA), a set of federal laws protecting the privacy of students in the United States, governs the sharing of academic documentation between institutions. For details on FERPA, see AACRAO's many FERPA-related resources,[14] as well as the U.S. Department of Education's FERPA web page.[15]

---

[14] *See* ‹www.aacrao.org/ferpa›.

[15] *See* ‹www.ed.gov/policy/gen/guid/fpco/ferpa/›.

Verification Process for Documents from non-U. S. Institutions

As discussed in Chapter Ten, "International Transfer Credit Evaluation and Methodology," in some countries the process of issuing and verifying academic documents is similar to the system in the United States, with privacy laws governing records, electronic systems for recordkeeping, computer-generated academic records, and a system for the student to request records to be transmitted to another institution. Likewise it is easy in some countries to contact officials at higher education institutions by email and through web-based applications in English to inquire about the authenticity of documents. On the other hand, there are many countries where documentation practices are much different than in the United States, and where it can be very difficult to make contact with the institution and have documents sent directly to another institution. *The AACRAO International Guide: A Resource for Education Professionals* (AACRAO 2012) is an excellent source for information and guidance on the process of reviewing and seeking verification of documentation from institutions outside of the United States.

STEP 6: KEEP A RECORD OF THE VERIFICATION REQUEST.

Once you have sent the verification request, put a copy of it in the applicant's file. Start a "Verification Requests" file for copies of request letters with attached copies of the questionable documents. Cross-reference the files so that you can easily retrieve the applicant's file when the response is received.

STEP 7: FOLLOW UP PROMPTLY AND APPROPRIATELY WHEN A RESPONSE IS RECEIVED.

The receipt of a verification letter is the first step in the resolution of a tense and difficult situation involving the institution and the applicant or student. Take prompt and appropriate action based on the reply. If the documents are verified as being fraudulent, follow-up should be immediate, according to established procedures and guidelines for the consequences to applicants or students who submit falsified documents. If the response is ambiguous or not clear, the evaluator must determine the best way to proceed. Would another round of communication with the issuing institution be fruitful? Is there another avenue that can be pursued?

STEP 8: REACH OUT TO YOUR PROFESSIONAL NETWORK TO DISCUSS YOUR VERIFICATION QUESTIONS AND SHARE NEWS OF YOUR VERIFICATION SUCCESSES.

Word needs to circulate whenever we receive authoritative, conclusive confirmation of fraudulent documents, particularly to colleagues in the local area where an applicant who submitted fraudulent documentation to your institution might also be applying. We can all help each other keep informed and vigilant through our professional networks.

Considerations for Policies on Fraud

To help maintain vigilance against fraud, proactive policies and clear, viable procedures can be effective tools in fighting fraud. The

145

following are some things to consider in establishing or adjusting policies on handling cases involving fraud.

- Define fraud. Identify the types of fraud to which the institution is vulnerable and the various scenarios in which fraud can play a part. Examine cases of fraud that the institution has experienced or that other institutions have encountered. What could/should have been done to prevent the problem? What was learned as a result?

- Identify the market value of the institution, particularly to international students. What is attractive about it, and why would fraudsters want to capitalize on this? What is the reputation of the institution; is it prestigious or an easy target?

- Review the institutional policies on student and faculty/administrator behavior (*e.g.*, academic dishonesty, honor code, code of conduct, code of ethics). Are any of these relevant to the type of fraud that the admissions office might see?

- Identify the various offices or departments within the institution that should be involved in discussions about policies on handling fraud cases.

- Work with the institution's legal counsel to become informed about federal, state, county, and city laws and ordinances that would be appropriate for potential cases.

- Communicate a procedure or protocol to be followed in fraud cases to all those who might deal with such cases. Who does what? What is the procedure, step-by-step? Should it be the same in every case? Is there an appeal process if the applicant disputes the findings? What is the procedure for that?

- Develop a team to coordinate anti-fraud efforts across the institution and to educate, inform, and train others, proactively function as "watchdogs" and monitor the Internet for usage of the institution's name, assist with questions, prepare cases for review and judgment, track results, and review and critique policy.

- Publish institutional policies and procedures, and consequences for breaking the rules in clear, concise, unambiguous language, and in easily-accessible locations, such as application packets, publications, and online.

- Incorporate a section in the institution's application materials that must be signed by the applicant, attesting to truthfulness, completeness, accuracy of information provided; understanding that institutions issuing the documents submitted may be contacted for authentication of the documents, or further information relevant to the student's education there; and agreeing to abide by relevant policies, regulations, etc. and accepting consequences if rules are broken.

- Act quickly when a case of questionable documentation is uncovered. Be a confident and assertive first responder, with appropriate policies and procedures to support findings.

- Seek the advice of experienced, expert, and neutral third parties if help is needed, in accordance with legal counsel.

- Keep a record of cases involving fraud. Cross-reference information and notes between various files so that data is easily retrievable. Note general information in generic files, and information specific to a particular student or applicant in the individual's file. This recordkeeping is useful should the person ever apply again.

■ Review institutional policy regularly, adjusting it to incorporate what is learned from each case. Each scenario presents a different set of circumstances, with new twists and perspectives. Review institutional policy regularly and tweak it as appropriate.

Best Practice is the Key: Being Informed, Remaining Vigilant, Verifying Documents

To safeguard the authenticity of our institutions, as well as to continue to attract quality applicants from U.S. institutions and well-qualified international students who contribute to the vitality, diversity, and quality of U.S. higher education, it is imperative that we follow principles of best practice in the admission of transfer students and the review of their academic records. This requires that we become informed about the unfortunate reality of document fraud in the admissions and transfer credit evaluation process, that we continue to learn through professional development opportunities and networking, that we exercise vigilance in reviewing documentation from transfer applicants, that we seek verification of suspicious or irregular documents, and that we share our experiences with the document verification process with our colleagues. The integrity of our institutions is on the line. There is too much at stake

to disregard or fall short on our responsibilities in the transfer process.

Resources on Fraud

AACRAO RESOURCES

American Association of Collegiate Registrars and Admissions Officers. 2006. *Guide to Bogus Institutions and Documents*. Washington, D.C.: American Association of Collegiate Registrars and Admissions Officers.

Ezell, A. 2002. Degree diploma mills—past, present, and future. *College and University*. 77(3): 39–47.

———. 2005. Transcript fraud and handling fraudulent documents. *College and University*. 80(3): 49–55.

———. 2007. *Accreditation Mills*. Washington, D.C.: American Association of Collegiate Registrars and Admissions Officers.

———. 2008. *Counterfeit Diplomas and Transcripts*. Washington D.C.: American Association of Collegiate Registrars and Admissions Officers.

OTHER RESOURCES

Bartlett, T., and S. Smallwood. 2004. Degrees of suspicion: Psst. wanna buy a Ph.D.? *The Chronicle of Higher Education*. 50(42): A9. June 25. Retrieved May 14 from: <http://chronicle.com/article/Psst-Wanna-Buy-a-PhD-/24239>.

Bazley, Thomas D. 2005. Degree mills: The billion-dollar industry that has sold over a million fake diplomas (book review). *College and University*. 80(4): 49–50.

Bear, J., and A. Ezell. 2005. *Degree Mills: The Billion-Dollar Industry That Has Sold Over a Million Fake Diplomas*. New York: Prometheus Books.

———. 2012. *Degree Mills: The Billion-Dollar Industry That Has Sold Over a Million Fake Diplomas, Updated Edition*. New York: Prometheus Books.

Bear, M., and T. Nixon. 2006. *Bears' Guide to Earning Degrees by Distance Learning*. Ten Speed Press.

Carnevale, D. 2004. Don't judge a college by its internet address. *The Chronicle of Higher Education*. November 26. Retrieved May 14, 2010 from: <http://chronicle.com/article/Dont-Judge-a-College-by-Its/8748/>.

Contreras, A. 2001. International diploma mills grow with the internet. *International Higher Education*. 24(Summer). Retrieved May 14, 2010 from: <www.bc.edu/content/dam/files/research_sites/cihe/pdf/IHEpdfs/ihe24.pdf>.

———. 2002. How reliable is national approval of university degrees? *International Higher Education*. 29(Fall). Retrieved from: <www.bc.edu/content/dam/files/research_sites/cihe/pdf/IHEpdfs/ihe29.pdf>.

———. 2003. *More Shenanigans: Fake Accrediting in the International Marketplace. A Case Study in Foreign Degree (Dis)approval*. Available at: <https://htmldbprod.bc.edu/prd/f?p=2290:4:0::NO:RP,4:P0_CONTENT_ID:100562>.

Council for Higher Education Accreditation. *Degree Mills and Accreditation Mills* (web pages). Washington, D.C.: CHEA. Available at: <www.chea.org/degreemills/>.

Gollin, G. 2003. *Unconventional University Diplomas from Online Vendors: Buying a Ph.D. from a University that Doesn't*

Exist. August. Overview of how diploma mills operate. Retrieved May 14, 2010 from: <www.hep.uiuc.edu/home/g-gollin/diploma_mills.pdf>.

Hallak, J., and M. Poisson. 2007. *Corrupt Schools, Corrupt Universities: What Can Be Done?* Paris, France: UNESCO International Institute for Educational Planning. Available at: <http://unesdoc.unesco.org/images/0015/001502/150259e.pdf>.

Noah, H., and M. Eckstein. 2001. *Fraud and Education: The Worm in the Apple*. Lanham, MD: Rowman & Littlefield Publisher, Inc.

Oregon Office of Student Access and Completion, Office of Degree Authorization. 2010. *Diploma Mills*. Available at: <www.oregonstudentaid.gov/oog-diploma-mills.aspx>.

Transparency International. *Corruption Perceptions Index 2009*. Retrieved from: <www.transparency.org/research/cpi/overview>.

U. S. Federal Trade Commission. 2005. *Avoid Fake Degree Burns by Researching Academic Credentials*. Available at: <www.business.ftc.gov/documents/bus65-avoid-fake-degree-burns-researching-academic-credentials>.

———. 2006. *Diploma Mills: Degree of Deception*. Available at: <www.consumer.ftc.gov/articles/0206-diploma-mills>.

U. S. Department of Education. 2010. *Diploma Mills and Accreditation*. Available at: <www2.ed.gov/students/prep/college/diplomamills/diploma-mills.html>.

———. 2010. *Family Educational Rights and Privacy Act*. Available at: <www2.ed.gov/policy/gen/guid/fpco/ferpa/index.html>.

University of Illinois at Urbana–Champaign. 2010. *Information Resources Concerning Unaccredited Degree-Granting Institutions* (a web-based compilation of various resources, including news items and public legal documents by Prof. George Gollin). Available at: <www.hep.uiuc.edu/home/g-gollin/pigeons/>.

148

TRANSFER HANDBOOK

PROMOTING
STUDENT
SUCCESS

Regulations

THE

TRANSFER HANDBOOK

PROMOTING
STUDENT
SUCCESS

CHAPTER TWELVE

FERPA and Reverse Transfer

MICHELLE BLACKWELL

Director of Reverse Transfer,
University of North Carolina General Administration

FERPA and Reverse Transfer

Over the past few years many universities and community colleges have been partnering to develop reverse transfer (RT) agreements to aid students in achieving their goals of an associate degree. In July 2011, Texas was one of the first states to legislate a reverse articulation for the awarding of an associate degree, and since then other states have followed. In November 2012 the Lumina Foundation partnered with USA Funds, the Kresge Foundation, and the Gates Foundation to offer grants to states to create statewide "Credit When It's Due" or RT programs. RT in this context is typically defined as the sending of a student's transcript record from a university back to the community college (where the student transferred from initially) to then evaluate it for a potential associate degree. The reverse transfer process involves developing agreements between universities and community colleges for policies and procedures in order to award the associate degrees.

When implementing a reverse transfer project it is critical to ask how and if the student's permission is needed to release the transcript records to the prior institution. Determining this requires a thorough understanding of the Family Educational Rights and Privacy Act (FERPA). FERPA gives students who reach the age of 18, or who attend a postsecondary institution, the right to inspect and review their own education records. Students also have some control over the disclosure of personally identifiable information from these records. FERPA applies to all educational agencies and institutions that receive funding under most programs administered by the Secretary of Education. Almost all postsecondary institutions, both public and private, generally receive such funding and must, therefore, comply with FERPA (AACRAO 2013, 1). Institutions may not disclose information contained in education records without the student's consent except under certain conditions.

FERPA Rules and Regulations

FERPA defines a student as "any person with respect to whom an educational agency or

153

institution maintains education records or personally identifiable information, but does not include a person who has not been in attendance at such agency or institution" (20 U.S.C. 1232g(a)(6)). The term "educational agencies or institutions" generally refers to local education agencies (LEAs), elementary and secondary schools, schools operated by the Bureau of Indian Education, and postsecondary institutions (75606 Federal Register / Vol. 76, No. 232 / Friday, December 2, 2011 / Rules and Regulations).

FERPA defines "education records" as "those records that contain information *directly related* to a student and which are *maintained by an educational agency or institution or by a party acting for the agency or institution*" (FERPA General Guidance for Students, U.S. Department of Education; emphasis added). An "education record" entails any information about the student maintained in any way, including:

- Handwriting
- Video or audio tape
- Computer media
- Film
- Print

Institutions may not disclose information contained in education records without the student's consent, except under certain conditions. FERPA states: "The parent or eligible student shall provide a signed and dated written consent before an educational agency or institution discloses personally identifiable information from the student's education records" (34 C.F.R. 99.30). LeRoy Rooker, Senior

Fellow at AACRAO and former Director of the Family Policy Compliance Office, has stated on many occasions that the student must have an active role in releasing his or her record.

The exceptions under which the student's record may be released without his or her consent include the following:

- The disclosure is to other school officials, including teachers, within the agency or institution whom the agency or institution has determined to have legitimate educational interests (34 C.F.R. 99.31).
- The disclosure is, subject to the requirements of §99.34, to officials of another school, school system, or institution of postsecondary education where the student seeks or intends to enroll, or where the student is already enrolled so long as the disclosure is for purposes related to the student's enrollment or transfer (34 C.F.R. 99.31).
- Authorized representatives of the officials or agencies headed by officials listed in §99.31(a)(3) may have access to education records in connection with an audit or evaluation of Federal or State supported education programs, or for the enforcement of or compliance with Federal legal requirements that relate to those programs (34 C.F.R. 99.35).

In the case of reverse transfer, many campus officials have asked and consulted with Rooker to determine whether a student's record can be sent back to an institution the student transferred from under the exceptions above. He has responded that these exceptions *do not apply* given that this education record is not for the purpose of the student transferring back to the prior institution. Furthermore, the purpose of the evaluation is to review for the potential awarding of a degree, not for compliance of regulations or research areas under the conditions. The conclusion is that *an individual must actively provide consent for the release of his or her records.* Given the above regulations, institutions must provide a way for the student to actively consent to the release of his or her record for the reverse transfer process.

Sample Scenarios

To help clarify the range of scenarios, below are some examples of how FERPA should be applied to reverse transfer.

EXAMPLE A : EMAIL NOTIFICATIONS

An institution sends an email a student stating that his or her records will be sent to the other institution unless otherwise notified by the student. Would this constitute an acceptable FERPA release? In this instance the student's consent defaults to mere participation and does not allow the student to actively approve releasing the record. Instead, the student should be asked for explicit authorization, which allows them to respond by email (one that clearly identifies the student) with an e-signature that he or she wishes to release the record.

EXAMPLE B : ADMISSIONS APPLICATION

An institution adds a consent for release of education records as part of the admissions application, requiring the student's signature. Would this constitute an acceptable FERPA release? No, the student must be given a choice to actively respond yes or no to the consent. Therefore, while the admissions application is a convenient place to acquire consent, the student must be able to explicitly indicate "yes" or "no" on the application regarding the release of his or her record. A box to check on the admissions application would be an appropriate FERPA release.

EXAMPLE C : SIGNED RELEASE

An institution asks its students to sign an authorization to release education records upon leaving the current institution and transferring to the new one. Is this an acceptable FERPA release? This is acceptable, but requires the transferring of the release document between the two institutions. Another option for consent and release would be establishing a place within the student's services account to opt in or out of the reverse transfer program. This area would also contain information about RT and the requirements for the records to be released.

Ensuring FERPA Compliance

Regardless of how the release of record is presented to the student, the key elements to include in the consent for release are clear and proper wording of the release, including:

- the records to be disclosed;
- the purpose behind the disclosure;
- to whom the disclosure will be made; and

155

a way for the student to indicate actively that he or she is willing to release the record.

Participating in the reverse transfer process is beneficial for both students and institutions. The student obtains a credential they have earned, but would not have otherwise received, and the institution gets credit for a student who has graduated. In order to run a successful reverse transfer program, it is important for the students to understand and be active in the process, and for institutions to comply with federal statutes.

156

THE

TRANSFER HANDBOOK

PROMOTING
STUDENT
SUCCESS

NCAA Regulations for Transfer Student-Athletes

ANDREW CARDAMONE

Associate Director of Academic and Membership Affairs,
National Collegiate Athletic Association (NCAA)

NCAA Regulations for Transfer Student-Athletes

The purpose of this chapter is to help registrars and enrollment management professionals understand the key tenets of NCAA transfer legislation. Registrars have an important role in NCAA institutional control and are integral to a student-athlete's progress toward a degree. Institutional control is an essential concept that links varsity athletics programs with higher education. Registrars help ensure an institution has controls in place on campus by performing the following functions, which include, but are not limited to:

- Monitoring student-athletes' enrollment and registration;
- Certifying progress toward degree legislation for student-athletes;
- Collecting and submitting graduation rates and Academic Progress Rate (APR) data (a team-based metric that accounts for the eligibility and retention of each student-athlete, each term);
- Certifying transfer student-athlete standards and requirements; and/or

- Evaluating prospective transfer student-athletes for admissibility, progress toward degree and transfer eligibility.

This chapter is not a substitute for the NCAA manual or the good judgment of the NCAA compliance professional(s) on campus. Rules, especially transfer rules, change, and new interpretations of the legislation are published frequently, so follow-up questions should always be brought to the institution's NCAA compliance team.

When completing an evaluation of a student-athlete's record, it is worth remembering that transferring from one institution to another is a crucial decision for student-athletes. They consider a variety of factors, including academics, athletics, campus life, and their personal situation. Transfer rules help student-athletes make rational decisions about the best place to pursue an education and compete in their sport. The information provided to a transfer student-athlete about

159

their potential eligibility will help them make a knowledgeable decision.

NCAA transfer legislation generally includes elements that promote graduation of the student-athlete. When NCAA committees and governance groups review or amend transfer legislation, improving graduation rates and using indicators of graduation are foremost in committee members' minds. The act of transfer usually results in student-athletes losing credits toward the degree of their choosing and may have ramifications related to their ability to practice, compete, and receive athletics-related financial aid.

Triggering Transfer Status

The NCAA has identified the common elements that make a student-athlete subject to the transfer regulations, known as "transfer triggers." These are the minimum amount of activity or enrollment at an institution that no longer permit the student-athlete to be considered a first-year student. These include:

- The student-athlete enrolls full-time at a two-year or four-year institution in a regular academic term (summer sessions do not count);
- The student-athlete reports for practice with the regular squad;
- The student-athlete practices or plays while enrolled part-time;
  or
- The student-athlete receives financial aid to attend a summer session at the institution (Division I only).

In any of these cases, the student-athlete must comply with the NCAA rules for transfer students.

Initial-Eligibility Certification

The same qualification rules that apply to a high school graduate entering college for the first time also apply to a student transferring to a Division I or II institution in order to play. The core courses the student-athlete took in high school, the grades and number of credits earned, and scores on standardized tests all combine to help determine whether she qualifies for certification, also called being a "qualifier." This status is determined by the NCAA Eligibility Center. A student-athlete's status as a qualifier, partial qualifier, academic redshirt, or non-qualifier will determine the specific transfer rules which apply to her.

Assessing "Qualifier" Status

Below are descriptions of the four certification statuses that a student-athlete may receive from the NCAA Eligibility center:

- **Qualifier**—A student who, for purposes of determining eligibility for financial aid, practice, and competition, has:
  - ▶ Graduated from high school;
  - ▶ Successfully completed the required core curriculum consisting of a minimum number of courses in specified subjects;
  - ▶ Obtained a specified minimum GPA in the core curriculum; and
  - ▶ Obtained a specified minimum SAT or ACT score.

160

- **Academic Redshirt (Division I)**—A student who has met some, but not all, of the academic requirements in Division I necessary to be a qualifier. An academic redshirt can practice on campus and receive financial aid from a Division I school, but cannot play for one academic year.
- **Partial Qualifier (Division II)**—A student who has met some, but not all of the academic requirements necessary to be a qualifier. A partial qualifier can practice on campus and receive financial aid from a Division II school, but cannot play for one academic year.
- **Non-Qualifier**—A student who has not graduated from high school or who, at the time specified in the NCAA rules, has not successfully completed the required number of core-curriculum courses or has not presented the required GPA and/or SAT or ACT score required to be a qualifier. A non-qualifier cannot practice, play, or receive athletically related financial aid from a Division I or II school during their first academic year in residence.

The Basic Transfer Rule

Generally, if a student-athlete (international or domestic) transfers from a two-year or four-year institution, he must abide by one basic transfer rule: the student-athlete must spend one academic year in residence at the new institution before being eligible to compete. However, certain elements, including the student-athlete's transfer pathway and GPA, may affect eligibility.

Two-Year (2–4) Transfers

If a student-athlete is transferring from a two-year school, and never previously attended a four-year school, he is known as a "2–4" transfer. The rules regarding this type of transfer vary slightly among the NCAA's three divisions.

Tables 10–13 break down the different types of student athlete eligibility, according to division, and help to determine to what degree the student-athlete can take part in the athletic program.[16]

Four-Year (4–4) Transfers

If a student-athlete enrolled at a four-year school wants to transfer to another four-year school, this scenario is referred to as a 4–4 transfer. A 4–4 transfer generally is not eligible to play at the new four-year school until she has spent an academic year-in-residence at the new school. However, some exceptions may allow the student-athlete to play right away. Conference rules may also play a factor in the eligibility of 4–4 transfers, making it important to work with the institution's compliance office to confirm the application of these regulations.

EXCEPTIONS FOR DIVISIONS I AND II

The following exceptions apply to student-athletes who have obtained Qualifier status in Divisions I and II. Qualifiers are allowed to use exceptions during the first year after they enroll at the new school.

161

---

[16] Division II two-year transfers: Please note the effective date of legislation as it is crucial to understanding eligibility.

Table 10. Division I Eligibility for Two-Year Transfers

Qualifiers	

At the two-year school, did the student-athlete:
- Complete at least one semester or quarter as a full-time student (excluding summer sessions)?
- Complete an average of 12 semester or 12 quarter-transferable degree credit hours for each full-time term?[1]
- Earn a minimum 2.500 GPA in those transferable credit hours?

If **Yes** to all, the student-athlete	If **No** to at least one, the student-athlete
■ Can practice ■ Can receive athletics-related financial aid ■ Can play right away during the first year [2,3]	■ Can practice ■ Can receive athletically related financial aid ■ Cannot play until a full academic year of residency is completed [2]

Non-Qualifiers	

At the two-year school, did the student-athlete:
- Complete at least three semesters or four quarters as a full-time student (excluding summer sessions)?
- Graduate? (A student-athlete must earn 25 percent of the credit hours at the two-year school that awards the degree.)
- Complete 48-semester or 72-quarter transferable-degree credit hours *and* earn a minimum 2.500 GPA in those transferable credit hours? The transfer credits MUST include:
  - ▶ Six-semester or eight-quarter hours of English
  - ▶ Three-semester or four-quarter hours of math
  - ▶ Three-semester or four-quarter hours of natural/physical science[1]

If **Yes** to all, a student-athlete	If **Yes** to all (with a GPA 2.00–2.49), the student-athlete	If **No** to at least one, the student-athlete
■ Can practice ■ Can receive athletically related financial aid ■ Can play right away during the first year [2,3]	■ Can practice ■ Can receive athletically related financial aid ■ Cannot play until a full academic year of residence is completed [2]	■ Cannot practice ■ Cannot receive athletically related financial aid ■ Cannot play until a full academic year of residence is completed [2]

[1] In all sports, not more than two credit hours of physical education activity courses may be used to fulfill the transferable degree credit and grade-point average requirements, unless the student-athlete is enrolling in a physical education degree program or a degree program in education that requires physical education activity courses.
[2] Additional progress-toward-degree rules from the NCAA, the conference, or the school may affect eligibility.
[3] Baseball and basketball mid-year enrollee: In Division I, a transfer student-athlete in the sports of baseball and basketball who initially enrolls at the certifying institution as a full-time student for the spring term shall not be eligible to compete until the next academic year (*i.e.*, fall term).

Student-Athlete's First Transfer

The one-time exception is the most common 4–4 transfer exception used by student-athletes. This exception "permits a student-athlete at a four-year college or university to transfer to another four-year college or university without being required to sit out a year in his or her sport" (Rosen 2006). If the student-athlete has not previously transferred from a four-year school, the accepting institution might be able to use the one-time transfer exception for the student-athlete to play immediately at a Division I or II school.

To use this exception, the student-athlete must:

- Be playing a sport other than baseball in Division I, basketball in Division I, men's ice hockey in Division I, or football in Division I. Note: In football, this exception may be used if:
  - ▶ The student-athlete transfers from a Football Bowl Subdivision school to a

Table 11. Division II Eligibility for Two-Year Transfers Enrolled Full-Time *Prior to* August 1, 2016

Qualifiers

At the two-year school, did the student-athlete:
- Complete at least one semester or quarter as a full-time student (excluding summer sessions)?
- Complete an average of 12-semester or 12-quarter transferable-degree credit hours for each full-time term?
- Earn a minimum 2.000 GPA in those transferable credit hours?

If **Yes** to all, the student-athlete	If **No** to at least one, the student-athlete
- Can practice; - Can receive athletically related financial aid - Can play right away during the first year	- Can practice - Can receive athletically related financial aid - Cannot play until a full academic year of residence is completed [1]

Partial Qualifiers

At the two-year school, did the student-athlete:
1. Complete at least two semesters or three quarters as a full-time student (excluding summer sessions)?
and
2A. Graduate? (The student-athlete must earn 25 percent of the credit hours at the two-year school that awards the degree.)
or
2B. Complete an average of 12-semester or 12-quarter transferable-degree credit hours for each term of full-time attendance at the two-year school *and* earn a minimum 2.000 GPA in those transferable credit hours? The transfer credits MUST include:
   - Six-semester or eight-quarter hours of English
   - Three-semester or four-quarter hours of math [2]

If **Yes** to 1 and either 2A or 2B, the student-athlete	If **No** to 1 or 2, the student-athlete
- Can practice - Can receive athletically related financial aid - Can play right away during the first year [1]	- Can practice - Can receive athletically related financial aid - Cannot play until a full academic year of residence is completed [1]

Non-Qualifiers

At the two-year school, did the student-athlete:
1. Complete at least two semesters or three quarters as a full-time student (excluding summer sessions)?
and
2A. Graduate? (The student-athlete must earn 25 percent of the credit hours at the two-year school that awards the degree.)
or
2B. Complete an average of 12-semester or 12-quarter transferable-degree credit hours for each term of full-time attendance at the two-year school *and* earn a minimum 2.000 GPA in those transferable credit hours? The transfer credits MUST include:
   - Six-semester or eight-quarter hours of English
   - Three-semester or four-quarter hours of math [2]

If **Yes** to 1 and either 2A or 2B, the student-athlete	If **No** to 1 or 2, the student-athlete
- Can practice - Can receive athletically related financial aid - Can play right away during the first year [1]	- Cannot practice - Cannot receive athletically related financial aid - Cannot play until a full academic year of residence is completed [1]

[1] Additional progress-toward-degree rules from the NCAA, the conference, or the school may affect whether the student-athlete can play.
[2] Remedial English and math courses may not be used to satisfy this requirement.

Table 12. Division II Eligibility for Two-Year Transfers Enrolled Full-Time *On or After* August 1, 2016

Qualifiers

At the two-year school, did the student-athlete:
- Complete at least one semester or quarter as a full-time student (excluding summer sessions)?
- Complete an average of 12-semester or 12-quarter transferable-degree credit hours for each full-time term?[1]
- Earn a minimum 2.200 GPA in those transferable credit hours?

If **Yes** to all, the student-athlete	If **No** to at least one, the student-athlete
• Can practice • Can receive athletically related financial aid • Can play right away during the first year[2]	• Can practice • Can receive athletically related financial aid • Cannot play until a full academic year of residence is completed[2]

Partial Qualifiers

At the two-year school, did the student-athlete:
1. Complete at least two semesters or three quarters as a full-time student (excluding summer sessions)?
   and
2A. Graduate? (The student-athlete must earn 25 percent of the credit hours at the two-year school that awards the degree.)
   or
2B. Complete an average of 12-semester or 12-quarter transferable-degree credit hours for each term of full-time attendance at the two-year school *and* earn a minimum 2.200 GPA in those transferable credit hours?[1] The transfer credits MUST include:
   ► Six-semester or eight-quarter hours of English[3]
   ► Three-semester or four-quarter hours of math[3]
   ► Three-semester or four-quarter hours of natural/physical science

If **Yes** to 1 and either 2A or 2B, the student-athlete	If **No** to 1 or 2, the student-athlete
• Can practice • Can receive athletically related financial aid • Can play right away during the first year[2]	• Can practice • Can receive athletically related financial aid • Cannot play until a full academic year of residence is completed[2]

Non-Qualifiers

At the two-year school, did the student-athlete:
1. Complete at least two semesters or three quarters as a full-time student (excluding summer sessions)?
   and
2A. Graduate? (The student-athlete must earn 25 percent of the credit hours at the two-year school that awards the degree.)
   or
2B. Complete an average of 12-semester or 12-quarter transferable-degree credit hours for each term of full-time attendance at the two-year school *and* earn a minimum 2.200 GPA in those transferable credit hours?[1] The transfer credits MUST include:
   ► Six-semester or eight-quarter hours of English[3]
   ► Three-semester or four-quarter hours of math[3]
   ► Three-semester or four-quarter hours of natural/physical science

If **Yes** to 1 and either 2A or 2B, the student-athlete	If **No** to 1 or 2, the student-athlete
• Can practice • Can receive athletically related financial aid • Can play right away during the first year[2]	• Cannot practice • Cannot receive athletically related financial aid • Cannot play until a full academic year of residence is completed[2]

[1] In all sports, not more than two credit hours of physical education activity courses may be used to fulfill the transferable degree credit and GPA requirements, unless the student-athlete is enrolling in a physical education degree program or a degree program in education that requires physical education activity courses.
[2] Additional progress-toward-degree rules from the NCAA, the conference, or the school may affect whether the student-athlete can play.
[3] Remedial English and math courses may not be used to satisfy this requirement.

Table 13. Division III Eligibility for Two-Year Transfers

At the two-year school, did the student-athlete practice or play in intercollegiate sports?

If **Yes**, the student-athlete:	If **No**, the student-athlete:
■ Can practice and compete provided that they would have been considered academically and athletically eligible had they stayed at the two-year school	■ Can practice ■ Can play right away after transferring

Football Championship Subdivision school and has at least two seasons of competition remaining (work with the compliance office to confirm seasons of competition remaining);

or

▶ The student-athlete transfers from a Football Championship Subdivision school that offers athletics scholarships to a Football Championship Subdivision that does not offer athletics scholarships.

● Leave the previous four-year institution in good academic standing and have been academically eligible had they stayed at that institution;

and

● Have a written release agreement from the previous institution stating that the institution does not object to the receiving institution allowing an exception to the transfer residence requirement (it is necessary to work with the compliance office to confirm the written release).

▶ If the release is denied, the student-athlete may be entitled to a hearing conducted by an institutional entity or committee outside of the athletics department (*e.g.*, the office of student affairs; office of the dean of students; or a committee com-

posed of the faculty athletics representative, student-athletes, and non-athletics faculty/staff members).

▶ In Division I, if the student-athlete's request for a written release is not provided within seven business days of the previous institution receiving the request, the release shall be granted by default, and the previous institution shall provide a written release to the student-athlete.

Student-Athlete Returns to First School without Participating at the Second School

The student-athlete may use this exception to go back to the initial school in Division I or II if he did not practice or play at the second school.

Student-Athlete's Sport is Discontinued or Not Sponsored at the Previous School

If the student-athlete's previous school dropped his sport from its program or never sponsored it while he was a student, the student-athlete may be able to use this exception to transfer to a Division I or II school. (Again, it is necessary to work with the compliance office to confirm the sponsorship or discontinuation of the student-athlete's sport at the previous institution.)

165

If the student-athlete has never been recruited by the Division I or II school he plans to attend, this exception may be used if:

- He has not received an athletics scholarship;

  and

- He has not practiced beyond a consecutive 14-day period at any school or participated in intercollegiate competition before the transfer.

Student-Athlete Did Not Practice or
Play in Their Sport for Two Years

If the student-athlete did not participate in his sport for the two years immediately before the transfer, the student-athlete may be able to use this exception to transfer to a Division I or II school.

This exception may be used if the student-athlete:

- Did not practice beyond a consecutive 14-day period or play in intercollegiate sports for two years before practicing or playing for the new school;

  or

- Did not practice or play in non-collegiate amateur competition while he was enrolled as a full-time student during the two-year period.

EXCEPTIONS FOR DIVISION III

If the student-athlete is transferring to a Division III institution and has never practiced or competed in intercollegiate athletics, she may be eligible to play right away upon transfer.

However, if the student-athlete did participate at her first school, the student-athlete may be immediately eligible only if she would have been both academically and athletically eligible had she stayed at her first school.

If the student-athlete transferred from a school that did not sponsor her sport while she attended that school, the student-athlete may be immediately eligible if she has successfully completed 24-semester or 36-quarter transferable-degree credit hours and attended the previous institution for at least two full-time semesters or three full-time quarters (excluding summer sessions).

Graduate Student/Post-Baccalaureate Participation

DIVISION I

A graduate transfer student-athlete who is enrolled in a graduate or professional school of an institution other than the institution from which he previously received a degree may participate in intercollegiate athletics if he fulfills the conditions of the one-time transfer exception and has eligibility remaining on his five-year clock.

A graduate student who does not meet the one-time transfer exception because they play the sport of football, basketball, baseball, or men's ice hockey, may be able to compete if:

- They fulfill the remaining conditions of the one-time transfer exception (*see* page 162);

- They have at least one season of competition remaining; and

166

Table 14. Glossary of Terms

One Academic Year-in-Residence	The length of time a student-athlete must spend at the new institution before he or she can compete; sometimes referred to as "sitting out." For an academic year-in-residence to count, the student-athlete must sit out only at the institution where he or she intends to compete and must be a full-time student. This requirement cannot be met by attending the institution part-time or by not being enrolled in the institution at all. For a semester or quarter to count toward the one academic year-in-residence, the student must be enrolled full-time (generally at least 12-credit hours) before the 12th day of class.
Full-Time Enrollment	Each institution determines the meaning of full-time status on its own. Typically, a full-time student is enrolled for at least 12-credit hours in a term. However, some institutions define a full-time student as someone who takes fewer than 12-credit hours in a term.
Transferable Credit Hours	Credit hours from prior institutions that an institution will accept toward a degree. Each institution determines internally how many and which credit hours are accepted.
Progress Toward Degree	Legislation designed to ensure student-athletes are moving toward earning a college degree at a reasonable pace. Each institution determines how many credits should be taken within a given time period to be considered meeting progress toward a degree. The institution applies the same definition to all its students. In addition, a student-athlete must meet NCAA and conference rules that govern whether appropriate progress is being made toward earning a degree.
Five-Year Clock	In Division I, the first time a student-athlete enrolls in any two-year or four-year institution as a full-time student, they begin a five-year period of eligibility. They have five calendar years from initial collegiate enrollment to play four seasons of competition—even if they are not enrolled in an institution at all or only attend an institution part-time within that time frame.
10-Semester/15-Quarter Clock	In Division II and III, student-athletes have 10 semesters or 15 quarters in which to complete all seasons of competition. They use one of the 10 semesters or 15 quarters every semester or quarter they attend a two-year or four-year college, are enrolled full-time or part-time, and compete. Unlike Division I, they are not charged during a term in which they are not enrolled in an institution or attend the institution part-time.

- Their previous institution did not renew their athletically related financial aid for the following academic year.

DIVISION II

A student-athlete who transfers and enrolls in a graduate program, professional school or second baccalaureate or equivalent degree program at an institution other than the institution she previously attended as an undergraduate may participate in intercollegiate athletics if she has eligibility remaining on her 10-semester/15-quarter.

DIVISION III

A student-athlete may *not* transfer to another institution and participate in athletics as a graduate or post-baccalaureate student.

167

Table 15. Resources

Division I Progress-Toward-Degree And Transfer Rules[1]	www.ncaa.org/sites/default/files/DI%20Academic%20Certification%20Progress%20Toward%20Degree%20and%20Two-Year-Four-Year%20College%20Transfers%20ONLINE.pdf
International Transfers	www.ncaa.org/sites/default/files/DI%20International%20Academic%20Issues%20for%20Initial%20and%20Transfer%20Eligibility.pdf
NCAA 2–4 Transfer GPA Calculation	www.ncaa.org/sites/default/files/TransferableGPA.pdf
Division II Two-Year Transfers	www.ncaa.org/sites/default/files/DII%20Two-Year%20College%20Transfers%20ONLINE_1.pptx
Division II Four-Year Transfers	www.ncaa.org/sites/default/files/DII%20Four-Year%20College%20Transfers%20ONLINE.pptx
Advanced Division III PTD and Transfer Issues	www.ncaa.org/sites/default/files/DIII%20Eligibility%20Advanced%20Application-ONLINE.PPTX
Guide to the College Bound Student-Athlete[2]	www.ncaapublications.com/productdownloads/CBSA15.pdf
Transfer Guide[3]	www.ncaapublications.com/productdownloads/TGONLINE2014.pdf

[1] including 4-2-4 transfers
[2] initial-eligibility rules resource intended for parent and high school student audience
[3] transfer rules resource intended for college student audience

Assistance from the NCAA Staff

Transfers can be complicated, and each institution differs in their organization of degree programs. Situations may arise where a difference of opinion exists between the registrar and the athletics compliance staff or confirmation is needed on the understanding of a specific NCAA rule. There are several options for assistance:

● The conference office has a compliance professional who serves as a resource for member institutions on conference rules and NCAA legislation. Generally, the conference compliance representative has experience with the application of transfer legislation from multiple institutions, so his or her perspective is valuable.

● The compliance office may also submit an interpretive request to the NCAA staff via the Requests/Self-Reports Online (RSRO) system. The NCAA has specific teams of staff members that focus on interpreting common areas of the legislation (*e.g.*, Eligibility and Transfer legislation in NCAA Bylaw 14). The staff will review a submission, follow up if any additional information is needed, and respond in writing. Generally, staff members in their respective bylaw areas discuss the case within a team of individuals who collectively have applied transfer legislation at multiple institutions and conference offices.

CHAPTER FOURTEEN

NAIA Regulations for Transfer Student-Athletes

ANGELA CRAWFORD
Manager of Marketing and Communications,
National Association of Intercollegiate Athletics (NAIA)

HEIDI HOSKINSON
Vice President, Academic Affairs (interim),
Friends University

NAIA Regulations for Transfer Student-Athletes

Today's college students are more mobile than ever before. One in three students will transfer during their collegiate career, and many will transfer multiple times before completing their degree (Gonzalez 2012). This dynamic increase in student mobility has confounded the traditional single-institution start and finish pattern and added a layer of complexity to providing comprehensive curricular, co-curricular, operational, and student support services. This is particularly true as colleges and universities support increasing numbers of transferring student athletes.

Institutions are implementing policy and service provisions in support of these students, including transfer articulation agreements, pipeline programs, "2 plus 2" models, reverse and lateral transfer options in addition to "swirling" enrollment consortiums, and other innovative enrollment, persistence, and graduation strategies (Lauren 2004). Many of these options are attractive to student athletes who often transfer from two- to four-year institutions.

Small colleges are increasingly attractive to transferring student-athletes. Often there are opportunities for increased playing time, access to student support services, and accessibility to full-time faculty who serve as mentors inside and outside of the classroom setting. Transfer admissions policies can be more accommodating, and entering seats more available. Transfer credit policies may also be kinder, allowing for additional credits to not only transfer in but also meet degree requirements.

College registrars find themselves at the epicenter of the transfer student explosion in higher education and are increasingly asked to keep institutional policy and record practices in sync with accrediting bodies, governmental agencies, and state and local educational systems as those systems grapple with student mobility on a large scale. Of particular interest are states which adopt public higher education system-wide course equivalencies and reverse transfer procedures that allow for the seamless movement of students within the

171

172

system. Increasingly, private non-profit institutions are developing similar arrangements with other private institutions as well as mirroring state system course equivalencies.

Opportunities and Challenges

Creating seamless transfer pathways for students is advantageous for a variety of reasons. Capturing a portion of today's large college transfer student population equates to increased revenue resources, assists in diversifying an institution's student body, and welcomes students who often have proven themselves capable in the college classroom (NSC 2012c). Graduation rates of transfer students are high: almost 60 percent of students who transfer from a two-year to a four-year institution graduate within four years and students who earn an associate degree prior to transferring graduate at a rate of 72 percent (NSC 2012c). Transferring student athletes bring experience and talent to athletic programs, in addition to being good additions to the classroom and overall campus community. They have proven to be efficient in the classroom, graduating on time at a rate of 65 percent, currently measured by the NCAA's Graduation Success Rate.

Similarly, implementing seamless transfer student pathways can have institutional consequences. In a federal and state regulatory environment that is increasingly using data-driven metrics to assess and evaluate institutional effectiveness, those institutions who welcome transfer students in greater numbers may be penalized as a result. This is particularly troubling in relation to the federal graduation rate which has, since its inception in the mid-1990s, excluded transfer students from its calculation (Selingo 2012). While institutional resources are often funneled toward first-year student programs and services, institutions with large transfer populations must make a commitment to providing enhanced support services that address the unique needs of this emerging sub-population of students (Handel 2011). Transferring student-athletes can also be a strain on institutional resources by their need for support in the areas of transfer admission requirements, navigating transfer eligibility rules, assessing transfer credit equivalencies, seeking academic advising, and making a plan for career exploration and professional development following their competitive career (Nile 2011).

Emerging Trends

The opportunities and challenges presented by the increasing prevalence of transfer students in higher education today are forcing institutions to think and behave in different ways. Emerging trends include the establishment of transfer student centers, counseling and academic support services, and institutional partnerships that provide degree completion pathways in a variety of formats (Jacobs 2004).

Student-athletes are benefiting from more robust student services and resources dedicated to improving academic performance and student athlete graduation rates. While gains are being made institutionally, a disturbing athletic trend is emerging as a growing number of coaches, particularly in the NCAA but also the NAIA, choose to harness the power of current transfer rules to restrict student mobility and keep talented players from playing for rival teams (Bishop, 2013). Stricter transfer policy proposals have also surfaced in NCAA, NAIA, and athletic conference circles as well.

NAIA History

The National Association of Intercollegiate Athletics (NAIA) was founded in 1937 with the development of the first national intercollegiate basketball championship tournament. In 1953, the NAIA was the first collegiate association to invite historically black institutions into membership, and in 1980 the NAIA became the first collegiate athletics association to sponsor both men's and women's championships (Wilson 2005).

The NAIA and National Collegiate Athletics Association (NCAA) are independent associations with different rules, processes, and member schools. Both associations govern collegiate athletics for their respective member institutions, all of which are four-year colleges or universities. Sports governed by the NAIA compete in a single division, with the exception of men's and women's basketball, which competes in two divisions differentiated by scholarship levels. The NCAA offers three divisions, with Division I competition being most prominent in the media. NAIA schools tend to be small schools with average full-time enrollment around 1,800. The majority of NAIA schools are private and/or faith-based, though there are also many public schools.

In its more recent history, the NAIA has introduced the Champions of Character program, which emphasizes character development as a core component of the intercollegiate athletics experience. In 2010, the NAIA opened the NAIA Eligibility Center to determine the academic and athletic eligibility of every student-athlete wishing to compete in the NAIA for the first time.

Approximately 22 percent of the students who receive determinations from the NAIA Eligibility Center are transfer students. Of those transfer students, about 20 percent are freshmen (have earned 30 or fewer semester credit hours) when they transfer, 34 percent are sophomores (have earned between 30 and 60 semester credits), 35 percent are juniors (have earned between 60 and 90 semester credits), and 11 percent are seniors (have earned more than 90 semester credits). On average, a transfer student-athlete to an NAIA school has attended 1.77 schools prior to transfer. The sports that see the most transfers (in descending order) are baseball, men's basketball, football, and men's soccer (Herrmann *et al.* 2013).

Campus Partners and Other Resources

ADMISSIONS

At most colleges, many student support service offices are involved in assisting transferring student-athletes. The admissions office is instrumental in assisting the student-athlete in completing the appropriate application paperwork, facilitating a campus visit, requesting official transcripts from other institutions,

173

and connecting the student-athlete with the financial aid office and often an academic advisor. Most institutions require an official transcript from all institutions the transferring student has attended. Some institutions also use the National Student Clearinghouse as a resource to determine where a student has attempted or completed coursework as a full- or part-time student.

REGISTRAR

At most colleges, the registrar reviews transfer coursework and makes equivalency determinations. These determinations may also be made by academic divisions, colleges, and/or schools via the use of academic catalog course descriptions, course syllabi, or other documentation provided by the transferring institution. Additionally, some colleges and universities allow faculty advisors, academic success coaches, or professional advising staff members to make course equivalency determinations through the process of advising. These determinations are often communicated to the registrar and noted on the student's academic record.

TRANSFER CREDIT POLICY

Most colleges have academic curriculum committees that are charged with establishing and reviewing institutional transfer credit policies. Those policies generally include, but are not limited to, determinations regarding how grades are calculated into transfer, institutional, and/or cumulative grade point averages; determinations regarding courses which can be used to meet degree and/or graduation requirements; determinations regarding

remedial coursework; facilitation of articulation agreements in reference to classification or other advanced academic standing; and determinations on overall transfer credit hour limits. Institutional rules must comply with appropriate accreditation standards, federal, state, and local regulations and are generally reviewed by those external bodies as a part of compliance reviews or accreditation visits.

FINANCIAL AID

In addition to specifically articulated transfer credit rules, many colleges have institutional financial aid eligibility rules. These rules are often in addition to NAIA financial aid and scholarship rules, and transferring student athletes must meet both institutional and NAIA rules in order to be eligible for aid. The U.S. Department of Education establishes overall federal financial aid policy, and colleges must comply with those regulations. Institutional aid rules can vary widely and may be more stringent than federal aid policies, particularly in association with institutional scholarship or loan funding.

NAIA financial aid rules can be complex. For more information about scholarship and financial aid rules, contact the NAIA national office (contact information appears at the end of the chapter). Under no conditions may anyone provide direct financial assistance to a student-athlete. Financial aid to either prospective or enrolled student-athletes must come through normal institutional channels. It must be administered by the institution using the same policies and procedures established for all students. The amount of athletic aid may not exceed the actual costs for tuition, mandatory fees, books, supplies, and room and board. The NAIA has established limits on the amount of institutional aid awarded to varsity athletes on a per sport basis. All aid that is funded, controlled, or allocated by the institution counts toward the limit established for a particular sport. Institutional funding does not include some federal grants and loans as they are not controlled by the institution. Exceptions to the limit policy include aid for academically gifted student-athletes and junior varsity participants. As the regulations and rules for financial aid are not always straightforward, it is advisable to consult a financial aid professional or an NAIA representative when questions arise.

NAIA LEGISLATIVE SERVICES AND ELIGIBILITY CENTER

Published on an annual basis, the *NAIA Official & Policy Handbook* is a comprehensive policy guidebook for NAIA rules and regulations. In addition to this publication, the NAIA provides a wealth of additional resources, including administrative staff, in its Legislative Services department. This department assists member institutions with policy and rule interpretation in addition to providing training regarding the execution of athletic and eligibility activities at the institutional level. In addition, the Association periodically publishes Legislative Briefs, which provide clear explanations of NAIA rules for members of the NAIA community.

It is important to note here that NAIA eligibility and other athletic rules may conflict at times with institutional rules, particularly in relation to academic policy, an area where institutions have significant leeway to determine their own rules. There are also times when the interpretation of a rule may be questioned as it relates to specific institutional situations. In those cases, it is important to work in collaboration with both the Eligibility Center and, if necessary, Legislative Services to understand the due process and appellate processes available when such conflicts arise.

Recruiting and Contact Rules

The NAIA defines a prospective student as any individual who has never identified with an institution or whose previous collegiate identification was with another collegiate institution. A student becomes identified with an institution upon representing the institution in an intercollegiate contest or enrolling in 12 or more institutional credit hours as reported by the institution's registrar on an official transcript based on the institution's official census date (summer session not included). An individual remains a prospective student until the student (a) practices with an institution's team during the 24-week season or (b) identifies with an institution. An individual's status as a prospective student is not impacted by age, grade level, college acceptance, or signed commitment.

Coaches are free to contact prospective students up until the point where the athlete draws equipment and engages in organized pre-school practice at another institution. Coaches may not initiate contact with a pro-

175

spective student once they register and/or enroll at another four-year institution. It is permissible to contact a student who is currently enrolled at a two-year institution once the student completes the academic year in which the student uses his/her first season of competition. The student does not need to have competed, only enrolled, at his or her current institution for the regulation regarding contact to apply.

A prospective student enrolled at another institution may contact members of a coaching staff at any time. However, the athletics director or faculty athletics representative must notify the institution where the athlete is presently enrolled within ten days following the first contact. A coach or another representative of a member institution may respond to a contact by an athlete only after the enrolled athlete's institution has been properly notified.

Initial emails, voicemails, and texts left by a prospective student for a member of the athletics department that are not responded to, addressed, or returned are not considered communications requiring notification. If at any point the prospective student-athlete makes contact with the athletics director, faculty athletics representative, or coach and is not ignored in the same manner described above, notification must be made in writing to the prospective student's enrolled institution within ten days of the contact.

Prospective students are not permitted to practice or compete with an institution's team prior to the beginning of the 24-week season, regardless of the student's stated com-

mitment to the institution. This prohibition includes practice and competition (including foreign tours) during the summer prior to the student's identification with the institution.

Prospective students are allowed to engage in informal conditioning activities with continuing student-athletes. However, this conditioning cannot be organized, directed, or required by any member of the coaching staff, including strength coaches.

Prospective students may attend camps hosted by an NAIA coach because a prospective student's participation in such a camp is not considered to be practicing with an institution's team (NAIA 2013a). A camp is considered legitimate if the camp is open to the public, and prospective students may participate if they pay a rate equivalent to all other similarly situated attendees.

Residency Rules

How soon a student can participate in athletic competition at their new institution is governed by residency rules, separate from recruiting and contact rules, that apply specifically to transfer students.

As stated on the NAIA Eligibility Center website:

- NAIA residency requirements govern how soon a transfer can play and depend on whether the student is transferring from a four-year or two-year college.
- If the student participated in an intercollegiate contest in his or her sport at a four-year school, the student must wait 16 weeks before participating in that sport unless the student:

176

- Has a written release from the athletic department at the immediately previous four-year college.
- Has a minimum 2.0 GPA from all previous institutions combined.
- Meets all additional academic requirements and any conference-specific requirements for transfers.
- A student transferring from a two-year school has no residency requirement. If, however, the student has participated at a four-year college prior to attending a two-year school, the student must have a written release from the athletic department of the four-year institution.

The *NAIA Transfer Eligibility Statement* walks through a detailed situation analysis to help determine whether a student-athlete will need to meet the residency requirement before participating in athletic competition.

Definition of an NAIA Transfer Student Athlete

A student becomes identified with an institution upon representing the institution in an intercollegiate contest or enrolling in 12 or more institutional credit hours as reported by the institution's registrar on an official transcript based on the institution's official census date (summer session not included).

A student-athlete is a transfer student if he or she has identified following high school graduation. Transfer student status may be defined differently by the NAIA than by a college or university. However, the NAIA definition supersedes the institutional one when making a determination of initial eligibility to play. Institutions may categorize transfer students as they wish or as defined by any institutional, local, state, or federal reporting requirements as necessary. Such internal institutional designations should not interfere with the eligibility determination process.

Transfer Forms

All transfer students are required to complete NAIA forms related to their status as a transfer student. All transfer forms used by the NAIA national office are located online.[17] The two primary forms are the *Transfer Player Eligibility Statement* and the *Competitive Experience Outside Intercollegiate Athletics* form. Each form provides additional explanation for when and how to use the form.

The *Transfer Player Eligibility Statement* is to be filled out by the faculty athletics representative (assisted by the transfer student) only once at any NAIA institution. This form must be completed prior to participation for all students who previously identified with an institution of higher learning, even if the student has received an NAIA Eligibility Center determination for the current academic term.

The *Competitive Experience Outside Intercollegiate Athletics* form is not required for students who have received an eligibility determination from the NAIA Eligibility Center for the current academic term.

A student will be charged one season of competition for each 12-month period in which the student competes in charge-

---

[17] See ‹www.naia.org/ViewArticle.dbml?DB_OEM_ID=27900&ATCLID=205327005›.

able competition. This includes both intercollegiate competition and elite-level, non-intercollegiate competition. A student who competes in both intercollegiate and non-intercollegiate competition will only be charged one season of competition if all competition occurs in the same 12-month period. The NAIA Competitive Experience Committee—made up of NAIA athletic directors, faculty representatives and conference commissioners—defines "chargeable" competition as competition at the same level or above that which is available to student-athletes at NAIA schools.

The institution does not need to review any competition that occurred prior to a student's NAIA Eligibility Center determination. The faculty athletics representative is required to complete the *Competitive Experience* Form and submit the completed form to the conference/A.I.I. Eligibility Chair before the student is eligible to participate.

It is the responsibility of the certifying institution to properly research a student-athlete's experience to the best of its ability, utilizing all areas of research including, but not limited to, interviewing the student, checking the NAIA Eligibility Center's Directory of Competitive Experience, conducting internet research, and contacting league administrators, etc. (NAIA 2014).

National Student Clearinghouse

The NAIA Eligibility Center uses the National Student Clearinghouse (NSC) to aid in the review of a transfer student's academic background. The NSC's enrollment database includes students' domestic academic history and an NAIA-approved online, third-party transcript submission service.

NSC is consulted by the Eligibility Center for every case that is not a "standard" case (*i.e.*, the student enrolled full-time at the NAIA school in the first possible regular term following high school graduation). NSC is consulted even in situations in which the Eligibility Center is able to account for every term after high school graduation with full terms of attendance, since it is possible the student forgot to include on his or her registration profile a school attended part-time or during a non-term.

Enrollment that the student did not originally list on his or her profile is sometimes found during the NAIA Eligibility Center's information gathering step, in a NSC database inquiry, listed as transferred credit on a transcript, or in an internet search. When additional enrollment is discovered, the Eligibility Center contacts the student to discuss his/her enrollment history and requests additional transcripts. If the student insists he or she never attended the school, the Eligibility Center will require confirmation of non-enrollment.

Non-enrollment is verified in one of the following ways:

- Letter of non-enrollment: A letter from the registrar at the institution indicating the student does not have any transcript on file.
- Recorded verbal confirmation: Non-enrollment may also be confirmed via phone by speaking with the institution's registrar and recording the conversation.

178

If the school confirms a transcript is available, an official transcript must be sent to the NAIA Eligibility Center.

Admissions Application and Eligibility Center Registration

Most colleges have similar admissions applications that are likely available online to complete and submit to the admissions office. General information that a student will be asked to provide may include name, address, city, state, zip code, phone number, personal email, interest areas, high school information including official transcript, prior college information including official transcript(s), interest areas including major and athletic team, parental information (if applicable), and, if applicable, a personal statement/essay.

Some institutions require the payment of an application fee, and some waive the fee for incoming student-athletes or transfer students. Most institutions require that official transcripts are sent directly from the transferring institution to the new institution, and today, such ordering can be done online.

In addition to completing the institutional admissions application, all transfer student-athletes must register with the NAIA Eligibility Center. If a student is transferring from one NAIA school to another or has participated previously at an NAIA school, Eligibility Center registration is not required.

FERPA Considerations

Registrars at NAIA schools may have occasion to contact registrars or admissions officers at other NAIA institutions or NCAA institutions. Current FERPA regulations permit such contact between school officials who are acting with a "legitimate educational interest" as defined by the FERPA regulation. This contact allows for sharing of institutional documentation between institutions, to include academic transcripts, admissions application documents, or other educational records. Each NAIA conference also has a conference registrar who serves as a resource to assist member schools in applying NAIA rules to institutional situations and in dealing with complex eligibility or academic record issues.

It is always good practice to review institutional FERPA guidelines with the athletics directors, coaches, and other athletic personnel to ensure understanding and compliance.

Conference Rules

NAIA athletic conferences have the ability to enact conference eligibility rules in addition to those enforced by the NAIA. Conference rules cannot be less stringent than NAIA rules and are often stricter. Transfer student athletes must meet any and all eligibility rules at the institutional, conference, and national association level in order to participate.

Key Transfer Eligibility Rules

At the NAIA's annual business meeting, rule changes are considered and the membership votes in accordance with Association guidelines. To ensure that the institution is referencing the most up-to-date rules, it is crucial to work from the latest version of the *NAIA Official Policy Handbook*.

179

24/36-HOUR RULE

A student must show steady and successful academic progress to participate in athletics in accordance with NAIA eligibility rules. The NAIA's 24/36-Hour Rule is a core eligibility requirement. However, calculating the 24/36-Hour Rule can be tricky.

General Rule

A student-athlete is eligible under the 24/36-Hour Rule if he or she satisfies the following:

- Semester system: student must have earned at least 24 institutional credit hours in his or her two most recent terms of attendance
- Quarter system: student must have earned at least 36 institutional credit hours in his or her three most recent terms of attendance

Note: If the institution uses a different academic model (*e.g.*, trimester, three-term semester, etc.), it is important to contact the faculty athletics representative or NAIA Legislative Services for further clarification.

Definition of Term of Attendance

A term of attendance is any academic term (*e.g.*, quarter, semester) in which the student becomes identified at an institution (summer sessions are excluded). A student becomes identified at an institution through either of the following methods:

- Representing an institution in an intercollegiate contest, or
- Enrolling in 12 or more institutional credit hours (minimum of nine attempted at the NAIA member institution) as reported on the official transcript based on the institution's census date.

For a student who withdraws from an institution during a term, the key factor is not the date of withdrawal, but rather how the coursework is represented on an official transcript based on the institution's census date. If enrollment in 12 institutional credit hours is recorded on the transcript, it will be considered a term of attendance, even if the withdrawal is noted. Please note that institutional policy determines how withdrawals are recorded on a transcript.

Non-Term Hours

Non-term hours may also be used to satisfy the 24/36-Hour Rule, with some limitations. A non-term is any term which does not meet the definition of a term of attendance as defined above. The primary examples of non-terms are summer sessions, winter intersessions, or any term in which a student enrolls in less than 12 institutional credit hours.

There are two qualifications to using non-term hours to satisfy the 24/36-Hour Rule.

- Only non-term hours earned since the second most recent term of attendance are eligible. Any hours earned prior to the second most recent term cannot be used to meet the 24/36-Hour Rule. For example, a student wishes to compete in fall 2014. She identified at her NAIA institution in the fall 2013 and spring 2014 semesters. She earned six institutional credit hours in summer 2013. These six non-term hours cannot be used towards the 24/36-Hour Rule for fall 2014 eligibility because they were earned prior to her second most recent term of attendance (fall 2013).

- No more than 12 non-term hours may be used to satisfy the 24/36-Hour Rule. A good rule of thumb to remember is if a student did not earn at least 12 institutional credit hours within the terms of attendance themselves, the student cannot satisfy the rule. For example, a student identified in fall 2013 and earned six institutional credit hours. The student identified in spring 2014 and earned five institutional credit hours. The student cannot satisfy the 24/36-Hour Rule for fall 2014 because a maximum of 12 non-term hours can be applied.

Conclusion

This information should help you begin to navigate the 24/36-Hour Rule. Remember these steps:

- Begin by identifying the student's most recent terms of attendance (two semesters or three quarters).
- If the student earned a total of 24 semester/36 quarter institutional credit hours over those terms, he or she meets the requirements of the 24/36-Hour Rule.
- If not, up to 12 non-term hours may be applied to help the student satisfy the 24/36-Hour Rule (NAIA 2013b).

PROGRESS RULE

The two core NAIA continuing eligibility requirements, the 24/36-Hour Rule and the Progress Rule, are often mistaken for one another. However, they represent separate concepts and are to be applied independently. The following explains the Progress Rule and its relationship to the 24/36-Hour Rule.

The main goal of the Progress Rule is to ensure a student-athlete is progressing towards earning a degree. To ensure this progress, a student-athlete must have earned a minimum number of institutional credit hours prior to participating in each additional season of competition. The progress rule does not apply to a student-athlete's first season in a sport.

To satisfy the Progress Rule, a student-athlete must have earned 24 semester/36 quarter institutional credit hours prior to the start of his or her second season of competition. Prior to a student-athlete's third season of competition, he or she must have earned 48 semester/72 quarter hours of institutional credit. Finally, a student-athlete must have earned 72 semester/108 quarter institutional credit hours prior to his or her fourth season of competition. The Progress Rule has one additional requirement in the student's fourth season of competition: at least 48 semester/72 quarter hours must be in general education or the student's major field of study.

Transfer Students

Transfer students can use certified institutional credit hours earned at their previous institution(s) to meet this requirement only for their first term of attendance at their new institution. After the student has been identified at the NAIA institution for one term, thereafter only credit hours recognized by the

181

Table 16. Progress Rule Requirements: Hours Earned, by Season in Sport

	Minimum Requirement	
	Semester Hours Earned	Quarter Hours Earned
First Season	n/a	n/a
Second Season*	24	36
Third Season (GPA requirement applies)	48	72
Fourth Season (GPA requirement applies)	72[a]	108[b]

* A freshman who identifies after the first term in the fall can meet the Progress Rule for the second season if he or she has earned 12 semester or 20 quarter hours.
[a] with 48 general education/major credits
[b] with 72 general education/major credits

student's current institution and appearing as cumulative earned hours on the student's NAIA transcript shall apply.

For example, Sally attended Old Institution in 2013–2014, where she played soccer. At Old Institution, Sally earned 24 institutional credit hours, including one three-hour course in which she earned a D. Over the summer of 2014, Sally transfers to New Institution, which does not transfer in any course passed with a D. In her first term of identification (fall 2014), all institutional credit hours from all past institutions are counted, meaning Sally satisfies the Progress Rule to play in her second season. However, after her first term of attendance is completed (fall 2014), from then on only courses recognized by New Institution may be counted toward the Progress Rule. The three hours that did not transfer to New Institution no longer count toward satisfaction of the Progress Rule.

There is one exception to the Progress Rule. A freshman who identifies after the first term

in the fall can meet the Progress Rule for the second season if he or she has earned 12 semester/20 quarter hours. This applies only to the student's second season of competition. By the start of the third season, the regular Progress Rule applies.

GRADE POINT AVERAGE REQUIREMENT

To participate in a third and/or fourth season in a sport, all students must have and maintain a total cumulative GPA of at least 2.000 on a 4.000 scale. The GPA is calculated differently for students continuing to identify at an institution and entering transfer students. For students with continuing identification, the official institutional policy is used for calculating the cumulative grade point average. For transfer students, all quality points achieved are divided by the total number of hours attempted for all courses listed on all official transcripts from all institutions previously attended.

Table 17. Comparison of the Progress Rule and the 24/36-Hour Rule

	Progress Rule	**24/36-Hour Rule**
Intent	To ensure a student's academic progress corresponds with the student's athletic experience.	To ensure a student is enrolled and passing institutional credits in a manner consistent with full-time enrollment.
Rule Trigger	The Progress Rule is triggered by the seasons of competition with which a student is charged.	The 24/36-Hour Rule is triggered by the terms of attendance with which a student is charged.
Repeat Courses	Institutional credits from previously passed courses will apply if accumulated on the transcript. The Repeat Course Rule (Art V, Sec C, Item 12) does not apply to the Progress Rule.	Courses previously passed with a D or better cannot count toward satisfying the 24/36-Hour Rule.
Non-term Hours	The Progress Rule does not limit the number of non-term institutional credit hours a student may accumulate for eligibility purposes.	A student may use no more than 12 non-term institutional credit hours to satisfy the 24/36-Hour Rule
Transfer Credit	After a student's first term of attendance at the NAIA institution, only institutional credit hours recognized by the NAIA institution apply.	All institutional credit hours earned during an applicable term of attendance and up to 12 applicable non-term hours (regardless of issuing institution) can be applied to satisfy the 24/36-Hour Rule.

Institutional Credit Hours

Institutional credit is the NAIA standard for determining whether accumulated credit hours apply toward a student's eligibility. The purpose of creating this standard is to ensure that courses which are given similar weight by the offering institution are viewed equally, regardless of course title or how the course may be treated by subsequent institutions. Whether a course is considered remedial or developmental is technically irrelevant; what is important is whether the individual course meets the definition of institutional credit.

At the 2012 National NAIA Convention, NAIA membership voted to amend the definition of "institutional credit" in Article V, Section B, Item 9 (*NAIA Official Policy Handbook*, 42). Credit hours only meet this new definition when the hours appear on the transcript as earned credit and the course has

a grade (A-F, Pass/Fail, S/U, etc.). The credits must appear in a category titled "earned" to be considered institutional credit.

The definition of institutional credit is important for two purposes:

- When determining courses in progress for satisfaction of identification and the 12-Hour Enrollment Rule (*see* "Identification and 12-Hour Enrollment Rule" below); and

- When determining a student-athlete's eligibility under the 24/36-Hour Rule. Typically institutions do not recognize remedial courses taken at a previous institution, which may result in those courses not being considered if the definition of institutional credit is not fully understood by the student and academic advisors at the institution.

183

IDENTIFICATION AND 12-HOUR ENROLLMENT RULE

Under the rules for identification and the 12-Hour Enrollment Rule, a student must be enrolled in at least 12 institutional credit hours (minimum of nine hours at their NAIA institution) in the semester of their participation in athletics. A course in progress qualifies as institutional credit if the course would appear on the transcript with a grade and credit hours earned upon completion of the course.

It is important to note that for the purposes of identification and the 12-Hour Enrollment Rule, a student's performance in the class is irrelevant. The student simply has to be enrolled in 12 institutional credit hours to meet both rules.

Case Example: A student is enrolled in 12 credit hours, but three of those hours will not appear on the transcript or will not be considered "earned credit hours" by the institution when completed. Is the student identified, and does the student satisfy the 12-Hour Enrollment Rule?

Ruling: No. The three credits that will not appear on the transcript as earned credit hours do not meet the definition of institutional credit. The student is viewed as being enrolled in only nine institutional credit hours, is not identified, and cannot compete for failure to meet the 12-Hour Enrollment Rule.

Case Example: A student enrolls in 15 credits. Prior to the institution's official census date, the student withdraws from one three-credit course that is considered institutional credit. One course (three credits) the student is enrolled in will not appear on the transcript as earned hours when completed. Does the student satisfy the 12-Hour Enrollment Rule?

Ruling: No, beginning from the time when the student dropped the course. After dropping the course, the student was enrolled in only nine institutional credit hours.

However, initially the student was enrolled in 12 institutional credit hours, meaning at that time he satisfied the 12-Hour Enrollment Rule and could have competed. As soon as he dropped the course, he no longer met this rule and was required to cease competition immediately. In this case, the student is charged a season of competition and a term of attendance (student identified by representing the institution in competition). If no competition occurred, the student is not considered to have identified with the institution since only nine institutional credit hours appeared on the institution's transcript after the census date. The student would not be charged a term of attendance.

24/36-HOUR RULE

Institutional credit hours come into play not only in determining if a student is identified and charged a term of attendance, but are also used to determine eligibility under the 24/36-Hour Rule. The student must have passed 24 institutional credit hours in his or her previous two semester/three quarter terms of attendance. Institutional credits are accepted for this purpose only after the instructor submits the completed course grade in the normal manner to the institution's registrar for posting on the transcript.

184

Case Example: A student enrolls in 15 credits. One course (three credits) the student is enrolled in will not appear on the transcript as earned hours when completed. Does the student satisfy the 12-Hour Enrollment Rule? How are the credits counted toward the 24/36-Hour Rule?

Ruling: The student is considered identified and satisfies the 12-Hour Enrollment Rule. However, only 12 credits meet the definition of institutional credit, meaning only these 12 hours count toward the 24/36-Hour Rule when calculating eligibility in future terms. The credits that do not appear on the transcript are not considered institutional credit since earned credit does not appear on the transcript (NAIA 2013c).

Gaps and Competitive Experience

The *Competitive Experience Outside Intercollegiate Athletics* form provides a breakdown of the competitive experience rule and to whom the rule applies. In accordance with NAIA Bylaws Article V, Section B, Item 18b, a student is charged a season of competition for participating in elite-level, non-intercollegiate competition occurring on or after the first day of the thirteenth month following high school graduation. The *Competitive Experience* Form must be completed for any student who meets either of the following criteria:

- Student has a break in continuous, full-time enrollment. This includes but is not limited to:
  - Students who are not required to register with the NAIA Eligibility Center, are continuing at the same NAIA institu-

tion, and had a break in identification (*i.e.*, took time off from school or enrolled in part-time coursework).
  - Students who are not required to register with the NAIA Eligibility Center, are transferring to an NAIA institution, and had a break in full-time enrollment prior to identification at the NAIA institution.
- Student transfers from a non-NAIA institution and is not charged a season of competition for every year in which student enrolled full-time at a non-NAIA institution. If a student is not charged a season of competition during each year enrolled full-time at a non-NAIA institution, the student's non-intercollegiate participation in that year(s) is subject to a competitive experience review. This includes but is not limited to:
  - Students who are not required to register with the NAIA Eligibility Center and were not charged any seasons of competition while enrolled full-time at a non-NAIA school.
  - Students who are not required to register with the NAIA Eligibility Center and were charged season(s) of competition while enrolled full-time at a non-NAIA school, but not for every year in which the student was enrolled full-time at a non-NAIA school.

International Transfer Students

The NAIA Eligibility Center has published extensive resources on the PlayNAIA.org website pertaining to international students.

185

Prior to beginning the eligibility process for an international student, it is necessary to review the documents published with the student-athlete.

DOCUMENTS/RECORDS REQUIRED

Because the academic system of every country is unique, the NAIA Eligibility Center International Team in consultation with the NAIA's International Students Records Advisory Committee (ISRAC) has published academic standards used in making eligibility determination for the students educated in each country seen in the NAIA Eligibility Center.[18] Each country's guide includes an educational timeline, documents that do and do not meet high school graduation requirements, grading scale used in high school, procedures for calculating the high school cumulative GPA, how class ranking is determined, and the types of institutions that are considered postsecondary. It should be noted that the published standards are specific to the high school level of education in each country.

Further, the NAIA Eligibility Center has also published a guide of *International Documents Required by Country* with instructions regarding the specific documents required for each country.[19] Included on page one of this document is an explanation of how records must be received by the Eligibility Center to be considered official. Third-party credential evaluations are not used in the NAIA's review. Instead, official, original language documents (accompanied by literal English translations)

are always required. The NAIA Eligibility Center conducts its own in-house evaluation of records.

APPLYING INTERNATIONAL RULES TO CREDIT CONVERSIONS AND TERMS OF ATTENDANCE

Transfer credit from international universities determined to be comparable to regionally accredited U.S. institutions are converted to U.S. comparable credits to apply NAIA transfer student rules. Credits from institutions not considered comparable to U.S. regionally accredited institutions do not count as transfer credits or apply towards credits earned in the eligibility process. If a student has identified in less than two terms of attendance, then the student needs to meet the initial freshmen eligibility requirements outlined in the published standards noted above.

The rules that apply to international transfer students are the same as those that apply to domestic students; the difference is the conversion of credits into a U.S. system prior to applying the eligibility rules. The NAIA converts international credits based on the notion that a full U.S. course load is approximately 30–36 U.S. credits for one year (or roughly 15–18 credits per semester). One year of attendance at an international university or postsecondary institution counts as two semesters or three quarters for the purposes of computing used and remaining eligibility. After the credits are converted, the NAIA Eligibility Center determines for how many semesters (quarters) the student identified (either through intercollegiate athletics or through enrollment in a sufficient course

---

[18] See ‹www.playnaia.org/page/intldirectory.php›.

[19] See ‹www.playnaia.org/d/international/International_Documents_Required_By_Country.pdf›.

load), resulting in a determination of how many terms of attendance a student has used and thus has remaining.

BACHELOR'S DEGREES

Students who have completed the requirements for a bachelor's degree that is comparable to a U.S. bachelor's degree are considered to have exhausted eligibility in the NAIA. Thus, the NAIA Eligibility Center determines whether or not the student's bachelor's degree (which could be a three-, four-, or five-year degree) is comparable to a U.S. bachelor's degree based on industry standards as outlined in AACRAO EDGE, an online database for credential evaluators.[20] There are many degrees that are considered comparable and thus exhaust eligibility (*e.g.*, England's three-year bachelor's degree or Scotland's four-year honours bachelor's), but there are also many other degrees that do not exhaust eligibility (*e.g.*, France's *licence* or Scotland's three-year ordinary bachelor's degree). The NAIA Eligibility Center requires actual documentation from the issuing institution (in the original language accompanied with a literal English translation) to make an evaluation of the comparability of the degree. No evaluation can be made verbally, through email, or without the proper documentation.

There is no age limit or penalty in the NAIA for taking time off from schooling. Students have ten terms of postsecondary attendance to complete their four seasons of competition. However, students can use their seasons of competition by playing in club, recre-

ational, professional, semi-professional, tournaments, etc., after one year from high school graduation if the level of play meets a certain level of competitiveness as determined by the NAIA's Competitive Experience Rule. For each season of competition that a student is deemed to have used, 24 U.S. credits are required prior to being eligible to play in her/his next sport season. For example, a student who has used three seasons of competition is required to earn 72 U.S. credits prior to being eligible to play in her/his fourth season. A student who takes ten years off from education after high school and has not played in any organized competition could still have all ten semesters remaining to compete in all four seasons of competition. Each student's athletic and academic history is carefully reviewed to determine remaining eligibility.

TIMELINES AND BEST PRACTICES

The NAIA Eligibility Center acknowledges the substantial hurdles that international students face in the admissions, visa, and eligibility processes, and it is recommended that students submit documentation in the required manner and finish their online Eligibility Center profile no later than two months prior to the start of classes. Students who wait to have records submitted, complete their online profile, or are added to an NAIA school's recruiting list for the Eligibility Center after June 15 are in danger of missing their fall season. It is recommended that NAIA schools do not issue I-20 visas until the student has completed the NAIA eligibility process to avoid surprises. Although students

---

[20] *See* ‹edge.aacrao.org›.

can accept scholarships, complete admissions procedures, attend classes, and even practice without an official determination, students cannot compete in the NAIA until they have a determination of eligible.

Students often misunderstand what is meant by university/postsecondary enrollment and may even be directly instructed not to disclose international university attendance by those assisting them in the process. However, it is crucial that any international university attendance (even withdrawals or incomplete attendance) be disclosed at the beginning of the NAIA Eligibility Center process. When international university attendance is discovered once the eligibility review begins, the student's determination is delayed, often substantially.

Dishonesty in the eligibility application process is not tolerated. False or misleading information is taken very seriously and can result in exhaustion of eligibility in the NAIA. Students are encouraged to contact the Eligibility Center International Team to discuss any questions they may have. Contact information is provided at the end of the chapter.

Transferring Student-Athletes to Other NAIA Institutions

The NAIA requires no official paperwork when a student-athlete decides to transfer out of an NAIA institution or transfer between NAIA institutions. Institutions providing service to student-athletes in that situation should consider the ease with which students can request transcripts and if possible assist students by using NAIA secure drop box fa-

cilities to facilitate faster delivery of official transcripts or other academic record documentation.

Graduate Transfer Students

NAIA rules regarding graduate transfer students differ from NCAA rules. In the NAIA, a student has 10 semester/15 quarter terms of attendance in which to complete four seasons of competition. Once a student has completed all academic requirements for graduation from a four-year school, the student is no longer eligible to compete in intercollegiate athletics.

The exception to this is when a student is enrolled in a graduate or professional school at the same institution where he or she earned an undergraduate degree. If this is the case, then the student may continue to compete in NAIA athletics, provided he or she has eligibility remaining. In short, this exception prohibits graduate transfer students from participating in NAIA athletics (NAIA Bylaws Article V, Section D, Item 5, Exception).

Legislative Appeals Process

REQUEST FOR REVIEW OF AN ELIGIBILITY CENTER DETERMINATION

After a student has received a determination from the Eligibility Center, an institution may file a Request for Review of that determination if there is an error, using the Request for Review of an Eligibility Center Determination Form. The form must be submitted by the athletics director or faculty athletics representative to the NAIA Eligibility Center.

A completed and signed form must specify the eligibility criteria in question; provide a rationale explaining why a different determination is warranted; and factual evidence to support institution's position as to why a different determination is warranted. The institution should provide verifying documentation when available. Documentation may vary based on the rule in question (for example, student's transcripts, information from sports experience source, records from previous institutions related to prior seasons of competition charged, etc.). If there is new academic information not previously submitted to the Eligibility Center, the records need to be sent officially. Requests for review must be submitted no later than 45 days from the date student's eligibility determination is posted.

APPEAL OF AN ELIGIBILITY CENTER DETERMINATION

After a student has received a determination from the Eligibility Center, an institution may file an appeal of that determination provided there is demonstrable evidence of:

- misapplication of NAIA rules;
- the decision having been reached in a capricious or arbitrary manner; or
- bias or discrimination in the decision-making process.

A completed and signed Appeal of an Eligibility Center Determination Form filled out by both the athletics director and faculty athletics representative must be submitted to the NAIA Eligibility Center. The appeal should specify the eligibility criteria in question; provide a rationale explaining the grounds for the appeal, and factual evidence to support the institution's position. The institution should provide verifying documentation when available. Documentation may vary based on the rule in question (for example, student's transcripts, information from sports experience source, records from previous institutions related to prior seasons of competition charged, etc.). If there is new academic information not previously submitted to the Eligibility Center, the records need to be sent officially. Appeal requests must be submitted no later than 45 days from the date student's eligibility determination is posted or 30 days from the date a request for review is complete.

MEDICAL HARDSHIP REQUEST

A medical hardship request is a request for an exception to the season of competition bylaw (Article V, Section B, Item 18), which allows a student to have a season of competition returned when the student has participated in a minimal amount of contests and suffers a season-ending injury or illness. Medical hardship cases deal only with seasons of competition and do not address terms of attendance.

A medical hardship can only be requested when a student has sustained a season-ending injury or illness, as verified by a medical doctor (M.D. or D.O.). The injury or illness must be beyond the control of the student or coach and incapacitate the student from competing further during the sport season. The student must not have participated in more than the allowable number of contests (described in Article V, Section M, Item 2b; varies per sport), excluding scrimmages. Medical hard-

189

ships cannot be requested for students who are incapacitated in the last regular-season contest or in postseason competition.

The Medical Hardship Request Form must be submitted by the athletics director or faculty athletics representative to the NAIA Legislative Services Office. A copy of the student's academic transcript must be included in the submission.

This process allows an NAIA institution to seek an exception to a NAIA rule or policy in exceptional circumstances. There are times in which unexpected or extenuating conditions occur that bar a student or institution from complying with NAIA rules. In such situations special consideration may be warranted, though a detailed exception may not be clearly defined in NAIA policy. An Exception to a Standard Rule grants an institution a one-time exception to a rule. There are not enumerated minimum grounds that must be satisfied for an institution to request an exception. An institution may submit a request if it believes that the circumstances call for a departure from regulations established by the membership.

A Request for an Exceptional Ruling to a Standard Rule Form must be submitted by both the athletics director and faculty athletics representative to the Conference Eligibility Chair. The Eligibility Chair will facilitate a review by the conference eligibility committee, and then forward the committee's recommendation to the National Eligibility Committee (NEC). The NEC will consider the

institution's submission and the conference's recommendation in making a final determination on the request.

Once an institution has decided to seek an exceptional ruling, the institution must create a packet of information specifying the situation and showing why an exception is warranted. The institution can provide any information it deems necessary to advocate its position and should provide verifying documentation when available. A copy of the student's official transcript must be included. There is no time limit for this request.

REQUEST FOR AN EXCEPTIONAL RULING TO A STANDARD RULE: LEARNING DISABILITY

The request follows the general Request for Exceptional Ruling process, but should include the additional documentation noted below.

A Request for an Exceptional Ruling to a Standard Rule Form must be submitted by both the athletics director and faculty athletics representative to the Conference Eligibility Chair. The Eligibility Chair will facilitate a review by the conference eligibility committee and then forward the committee's recommendation to the National Eligibility Committee (NEC). The NEC will consider the institution's submission and the conference's recommendation in making a final determination on the request.

In addition to the Request for an Exceptional Ruling to a Standard Rule Form, the following information should be included:

- Documentation/diagnosis of learning disability

- Most recent IEP/504 plan (if any)
- ACT/SAT test results, including subject sub-scores
- Past accommodations that were available (if any), and whether they were utilized
- High school transcripts
- College transcripts (if any)
- Planned schedule at NAIA school
- Individualized academic support plan prepared by NAIA institution. Plan should include services that will be provided for student and should be specifically tailored to particular student's disability.

There is no time limit for this request.

SELF-REPORT VIOLATION

Should any member of an institution's administration or athletics department become aware of an apparent institutional violation involving an athlete or institutional representative, it is the responsibility of the individual to notify the athletics director of the violation immediately. Upon becoming aware of an apparent violation within her institution, it is the responsibility of the athletics director and/or faculty athletics representative to initiate an internal investigation. A report should be created describing the violation and providing appropriate supporting documentation.

If the violation involves the use of an ineligible student-athlete, the student-athlete is prohibited from competing while the violation case is in progress. The institution will automatically be suspended from competing in NAIA postseason competition in the affected sport program until clearance is given by the National Eligibility Committee.

A Self-Report Violation Form must be submitted by both the athletics director and faculty athletics representative to the Conference Eligibility Chair. The Eligibility Chair will facilitate a review by the conference eligibility committee, and then forward the committee's recommendation to the appropriate national committee (National Eligibility Committee or National Conduct and Ethics Committee). The national committee will consider the institution's submission and the conference's recommendation in making a final determination on necessary sanctions.

The institution must create a packet of information specifying the violation, the situation that allowed the violation to occur, and any preventative or corrective measures the institution is taking. Supplemental or verifying documentation should be provided when applicable including the student's academic transcript (*e.g.*, conference eligibility certificates, statistics, statements from individuals involved, etc.).

There is no time limit for submission.

APPEAL OF COMMITTEE PREVIOUS RULING

An institution may request an appeal of a ruling made by the National Eligibility Committee, National Conduct and Ethics Committee, National Administrative Council, Competitive Experience Committee, or the Council of Faculty Athletics Representatives, provided the institution can show one of the following grounds have been met:

191

Table 18. NAIA Additional Resources

Resource	Location/Contact Information
Official Policy Handbook	www.naia.org/ViewArticle.dbml?DB_OEM_ID=27900&ATCLID=205327260
Eligibility Center	www.playnaia.org 816–595–8300 ECinfo@naia.org
Legislative Services Department	816–595–8180 legislative@naia.org
Legislative Rules Education	www.naia.org/ViewArticle.dbml?DB_OEM_ID=27900&ATCLID=205327261
International Students	www.playnaia.org/page/internationalresources.php

- there is new or additional evidence pertinent to the case that was not considered in reaching the initial decision;
- the decision reached was demonstrably capricious or arbitrary; and/or
- there was demonstrable bias or discrimination which influenced the decision.

A Request Appeal of Committee Previous Ruling Form must be submitted by the president, athletics director or faculty athletics representative to the NAIA President/CEO and NAIA Legislative Services office.

An individual may only appeal on his or her own behalf a ruling that includes the penalties listed in Article VI, Section C, Item 5, if the individual can show one of the above grounds has been met. The appeal must be submitted 30 days from notification of original committee's decision.

Conclusion

Transfer student-athletes are one-fourth of the total population of new NAIA student-athletes each year. Their influx is changing the small college campus community in many positive ways. Institutional student support services are working together to ensure smooth transitions; the NAIA is working with member institutions to ensure that eligibility determinations and rule interpretations are handled efficiently and effectively; and student-athletes are transitioning well to their new institutions. It remains incumbent upon institutional leaders, however, to continue to improve the experience of transfer student-athletes, to make transfer policies more student-friendly, to remove hurdles preventing seamless transfer opportunities, and to ensure that adequate academic support structures are in place to not only assist student-athletes in maintaining their eligibility status, but to successfully achieve their educational goal of degree attainment.

192

Partnerships

CHAPTER FIFTEEN

Reverse Transfer:
The Newest Pathway to Student Success

FRANK YANCHAK

University Registrar,
Franklin University

JACK MINER

Director of Operations,
The Ohio State University

Reverse Transfer: The Newest Pathway to Student Success

Reverse Transfer Defined

Reverse transfer is a process whereby academic credits for coursework completed at a four-year university are transferred back to a student's community college. When students transfer from community college to four-year institutions before earning their associate degree, they miss out on the multiple benefits of obtaining the degree. Through this new initiative, a student's achievements are recognized after they have transferred to a four-year school and have accumulated the credits needed to fulfill the two-year degree program requirements.

Reverse transfer represents an innovative initiative by colleges and state governments. It significantly assists students in the attainment of academic credentials and the benefits bestowed by those credentials.

Reverse transfer is specifically beneficial to students who have studied first at a two-year institution and then transferred to a four-year institution. In the same way that credits are transferred from the two-year to the four-year school at time of admission, at some point in the four-year college career, credits can be transferred back to the two-year school.

Many community colleges have rebranded themselves as a specific pathway to a bachelor's degree at a four-year institution. In some cases, this is through a specific partnership for articulation, whereby community colleges and four-year institutions create reciprocity partnerships that guarantee honoring of credit toward both degrees and program requirements (*see* Appendix B: Sample Articulation Agreement, on page 253). The prevalence of these partnerships in recent years has led to a significant emphasis on the transfer of students and their credits from institution to institution.

Statewide Reverse Transfer Initiatives

In many cases, these reverse transfer initiatives originate through a larger statewide policy. In many states, legislators and higher education governing agencies have initiated opportunities to create a stronger bond between two-

197

year and four-year institutions. The ultimate goal is to create a smoother path for transfer so that students can obtain a degree. State legislators look at these transfer partnerships as an opportunity to increase enrollment at their publicly-funded higher education institutions and as a service to their constituents. The opportunity to decrease student debt while increasing college affordability and completion rates are great examples of ways that legislators can use public policy initiatives to impact the daily lives of their constituents.

These policies also have an impact on the economic stability and infrastructure of a state. More and more often, states are competing for industry and jobs with other states and localities. A common measure of a community's strength and competitiveness for economic growth and private investment is the education level of its citizens. By encouraging reverse transfer programs and enabling more students within a state to earn some form of degree or certification, both the state and the student benefit. The state can show industries and businesses looking to invest that the human capital and education infrastructure already exist to sustain a quality workforce.

Transfer initiatives and reverse transfer initiatives have grown quickly, in part due to the community of cooperation and sharing within higher education. That same sharing of initiatives and ideas extends across states through groups such as the National Conference of State Legislators. This organization provides professional resources for legislators and also provides an avenue to share best practices. As states have had success with reverse transfer

initiatives, legislators have in turn shared concepts and best practices across state lines.

As described in later parts of this chapter, statewide reverse transfer initiatives are beneficial because they can help define goals, terminology, policies, and practices across institutions that have their own governing bodies and cultures. In addition, statewide initiatives can provide common infrastructure and cooperation among institutions to share data and technology. In most cases, a statewide initiative can also provide funding either through direct grants or increased subsidies for existing enrollment.

Benefits for the Student

Transitioning from a two-year school to a four-year school can be difficult for some students due to changing environments, protracted terms of study, and an unclear path to a degree. Many students find the length of time discouraging. While at the two-year school, they have a milestone in mind—"once I receive X number of credits, I can transfer to a bachelor's program." Once they achieve that milestone and make the transfer, the next milestone of a bachelor's degree completion can seem distant. Achieving an associate degree award along that path can break up the journey into manageable segments and create a sense of accomplishment along the way.

The concept of associate degrees as a predictor of student success and eventual achievement of a bachelor's degree is often referenced as a justification for reverse transfer. While most would argue that these programs and partnerships are too new to truly gauge success, initial data from some of the first schools to adopt reverse transfer programs show about a 10 percent increase in retention and degree completion (Ekal and Krebs 2011). Further, at many four-year institutions, transfer students have a higher completion rate than the general student population. While these successes may carry forward, their influence may be temporarily inflated due to the increased attention currently being paid to the programs. The newness of reverse transfer may give students a stronger boost than when the programs become more common in the future. Further, the results may be impacted by other support services related to degree completion agendas such as increased academic advising and student contact.

One population of students who benefit greatly from reverse transfer are those who stop out or drop out of a four-year school before obtaining their bachelor's degree. These students leave without receiving any academic credential to show for their work. Thus, the awarding of an associate's degree can more accurately and fairly reflect their achievements.

The benefit can also be immediate for the student. The earning and receipt of a certificate or degree provides an immediate and practical benefit for working students. The student may be eligible for a new role because of the degree, increased wages, promotions, or new opportunities within their current role based on the receipt of an associate degree or certificate. Even though the knowledge and skillsets already exist and an academic transcript would show the applicable coursework, in many cases, without the

associate degree the opportunities would not be available to the student.

Benefits for the Institution

Many benefits to institutions exist pertaining to reverse transfer, namely increasing rates of completion of associate degrees. Furthermore, degree completion at a community college can result in increased revenue from the state, as many states are evaluating and redesigning their higher education funding formulas to integrate a stronger emphasis on degree completion. In addition, degree completion is viewed by ranking agencies and reviewers, and subsequently potential students, as a sign of effectiveness and value. A higher level of degree completion, including degrees granted through reverse transfer, reflects positively on the profile and reputation of the community college within the community and helps to attract future students.

Though less readily recognizable, policies regarding reverse transfer are extremely important for four-year institutions as well. The newly awarded associate degree or certificate can become a milestone for their students, which may help propel them towards success. Students participating in the reverse transfer process more actively engage with their advisor and become more aware of their own degree audit and academic progress. This awareness and attention to their academic career path facilitates degree completion and an ongoing relationship with advisors within the institution.

Another benefit of reverse transfer is the strong relationship between institutions. Enhanced communication between partner insti-

199

tutions through exchanging information and updates on students contacted creates stronger relationships for the offices involved. When both institutions see the benefits of reverse transfer, a clearly articulated vision for success can more easily be demonstrated to students. Ultimately, enhancing preferred partner and articulation agreements between institutions allows them to leverage those partnerships to recruit and retain more students. Unproductive competition between the two- and four-year schools should decline as articulation agreements are more fully fleshed out and as these new partnerships allow each of the schools to concentrate on the courses and programs where they excel, capitalizing on their established partnership with another institution, which will fill in any gaps for their students.

There are also benefits to the general population, as these partnerships, initially forged on the local level, eventually increase the number of Americans with stronger academic credentials, creating a more educated workforce across all disciplines and across all regions. The aggressiveness with which reverse transfer is pursued as a model in each state or region will ultimately lead to competitive advantages regarding economic investment in the given area. The presence of a more educated workforce can attract new industries and businesses to regions that would not have previously been considered optimal for development or investment.

Public Institution Model

Many public institutions that have moved towards a reverse transfer initiative have done

so at the urging or mandate of state policy makers and state government. In those cases, rewards or penalties have helped guide the adoption of a particular model.

As most funding models for higher education require reporting of student enrollment data to the state, within many states the governing body for higher education may provide the initial list of students eligible for reverse transfer. This is a function of existing student data spread throughout numerous databases to which the governing body has access. This information may include minimal data on each student and the courses they have taken or a more summative level of data similar to that reported to the National Student Clearinghouse (NSC).

Because the state has become a repository for this historic data, they can often query the data to produce a list of students currently enrolled at a particular four-year institution and who have also achieved some level of credit from a community college in the state. In this model, the governing body at the state level produces a list of potentially eligible students and shares it with the schools for their outreach.

Another alternative for selecting the student population is to query transfer credit data at the four-year institution. By reviewing how many credit hours are transferred from a community college and which community college those credits come from, four-year schools can develop a list of potential candidates for reverse transfer.

An additional avenue for institutions is to use existing data with the National Student Clearinghouse. NSC data provides a basic level of information but enough to begin outreach and analysis. Currently, NSC data provides courseload level and the number of terms a student was enrolled at a given institution. Either through the student tracker module or through partnership with NSC, community colleges are able to uncover the educational paths of their former students and begin to approach students who have completed additional coursework at a four-year institution. It is up to the community colleges to determine their own institutional mechanisms through which to discover individuals with enough credit to merit an associate degree.

Private Institution Model

Unlike the public institution model, private institutions do not receive funding for graduation rates and may not have the same capability to pull the raw data from a unique database. Still, community colleges may work with private institutions to provide the benefits of reverse transfer to the students. Institutions may first approach working with one another by determining necessary data. Once the institutions agree on the approach, the student population is queried from the transfer credit database at the four-year institutions. From this point, four-year schools will develop a list of potential candidates for the reverse transfer model and begin working with these students on the option of reverse transfer.

Supporting Reverse Transfer

A number of schools have identified best practices that either existed prior or were devel-

oped to facilitate the reverse transfer process. Some of the infrastructure investments were:

A DEGREE AUDIT SYSTEM

In instances where electronic degree audit systems are not in place, the amount of work to determine degree eligibility can be overwhelming. The lack of a degree audit system always increases the time dedicated to degree certification and is exacerbated by unclear articulation of transfer credit and credits earned from the four-year school. Degree auditing systems are helpful to both two-year and four-year schools involved in the process. While the two-year schools use the system to certify eligibility for a degree, the four-year schools often use the system to begin developing a data set to share with the community college.

XML DATA TRANSFERS AND ELECTRONIC TRANSFER CREDIT EVALUATION

The electronic exchange of transcript data has significantly increased the efficiency and ease of sharing information between institutions, which is incredibly valuable when processing reverse transfer credit. Schools that are able to share data electronically, import data, and perform electronic evaluation of the credit being transferred see higher return rates and a bigger return on their investment.

STATEWIDE DATA SYSTEMS

In some states, enrollment data collection is handled centrally, enabling four-year schools to save a significant amount of time. State higher education governing offices have the ability to create the initial data set of students

201

who are studying at a four-year school and who may be eligible for reverse transfer with a two-year school in the state.

ONLINE FERPA RELEASE COLLECTION

The collection of the Family Educational Rights and Privacy Act (FERPA) release can present one of the most cumbersome and territorially ambiguous issues in the process. Four-year schools that develop online systems, taking advantage of their existing student relationship, enjoy more successes in student responses along with a less complicated and convoluted path. Since the student is still enrolled at the four-year institution, the institution can use the online authentication process to obtain a FERPA release from the student. This security mechanism is similar to that used to authenticate students for information releases they request, such as transcript and enrollment verifications.

Student Processes

Once a student is identified as a potential candidate, schools may communicate by mail, email, or by word of mouth that he or she has obtained the credits necessary for an associate degree. Students then need to authorize their institution under FERPA regulations to release their transcript to the potential awarding institution. This can be done via paper or electronic form. After submitting their FERPA release, the student should be contacted by the community college with the results of the review. Certain aspects that may need to be addressed include whether a student may appeal any decision regarding transfer credit, as well as which

institution will make the final determination concerning articulation of transfer credit (*i.e.,* the two-year or the four-year school).

FERPA Considerations[21]

Triggers for reverse transfer can be different than traditional student transfer activities, resulting in FERPA considerations often being overlooked. Some institutions implement reverse transfer processes and fail to take FERPA into account, by sharing transcripts with their partner institutions without first obtaining the student's consent. Discussions with institutions that initially made this error reveal a number of pitfalls: the reverse transfer initiative is implemented without full review and analysis and/or the process is being driven or managed by staff or offices who are not normally involved in the issuance of transcripts or the transfer of credit. The models most compliant with FERPA regulations involve various offices, including academic affairs, registrar's offices, admissions offices, and transfer credit offices, who work as partners in developing a thoughtful process in advance of implementing a reverse transfer program. This allows the institution to develop the necessary infrastructure in advance.

When developing a reverse transfer partnership, it is important to determine the process for requesting a FERPA release from the student. First, institutions should agree on which institution should be initiating the request: the sending or receiving institution. Strong

---

[21] For more on this topic, see Chapter Twelve, "FERPA and Reverse Transfer," on page 153.

202

arguments exist for each option, although neither option has become the standard.

The principle behind the receiving institution requesting the FERPA release is that it is driving the process. The two-year school has developed a way to determine which students it would like to evaluate for a certificate or degree and compiled a list, either using their own databases or alternative sources of information, such as state higher education databases. The two-year school ultimately receives the more tangible benefits from reverse transfer, and therefore it can be argued that it should reach out to the impacted students to collect FERPA releases and send them to the four-year school to trigger the release of the transcript.

For many schools, the FERPA release is delivered in conjunction with the communication to the student(s) about the opportunity for the certificate or associate degree. In some of the strongest examples of partnerships between schools, the letter is branded jointly and signed by leadership at the two institutions who are sharing information.

In some cases, the sending institution (four-year school) collects the FERPA release information from the student. This model has several advantages, namely that at the time of the reverse transfer process, the students are more actively engaged with this school. Further, since the student is in the routine of receiving correspondence from this school, he or she is more likely to respond to the inquiry. Ultimately, these institutions have also felt comfortable taking on the burden of collecting the FERPA release information because they are also releasing the data. This model is

effective because it allows a relatively unfamiliar process to mimic existing procedures.

One emerging trend is a blanket, yet limited, FERPA release collected well in advance of the reverse transfer process. Community colleges may include this form in their initial application while four-year colleges may choose to include this release in their transfer applications. In both cases, the student is asked to sign off on the release of information to other colleges and universities for the purpose of reverse transfer. This model simplifies the reverse transfer process by allowing institutions to exchange data as necessary and contact the student at different points in the process, based on what would be most convenient and appropriate. For example, all of the degree audit analysis could be completed and the two-year school would be confident of their ability to award a certificate or degree before even making initial contact with the student. Because of fewer opportunities for interruption (*e.g.,* a student's lack of engagement), there would likely be a greater rate of issuance for associate degrees. However, this model runs contrary to the established conventions for transcript requests from outside of higher education. Offices have traditionally expected each transcript request to be unique and for a specified and limited purpose in order to guard against abuses of FERPA rights. In the case of reverse transfer, concern is that this model could lead to other abuses, including awarding certificates and degrees that students have not explicitly requested. As reverse transfer becomes more common, this FERPA release model is likely to become one of the more preferred methods. A potential precaution is that the four-year school/sending institution should collect the authorization since it carries the ultimate responsibility of protecting the data.

Residency Considerations

Another important consideration in reverse transfer is the two-year institution's residency requirements. Are the residency requirements waived to accommodate the student's ability to finish an associate degree? Who makes the decision, and does a policy in the academic catalog need to be amended? These issues must be communicated and discussed with the leadership and faculty at the community college. Making these decisions before starting the process is imperative to determine if reverse transfer is suitable for both institutions.

Territory Issues

One of the emerging issues for reverse transfer involves "territory," or which schools can award degrees through reverse transfer. One might simply ask if the student met the minimum residency requirements at the community college and whether he or she attended a minimum number of terms or earned a minimum number of credit hours. This establishes whether the specific institution can award a degree, but does not answer if that is the only school that may award a degree.

Students are increasingly building a college degree based on credits earned at a variety of institutions. This can result from more traditional multiple transfers where the student is only enrolled at one institution at a time, or

204

it can result from a student simultaneously enrolling in two institutions in order to pick and choose coursework. This may be a financial decision (one institution offering lower tuition/greater financial aid), a convenience decision (campus proximity/online options), course offering decision (specific courses being available at one school but not another), or even quality or pedagogy decisions (specific courses being perceived as more/less challenging at one institution). One of the most common trends seen currently is students who go to a four-year institution but return home in the summer to take coursework at a local community college, with the end goal of transferring those credits. This individual student may meet the residency requirement at multiple schools that could award an associate degree. Additionally, should each school even be granted the right to award a degree? This question becomes even more complicated when the coursework could make the student eligible for different titled degrees or certificates in different disciplines.

Another potential issue is that some four-year institutions offer associate degrees in addition to bachelor's degrees. If the end result is for a student to receive an associate degree, and he or she meets the requirements for the associate degree at a four-year school in addition to the two-year school he or she attended, should both be able to award associate degrees?

One intricacy is that many four-year public institutions have their own regional, extended, or branch campuses that offer associate degrees and are seen as feeder locations for the main campus. Some students, through normal matriculation, would earn an associate degree and then go on to earn a bachelor's degree from the main campus. In this scenario, why should the four-year institution be prevented from awarding an associate degree to everyone who moves from a regional campus to the main campus and achieves the specified hours? This would lead to an institutional increase in degree completion and eligibility for state funding.

Cost and Revenue Considerations

Many of the benefits of reverse transfer are to be expected: increased graduation rates, an increased institutional profile, and a better-educated community. However, schools also gain a real revenue benefit for participating in reverse transfer programs. A number of states have begun to transition the funding formulas for public colleges and universities away from enrollment and towards completion. These new "completion agendas" in many states incentivize increasing the number of degrees and certificates a school awards by tying state support to those accomplishments. For a community college, this creates the incentive to not only award degrees through reverse transfer, but also to create stronger links to four-year institutions in order to ensure that students who go on to pursue a bachelor's degree elsewhere will be counted.

Because of this financial incentive, in most cases, the cost-benefit analysis regarding reverse transfer supports community colleges pursuing these programs. The relatively small amount of investment of staff time and re-

sources spent administering the reverse transfer process to award an associate degree is generally outweighed by the increased funding from the state.

The "completion agenda" and change in state funding models does not incentivize degree completion for a four-year school in the same way, as the benchmark for them is normally the bachelor's degree rather than the associate degree. In this case, the participation in the reverse transfer process does not generally result in increased state funding, as there are no new bachelor's degrees awarded as a result of the process. To further complicate the impact on the four-year institution, most reverse transfer partnerships waive any transcript request fees in order to ease the burden on the student and to increase participation in the program, resulting in additional work for the sending institution without monetary compensation. There are significant barriers associated with increasing participation by four-year schools that have not been fully explored and addressed. It is important for the leadership at the four-year institution to see the partnership as a long-term benefit. Increased partnership and communication between specific community colleges and universities will form a strong pipeline encouraging community college students to transfer into bachelor's degree programs.

To encourage greater participation in reverse transfer, the Lumina Foundation has issued grants to numerous states. Alongside other partners it created "Credit When It's Due: Recognizing the Value of Quality Associate Degrees," a grant to increase the

205

number of degrees awarded by community colleges. States including Arkansas, Colorado, Maryland, Minnesota, Ohio, and New York (among others) received grants to support their reverse transfer initiatives. These grants helped support the development of infrastructure at both the two-year schools and four-year schools and allowed the states to initiate the pilot program without cost to the individual student (*see* Chapter Eighteen, "Implementing Reverse Transfer in Ohio: A Case Study," on page 231).

Future of Reverse Transfer

Perhaps more than any other process in the admissions and registrar spectrum, reverse transfer is benefitting greatly from advances in efficiency. The quick pace at which programs are developed and move from clunky, initial roll-outs to efficient, well-structured programs is remarkable. These results are strongly influenced by the rate at which information can now be shared and the push across higher education to adopt and develop new reverse transfer policies. As new states and systems continue to develop programs, information and experiences are shared to help identify and create best practices.

The development of new reverse transcript procedures presents an opportunity for schools to evaluate current practices across many areas. For example, if choosing not to charge students for transcripts when transmitting data for the purpose of reverse transfer, should any type of transfers incur a charge? The issue of reverse transfer has also created a renewed interest in a single reposi-

tory for row-level data on students to support the process. Rather than going to each school to retrieve transcripts for reverse transfer, a school could go to a single repository or clearinghouse. Again, if this is a model for reverse transfer, why would the same model not be initiated for all transfer students and transfer transcripts? These are examples of larger questions that reverse transfer has helped bring to the surface.

Summary

Reverse transfer must be further developed to truly be considered valuable for higher education. The current programs have significant benefits for both the students as well as the institutions of higher learning involved. In many ways, the academic credentials should have always been available, but without clearly articulated policies, students have not been able to take full advantage of reverse transfer. In the short term, transfer students will benefit from a higher rate of issuance of associate degrees; in the long run, the benefit to colleges and universities, specifically due to the implementation of new efficient and robust policies, will be realized. Developing reverse transcript policy and practice has helped foster partnerships among colleges and universities and reduced the level of competition between two-year and four-year schools through increased cooperation, ultimately bolstering the philosophy that when a student succeeds, all of the schools who participate along the journey are responsible for that success.

Reverse transfer, combined with other transfer initiatives, will allow schools to focus on specific academic programs. Potentially, this will lead to an increase in the number of students who receive coursework from both a two-year school and four-year school not only because of the student's preference, but because of design by the schools involved. Two schools that are proximate to each other or who have strong distance components can begin to partner in order for one institution to offer specific courses or specializations that will apply at both institutions. This more robust program of offerings will be a natural extension of the model that students are already designing for themselves.

For offices of admissions, enrollment management, registrar, and transfer credit, reverse transfer will develop stronger relationships. This specific topic presents excellent opportunities for information sharing and collaborative creation of best practices in order to streamline general processes and better serve students.

207

THE

TRANSFER HANDBOOK

PROMOTING
STUDENT
SUCCESS

CHAPTER SIXTEEN

The Interstate Passport:
A New Framework for Transfer

CATHERINE WALKER

Passport Project Manager,
Western Interstate Commission for Higher Education

PATRICIA SHEA

Passport Principal Investigator; Director,
Academic Leadership Initiatives,
Western Interstate Commission for Higher Education

ROLAND SQUIRE

Registrar,
Utah State University;
Director, Passport Central Data Repository

The Interstate Passport: A New Framework for Transfer

The Interstate Passport Initiative was launched in October 2011 as a regional project of the Western Interstate Commission for Higher Education (WICHE), to address the problems of interstate student transfer. WICHE is one of four regional compacts that were established by the U.S. Congress in the early 1950s with the mission to support the expansion of educational access and excellence by sharing information and resources across the higher education community in the region.

Chief academic officers from two regional membership organizations based at WICHE—the Western Academic Leadership Forum (representing four-year institutions and related system and state agencies) and the Western Alliance of Community College Academic Leaders—convened in early 2011 to discuss the current barriers to, and identify opportunities for, a voluntary, multi-institution, multi-state initiative to facilitate friction-free student transfer and articulation leading to improved student success and com-

pletion. Particular obstacles faced by transfer students, especially when crossing state lines, include losing credits at transfer and having to repeat coursework after transfer.

Meeting participants identified several essential elements and characteristics of the proposed voluntary regional effort, which included: providing transparency and expediency to students, actively engaging faculty, and fostering institutional efficiencies. They further determined that the project should focus on a common set of learning outcomes as the new currency for block transfer of lower-division general education. In addition, the project aimed to devise a way for institutions to acknowledge students who successfully achieve the Passport's learning outcomes and to notate it on their student record for use in seamless block transfer to other participating institutions. The project would also include a feedback system to inform sending institutions about the academic progress of their Passport transfer students to assist in continuous improvement efforts.

211

Phase I

WICHE was awarded a two-year grant from the Carnegie Corporation of New York to conduct the pilot phase (Phase I) of the Passport. Five Western states—California, Hawaii, North Dakota, Oregon, and Utah—including 23 two- and four-year institutions participated. A Passport State Facilitator in each state worked closely with both the project staff and with institutions' faculty and other personnel. As part of Phase I, project staff compiled information on general education and transfer policies in the 16 WICHE states, examined transfer patterns and frequency within and between WICHE states, and also studied characteristics and data of transfer in general from a variety of national and regional sources.

Loss of credits is a major deterrent to student degree completion. Even with institutional efforts to produce clarity about the transfer process and inter-institutional articulation agreements that spell out degree requirements and pathways, transfer students still frequently encounter the obstacle of less-than-total transfer of credits for academic work completed at the sending institution. Monaghan and Attewell (2014) found that only 58 percent of transfer students are able to bring all or almost all (90 percent or more) of their credits with them; about 14 percent of transfers lose more than 90 percent of their credits; and the remaining 28 percent lose between 10 percent and 89 percent of their credits (*see* Chapter Two, "Lost Credits: The Community College Route to the Bachelor's Degree," on page 17). The authors conclude that there is a correlation between the num-

ber of credits that transfer and degree completion (Monaghan and Attewell 2014).

These data findings make a compelling case for improving the transfer process. Too many students are hampered on their pathway to degree completion by obstacles when they transfer, and unnecessary repetition of academic work costs time and money for students, institutions, and states. The Passport provides a common currency—learning outcomes and proficiency criteria—to facilitate student transfer between institutions within states and in other states.

Phase I of the Passport project, which concluded in April 2014, undertook development of learning outcomes in three lower-division areas: oral communication, written communication, and quantitative literacy. The nine knowledge and skill areas of the Passport learning outcomes map to the LEAP (Liberal Education and America's Promise) Essential Learning Outcomes developed by the American Association of Colleges and Universities and adopted at numerous institutions around the country (*see* Table 19, on page 213). Fifteen pilot institutions signed the Passport Agreement (Phase I) for a term of five years, agreeing to:

- acknowledge that the institution's lower-division general education learning outcomes in the three academic areas are congruent with the Passport learning outcomes;

- create their institution's Passport Block—a list of courses and other learning opportunities provided to students for achieving the Passport Learning Outcomes;

Table 19. Passport Content Areas Mapped to LEAP Essential Learning Outcomes

Passport	LEAP
◆ **Phase I** Foundational skills in: ■ Oral communication ■ Written communication ■ Quantitative literacy	**Knowledge of Human Cultures and the Physical and Natural World** *Focused by engagement with big questions, both contemporary and enduring* ★ Through study in the sciences and mathematics, social sciences, humanities, histories, languages, and the arts;
★ **Phase II** Knowledge concepts in: ■ Physical and natural world ■ Evolving human cultures ■ Human society and the individual ■ Creative expression Cross-cutting skills in: ■ Critical thinking (information literacy, inquiry and analysis, and problem solving) ■ Teamwork and value systems	**Intellectual and Practical Skills** *Practiced extensively, across the curriculum, in the context of progressively more challenging problems, projects, and standards of performance* ★ Inquiry and analysis ★ Critical and creative thinking ◆ Written and oral communication ◆ Quantitative literacy ★ Information literacy ★ Teamwork and problem solving **Personal and Social Responsibility** *Anchored through active involvement with diverse communities, and real-world challenges* ■ Civic knowledge and engagement—local and global ★ Intercultural knowledge and competence ★ Ethical reasoning and action ■ Foundations and skills for lifelong learning **Integrative and Applied Learning** *Demonstrated through the application of knowledge, skills, and responsibilities to new settings and complex problems.* ■ Synthesis and advanced accomplishment across general and specialized studies

■ award the Passport to students who satisfy their block's requirements;

■ for incoming transfer students, accept the Passport as a block, no longer needing to individually evaluate courses or curricula for articulation from other participating institutions; and

■ track Passport students' academic progress and report data to the Passport Central Data Repository (*see* "Passport Tracking System" on page 215).

Phase II

Phase II of the Passport was launched in October 2014 with support from the Bill & Melinda Gates Foundation and Lumina Foundation. Seven Western states—California, Hawaii, North Dakota, Oregon, South Dakota, Utah, and Wyoming—and more than two dozen institutions are participating with Passport State Facilitators overseeing the work in each state. During this two-year phase, the Passport will develop the lower-division general education learning outcomes in

213

six remaining knowledge and skill areas, again mapping to the LEAP Essential Learning Outcomes: physical and natural world; evolving human cultures; critical thinking; creative expression; human society and the individual; and teamwork and value systems. The project will also expand beyond the WICHE region to include as many as 12 institutions from six new states in the three other regional compacts (Midwest Higher Education Commission, New England Board of Higher Education, and the Southern Regional Education Board). In addition, the Passport tracking system developed during Phase I will be refined and updated to include all nine lower-division knowledge and skill areas.

During Phase II, project staff will work with the institutions' academic advisors and marketing specialists to disseminate information about the Passport to students and faculty. The Passport is scheduled for completion at the conclusion of Phase II in September 2016. Institutions in all the WICHE states and throughout the country will be invited to sign the Passport Agreement and employ this new framework to streamline the transfer process and improve degree completion.

Passport Learning Outcomes and Proficiency Criteria

The Passport transfer framework is based on learning outcomes, fulfilled through the satisfaction of the lower-division general education requirements. It allows for a cross-state "match" of these outcomes-integrated general education requirements for block transfer. The Passport is a *block* transfer that cannot

be unpacked. Students who earn a Passport at one participating institution and transfer to another one will have their learning achievement recognized; they will not be required to repeat courses at the receiving institution to meet lower-division general education requirements.

The first step in the process to develop the Passport's learning outcomes involves faculty members from participating institutions in a state developing a common set of learning outcomes for each knowledge and skill area. Faculty representatives from each state then bring their "state set" of learning outcomes for discussion and negotiation at an interstate meeting. The faculty team compares and contrasts the different state sets to arrive at the "Passport Learning Outcomes." Participating institutions are not required to alter their general education learning outcomes, but rather acknowledge that their learning outcomes *map to and are congruent with* the Passport Learning Outcomes.

The faculty teams also assemble a list of Proficiency Criteria, or the evidence of proficiency with the Passport Learning Outcomes at the transfer level that one might see in a student's behavior, performance, or work (*see* Table 20, on page 215). These are based on, built from, and determined by observable behaviors rather than subjective descriptors such as "appropriate" or "excellent." The Proficiency Criteria are not intended to mandate curriculum or assessment methods, nor do they constitute a comprehensive list that each student must demonstrate. Instead, they serve as guidelines for faculty to determine whether

Table 20. Excerpt of Oral Communication Passport Learning
Outcome and Attendant Proficiency Criteria

Learning Outcome Features	Passport Learning Outcomes	Transfer-Level Proficiency Criteria[1]
Preparation for Performance	Develop a central message supporting details by applying ethics, critical thinking, and information literacy skills. Organize content for a particular audience, occasion, and purpose.	Student speakers will be able to: ■ Select topics that are relevant to and important for a public audience and occasion; ■ Find, retrieve, and critically examine information from personal experience and published sources for credibility, accuracy, relevance, and usefulness; ■ Select and critically evaluate appropriate support materials; ■ Represent sources accurately and ethically; ■ Become fully informed about the subject matter; ■ Defend motive of the presentation; and ■ Apply organizational skills in speech writing that use the claim-warrant-data method of argument construction.

[1] Evidence of proficiency of the learning outcome appropriate at the transfer level. No single student is expected to demonstrate *all* of these Proficiency Criteria, nor is this intended to be a list of all possible criteria

a student has reached the desired transfer level of proficiency for the specific learning outcome through a variety of possible methods. Each Passport institution also identifies the list of general education courses and other learning opportunities that impart these learning outcomes at the transfer-level proficiencies, which constitutes the institution's "Passport Block."

Passport Tracking System

During Phase I of the project, a task force composed of registrars and institutional research representatives from the participating institutions were charged with devising the process for indicating the Passport on student records and the process for tracking Passport student success for comparison with non-Passport transfer students and native students. In undertaking this work, the task force was informed by background information related to the transcript and student record from AACRAO.

The task force recommended that institutions indicate that a student has achieved the Passport by choosing to use one or more of the following options as preferred by the participating institution's registrar:

● Adding a comment on the transcript using a standard format,

● Posting a pseudo course on the transcript, or

● Creating an additional record to accompany the transcript.

Registrars choose the option that best serves their institution and is most compatible with the institution's student information system.[22]

Passport institutions also agree to send aggregate data to the Passport Central Data Repository (CDR) annually on the academic performance of Passport and non-Passport transfer students for two terms after transfer.

[22] For a thorough explanation of the process and rationale see task force report, Recording and Tracking Passport Students: Guidelines for Registrars <www.wiche.edu/passport/awarding>.

The CDR sorts the data from the receiving institutions and forwards it to the relevant sending institutions for use in their continuous improvement efforts. The CDR also forwards aggregate data to the Passport Review Board (PRB) for its annual review of the overall performance of the Passport program. The PRB, whose members consist of the Passport state facilitators and higher education experts in academic quality, research, student affairs, and other areas of expertise, sets policy and reviews and approves new institutions/states for participation.

At the time of this writing, data has been requested from the Phase I institutions for the first year of operation, SY2013–14. Registrars have been asked to: (1) provide the total number of Passports awarded by the institution; (2) indicate the academic progress of transfer students—both Passport and non-Passport—in the 2014 spring semester; and (3) provide the number of native students who earned a Passport. Reporting on the academic progress of students entails reporting the number of credits of grades (*e.g.*, A, B, C, D, P, Did Not Finish, and F) earned at the receiving institution after transfer; the mean number of credits in which the student is enrolled at the receiving institution for each of the first two terms after transferring; and

the mean GPA, weighted for number of credits each student completed. In addition to providing information about the number of Passports awarded and how Passport students perform after transfer, particularly compared to non-Passport transfers, this first effort at data collection offers the opportunity to refine and improve the data collection process based on feedback from registrars and institutional researchers. The PRB is scheduled to issue its first annual report in spring 2015.

Summary

Academic leaders are developing strategies that address the "completion agenda," seeking ways to increase the proportion of the U.S. population with associate, bachelor's, master's, and doctoral degrees. The Passport offers an opportunity to focus on the quality and coherence of learning in lower-division general education across institutions in multiple states. Based on learning outcomes and transfer-level proficiency criteria, students achieve the Passport by demonstrating knowledge and/or skills. Implementation of the Passport is expected to save students, institutions, states, and taxpayers time and money as it streamlines and accelerates the transfer process, thereby reducing time to credential.

216

Case Studies

CHAPTER SEVENTEEN

Strengthening Community College Transfer to Highly-Selective Research Institutions:
A University of California Case Study

STEPHEN J. HANDEL
Associate Vice President, Undergraduate Admissions,
University of California
Office of the President

ADAM PARKER
Policy and Program Analyst,
University of California
Office of the President

SHAWN BRICK
Associate Director, Undergraduate Admissions,
University of California
Office of the President

LIZ TERRY
Policy and Program Analyst,
University of California
Office of the President

This article is based on the findings and recommendations of the University of California Transfer Action Team report, Preparing California
for Its Future: Enhancing Community College Transfer to UC, available at ‹http://ucop.edu/transfer-action-team/›.

Strengthening Community College Transfer to Highly-Selective Research Institutions: A University of California Case Study

On September 30, 2013, Janet Napolitano became the 20th president of the University of California (UC); in one of her first acts as president, she urged the Regents of the University of California to "reexamine how we interact with community college transfers" (Napolitano 2013). Citing statistics revealing that UC tapped only a small proportion of the geographic and racial/ethnic diversity of students attending the state's community colleges,[23] the President announced her intention to convene a UC "transfer action team" to address "not just the need, but also the steps needed to streamline the flow of community college students who transfer into the University of California."

This chapter describes the conditions that led to President Napolitano's call for a review of transfer at all UC institutions. The findings and recommendations from the President's Transfer Action Team's ("The Team") final report are delineated within this chapter, with special emphasis on those strategies that can be employed by any college or university interested in increasing success rates for transfer students working towards a four-year degree.

Background and Context

The Team, co-chaired by a member of the Academic Senate and the Vice President of Student Affairs, was convened in December 2013. It was composed of faculty, students, and staff tasked with identifying strategies to increase the success of transfer students from California's community colleges to one of nine UC undergraduate campuses. Five months later, the Team produced a high-profile report, *Preparing California for its Future: Enhancing Community College Transfer to UC* (University of California 2014).

UC's commitment to transfer stems from the California Master Plan for Higher Education (California State Department of Education 1960). The Master Plan delineates a set of responsibilities for each of California's higher education segments and also explicitly

---

[23] For example, UC admits 50 percent of its transfer students from only 19 of the state's 112 community colleges.

221

identifies transfer between California's community colleges and UC as a key goal of California's higher education system. California has invested heavily in a community college system as a way of making the bachelor's degree accessible to a broad range of Californians and as a means of supplying a statewide economy increasingly dependent upon a well-educated citizenry.

While UC's focus on transfer follows naturally from the California experience, it is unique nationally. While most highly-selective institutions admit relatively few transfer students from community colleges, nearly one-third of the students entering UC in any given fall term start at a California two-year institution (Dowd and Melguizo 2008). In addition, UC's place as a selective research institution means that its standards of admissions are rigorous, emphasizing pre-major preparation for transfer student success in upper-division courses (junior level and above). Transfer students who enter UC must be prepared to compete on an even par with students who enter UC as freshmen.

In fulfilling its charge, the Team delineated five characteristics that should be the core of efforts to strengthen the transfer pathway between community colleges and four-year institutions. They are:

● Two- and four-year institutions should strive for *simplicity* in the transfer process. Acknowledging that transferring in the middle of one's undergraduate career is inherently complex for many students, the Team stressed that whatever hurdles prospective applicants face in preparing for

222

transfer should be intellectual rather than administrative.

● The transfer process must be *transparent*. In a system stressing intellectual engagement and extensive preparation for transfer, the Team emphasized that the four-year institution must provide clearly-articulated pathways that delineate a roadmap for student transfer and completion of the baccalaureate.

● All institutional solutions adopted to improve transfer should be *strategic* and *sustainable*, helping foster long-term success for transfer students.

● Improving *student diversity* must be a key driver for a strengthened transfer process, especially given that community colleges are far more likely to enroll students that have been traditionally underrepresented in higher education, including low-income, first-generation, and underrepresented minority students (African American, American Indian, and Chicano/Latino students are classified as underrepresented at UC).

● Finally, access is not enough for a fully functioning transfer process; *timely degree completion* for all students must be the ultimate goal.

Findings and Recommendations

Although the Transfer Action Team's findings and recommendations primarily were focused on addressing specific issues influencing UC, many of the Team's findings and recommendations will be useful to college leaders, policy analysts, enrollment managers, and other student service professionals who are committed to strengthening the transfer pathway in their states, regions, or locales.

FINDING 1: *TRANSFER DEMAND IS DEPENDENT ON STUDENT PREPARATION AND FOUR-YEAR INSTITUTIONAL COMMITMENT*

Transfer student demand—just like demand at the freshman student level—is a function of student interest and preparation, which, in turn, is influenced by the programs, services, and mission of community colleges and four-year institutions. Transfer demand, often measured by application volume to any given four-year institution, is a pivotal marker of interest and must be analyzed with the same degree of seriousness given to first-year student enrollment. When such demand declines, community college and four-year institution leaders must look to the causes of this decline. Yet transfer demand remains a rarely discussed and little-researched area of enrollment management.

At the University of California, where transfer enrollment had sustained increases, a decline in applications of nearly 9 percent since 2011–12 brought increased scrutiny. The Team concluded that the drop in transfer applications was likely due to the cumulative effects of state budget cuts in response to the national economic downturn that began in 2008 (Bohn, Reyes, and Johnson 2013). Reduced enrollment, limited availability of courses needed for transfer, and insufficiently supported advising services likely combined to undercut both the number of students aiming to transfer and their progress toward becoming transfer eligible.

RECOMMENDATION 1: *CREATE MESSAGES AND RESOURCES THAT ENCOURAGE AND HELP PREPARE STUDENTS FOR TRANSFER*

To address the decline in UC transfer applications, while anticipating potential demand in the future as the economy improved, the Team recommended that UC's commitment to transfer students should be made more visible through the use of traditional and emerging technologies that:

- amplify UC's current messaging to prospective students, especially to students from underserved groups, encouraging them to prepare for and apply to UC;
- better identify and track prospective California community college applicants who may be good candidates for a UC degree; and
- reach out to students at strategic points both in high school and during their community college careers, helping them to prepare for transfer to UC from the first day they enter a community college (Grubb 2006).

The Team emphasized that in reaching out to prospective applicants, UC should develop resources that provide students with the information they need—*when they need it*—so that they can prepare effectively for transfer to a UC campus.

FINDING 2: *STUDENT DIVERSITY IS KEY TO A VIBRANT TRANSFER PROCESS*

While the decline in applications from California resident community college students was a relatively recent phenomenon, UC has

223

had long-standing difficulty in attracting students from some underserved groups to its campuses. Although UC excels in recruiting students who are first in their family to attend college and students from low-income backgrounds, the institution's record in attracting students from certain racial and ethnic minority groups is less impressive.

In analyzing the diversity of its transfer classes, the Transfer Action Team discovered that a large portion of transfer applicants to UC originated from a limited number of community colleges (University of California 2014a). Data revealed that half of all California community college transfer students entering UC come from only 19 of the state's 112 community colleges. Extraordinarily, two community colleges transfer more students to UC than the combined total of 46 other community colleges in the state. In drawing from so few of the state's community colleges—among the most diverse postsecondary systems in America—UC was hobbled in its ability to increase the diversity of its transfer classes.

To counter this stratification, the Team recommended that UC foster stronger relationships with community colleges that did not send significant numbers of transfer students to UC, recognizing that many of these colleges were not able to offer all of the transfer-preparation courses and services their students needed, and recommended UC support their efforts to enhance the transfer path from their institutions.

RECOMMENDATION 2: *INCREASE INSTITUTIONAL PROFILE THROUGHOUT ALL COMMUNITY COLLEGES AND SEEK PARTNERSHIPS WITH TRANSFER-FOCUSED COMMUNITY COLLEGES THAT ENROLL A DIVERSE STUDENT BODY*

Appreciating the benefits of enrolling a transfer class that encompasses the broad diversity of California, the Transfer Action Team recommended that UC create mechanisms ensuring that UC reaches out to every community college by:

- increasing its interaction with community college counselors and advisors. For the past two decades, UC has hosted a series of "Ensuring Transfer Success" counselor institutes, which are designed to communicate UC's transfer admissions requirements to these influential student advocates. The Team recommended that these events be offered throughout California.[24]
- developing a statewide strategy of onsite visits and use of technology to ensure a more consistent engagement with every California community college; this includes, at minimum, a commitment of at least one annual visit by UC admissions and outreach staff to all two-year colleges in California.

In addition to expanding UC's presence in all of California's community colleges, the Team concluded that in order to foster greater diversity, UC should develop specific partnerships with 30 community colleges that cur-

224

---

[24] Additional information on these institutes can be found at ‹http://admission.universityofcalifornia.edu/counselors/news-events/ets/›.

rently send few transfer students to UC yet enroll significant numbers of students from underserved racial/ethnic groups. These partnerships should provide these community college partners with extensive counseling resources, UC advising and outreach services for students, UC student ambassadors who have successfully transferred and can serve as peer mentors, and opportunities for faculty to create transfer-appropriate courses and align lower- and upper-division curricula.

FINDING 3: *STREAMLINE TRANSFER PREPARATION PATHWAYS*

Transparency is the third component of a vibrant transfer process. In a state that has 112 community colleges, 23 CSU campuses, and nine undergraduate UC campuses, prospective students are presented with a rich array of majors and degrees. Yet this can be especially bewildering for transfer students, particularly those without guidance on negotiating their transition between institutions, each possessing its own curricula, degrees, and academic rules and regulations (Handel 2013).

Research indicates that the low rate of transfer between community colleges and four-year institutions may be at least partially the result of the abundant number of academic programs and majors available at four-year institutions, coupled with insufficient guidance about how to evaluate competing educational choices (Goldrick-Rab 2007; Rosenbaum 2006). Reductions in student advising services at California community colleges, as noted earlier, exacerbate an already complex process that students must

negotiate. Students may not realize the implications of ill-advised course selections at their community college until they prepare to apply for transfer, at which point they are confronted with the fact that they have not, in fact, prepared adequately to transfer. Rosenbaum and his colleagues articulate the dilemma facing transfer students well: "First [transfer] students must be aware of what kind of help they need and when they need it. Second, they must be informed about how and where to get it. Third, they must actually go get it. Fourth, students must seek this information well in advance" (2006, 119–120).

Additional research reveals that students who are "transfer-directed"—that is, students who have a plan for transfer, even if a relatively tentative one—are more likely to successfully transition to a four-year institution and complete a bachelor's degree (Moore and Shulock 2011; Horn 2009). But such plans are more than the amalgamation of information: in conversations with UC transfer students solicited for this project, most believe there is sufficient information about transfer; what is lacking is the careful organization of that information in ways that help students plan for this transition, along with interfaces, such as web and mobile technologies, which better represent how students access and use college-planning information.

RECOMMENDATION 3: *STREAMLINE TRANSFER PREPARATION PROCESS TO ENSURE STUDENT COMPLETION*

Transparency, then, represents an emphasis on providing students with unambiguous academic pathways, along with sufficient guidance and information that help keep them on track from the first day they step on a community college campus. The Team concluded that although the transfer pathway may be difficult to negotiate, especially for students unfamiliar with higher education processes, efforts most likely to succeed in advancing transparency will:

- highlight the specific preparation requirements for student success at UC;
- leverage new technologies that place greater emphasis on transfer guidance and planning for students (as opposed to increasing the amount of information); guidance that, where possible, is personalized to address the needs of individual students; and
- reflect successful efforts by faculty at the sending and receiving institutions to align their curricula so that there are explicit and transparent academic pathways for students to follow.

FINDING 4: *CREATE TRANSFER-AFFIRMING CULTURES*

The degree to which students feel a sense of belonging on their chosen campus has been the subject of considerable research in the past three decades.[25] Students who find themselves positively attached to the work of the academy—often the result of opportunities that allow them to engage actively with faculty, staff, and peers—are far more likely to view their college experiences satisfactorily and to graduate.

---

[25] *See*, for example, Astin 1993; Tinto 1994.

At UC, surveys indicated that 81 percent of UC transfer students feel that they "belong" on their campus. This high level of commitment is eclipsed, however, by UC freshman students, 86 percent of whom feel a sense of belonging to the UC campus that they attend (University of California 2014b). Although the impressions of transfer and freshmen students are not radically different, they hint at some measure of relative dissatisfaction for transfers. These observations are consistent with research focusing on the satisfaction of community college transfer students nationally, despite additional evidence indicating that such students are likely to perform as well as or better than students who started college as freshmen at a four-year institution (Pascarella and Terenzini 2005).

Such institutional bonding, however, takes time, and transfer students have less of it than freshmen when they arrive on a four-year college campus. Kuh, Kinzie, Schuh, and Whitt describe the problem well:

> *Most institutions pay far more attention to new first-time first-year students than they do to transfer students. As a result, transfers often do not know enough about the resources available to them. Equally problematic, they have little by way of common academic and social experiences with their peers who started at the institution and cannot easily connect with other transfer students. Thus, they often feel disconnected from the institution* (2005, 255).

In response to the unique challenges facing community college transfer students, higher education leaders at two- and four-year institutions are beginning to identify the elements that encompass what has come to be known as a "transfer-affirming culture" (*See* College Board 2011; Handel and Williams 2012; Herrera and Jain 2013). This approach is designed to identify those factors—people, services, and resources—that propel community college students toward the baccalaureate degree.[26] Many of these students, especially those who come from families with no history of college attendance, lack the "transfer cultural capital" needed to negotiate the transfer process (Laanan, Strarobin, and Eggleston 2010). Such capital is the accumulation of knowledge and skills that are essential and unique to the transfer process. For example, transfer students—unlike college-bound high school graduates—must become adept at finding and interpreting articulation agreements, fashioning different course schedules that satisfy the lower-division requirements of multiple four-year institutions that they would like to attend, and estimating the extent to which their community college credit will satisfy requirements for a four-year degree.

RECOMMENDATION 4: *WELCOME STUDENTS WITH A "TRANSFER SUCCESS KIT"*

The Transfer Action Team concluded that four-year institutions can streamline the transition of transfer students by conducting a comprehensive review of its current transfer services, identifying programs or services where additional support is needed, and developing an organized package or "kit" of

transfer support initiatives. Culling the available research, this transfer success kit should include:

- guaranteed on-campus housing for transfer students, allowing them to participate in campus life, and offering a safe and stable environment for study and social integration;
- physical transfer centers or online, web-based "resource hubs" that link transfer students to the wider campus network of academic, research, and social opportunities;
- peer-to-peer mentoring and advising programs that provide new transfer students with the insight and guidance of individuals who have experienced the transfer transition;
- summer programs for admitted students that allow California community college transfers to immerse themselves in the four-year campus culture, meet with faculty and staff, participate in social and cultural events, and strengthen academic skills that will be needed for success in upper-division courses;
- mandatory orientation programs for transfer students. While an orientation is typical—and mandatory—for freshman students at most four-year colleges and universities, transfer student orientations are far less available and are often perfunctory; and
- transfer credit evaluation for every transfer enrollee that delineates how a student's community college credit will be applied to the bachelor's degree and guid-

---

[26] *See*, for example, McDonough 1997.

ance (or instructions on how to obtain guidance) about program planning for their first term and major program. This credit evaluation should be received well before a student must select courses for the first term at the four-year institution.

Strengthening the Transfer Pathway

A common thread throughout the Team's recommendations is a renewed partnership among four-year institutions and community colleges to strengthen the transfer pathway. Such a partnership, especially among publicly supported institutions, should include joint strategic planning opportunities to better align courses and majors across institutions, as well as providing a united voice for higher education in state political processes.

In addition to stronger partnerships with community colleges, four-year institutions must make community college students an explicit element of their overall strategic enrollment strategy. Recruiting community college students as backfill for an unsuccessful freshman enrollment plan is neither good practice for four-year institutions that may be saddled with transfers they never authentically intended to enroll, nor educationally sound from the standpoint of community college students not yet fully prepared for the upper division. Transfer must be a strategic and authentic part of the institution's mission and planning processes.

The Transfer Action Team report received national media coverage, not only for the comprehensiveness of its findings and recommendations, but also for the message it conveys to a constituency of students often overlooked in the national debate about higher education. Napolitano's *Preparing California for its Future* is an alert from the leader of one of the nation's most prominent public institutions that transfer must be included in any four-year institution's enrollment strategy—a strategy that will increase student diversity and create lower-cost college options for more American families.

CHAPTER EIGHTEEN

Implementing
Reverse Transfer in Ohio:
A Case Study

JASON L. TAYLOR
*Assistant Professor, Department of Educational
Leadership and Policy, University of Utah*

I want to acknowledge and thank several individuals and organizations that have supported this research. Thank you to Calista Smith and Anthony Landis at the Ohio Board of Regents who led the CWID grant in Ohio, and thank you to Debra Bragg, the PI for the CWID research as well as the many members of the CWID research team. Finally, I want to acknowledge the Bill & Melinda Gates Foundation and the Kresge Foundation for funding this research.

CHAPTER EIGHTEEN

Implementing Reverse Transfer in Ohio: A Case Study

In 2012, 12 states were awarded a grant to develop and implement reverse transfer programs as part of the Credit When It's Due (CWID) initiative, and three additional states joined the initiative in late 2013. This chapter reports the experience of reverse implementation and initial outcomes in Ohio through the CWID grant. To contextualize Ohio's experience, the chapter begins with a brief summary of the literature on transfer students and state transfer policy and is followed by a description of the CWID initiative. A presentation of the primary implementation strategies used to develop and implement reverse transfer policy under the CWID grant follows, along with an analysis of the five dimensions of reverse transfer implementation to report how implementation works in Ohio. The chapter ends with a description of initial results from implementation efforts and a discussion of successes and challenges in Ohio.

Background

The impetus for reverse transfer can be contextualized by the literature on transfer students

and transfer policy. National data show that about 78 to 80 percent of students who transfer from a community college to a university do so without an associate degree (Hossler *et al.* 2012; McCormick and Carroll 1997). If all transfer students were equally successful and obtained a bachelor's degree, this would not be a problem. However, data from the CWID Baseline Study show that of students potentially eligible for reverse transfer, approximately 50 percent had not earned a bachelor's degree from the university to which they transferred four years after their transfer (Taylor *et al.* 2013). Further, some evidence demonstrates that earning an associate degree prior to transfer is related to bachelor's degree completion. For example, the National Student Clearinghouse reports that 71 percent of students who transfer with the associate degree complete a bachelor's degree four years after transfer compared to 55 percent of students who transfer without an associate degree (2012).

Reverse transfer programs and policies emerged in the early 2000s, most notably at institutions such as the University of Texas-

231

Table 21. Ohio Institutions Participating in CWID

▪ Belmont College	▪ Kent State University-Stark	▪ Shawnee State University
▪ Bowling Green State University	▪ Lakeland Community College	▪ Sinclair Community College
▪ Central Ohio Technical College	▪ Lorain County Community College	▪ Southern State Community College
▪ Central State University	▪ Marion Technical College	▪ Stark State College
▪ Cincinnati State Technical & Community College	▪ Miami University	▪ Terra Community College
	▪ Miami University-Hamilton	▪ University of Akron
▪ Clark State Community College	▪ Miami University-Middletown	▪ University of Cincinnati
▪ Cleveland State University	▪ North Central State College	▪ University of Cincinnati-Blue Ash
▪ Columbus State Community College	▪ Northwest State Community College	▪ University of Cincinnati-Clermont
▪ Cuyahoga Community College	▪ Ohio State University	▪ University of Toledo
▪ Eastern Gateway Community College	▪ Ohio University	▪ Washington State Community College
	▪ Owens Community College	
▪ Edison Community College	▪ Rhodes State College	▪ Wright State University
▪ Hocking College	▪ Rio Grande Community College	▪ Youngstown State University
▪ Kent State University		▪ Zane State College

El Paso and the University of Massachusetts at Boston (Ekal and Krebs 2011). Only in the past few years have reverse transfer state policies emerged around the country (Bautsch 2013). In many ways, states' reverse transfer efforts are part of larger efforts to improve transfer access and student success. State policies such as common course numbering, statewide articulation agreements, transferable general education cores, transferable associate degrees, and articulation websites, among others, demonstrate how states continue to improve the transferability of credits among institutions of higher education (Anderson *et al.* 2006; Ignash and Townsend 2000; 2001; Cohen *et al.* 2012).

Credit When It's Due Initiative

The Credit When It's Due (CWID) initiative was "designed to encourage partnerships of community colleges and universities to significantly expand programs that award associate degrees to transfer students when the student completes the requirements for the associate degree while pursuing a bachelor's

degree" (Lumina Foundation 2012). The Lumina Foundation, along with four additional funders, released a competitive request for proposal and awarded grants in late 2012 to 12 states to develop and implement reverse transfer: Arkansas, Colorado, Florida, Hawaii, Maryland, Michigan, Minnesota, Missouri, New York, North Carolina, Ohio, and Oregon. Three additional states—Georgia, Tennessee, and Texas—joined the initiative in late 2013, for a total of 15 states.

The Ohio Context

The public system of higher education in Ohio is coordinated by the Ohio Board of Regents and includes 14 universities with 24 regional branch campuses, 23 community colleges, and over 120 adult workforce education and training centers across the state. Ohio is home to 111 private, not-for-profit and 31 private, for-profit colleges and universities, many of which belong to the Association of Independent Colleges and Universities of Ohio (AICUO) or the Ohio Foundation of Independent Colleges (OFIC).

232

Ohio has a long history of transfer and articulation efforts that provide the policy framework and context for reverse transfer. The first Ohio Articulation and Transfer Council was formed in 1990 and aimed to develop a transfer guarantee for students moving among public institutions within the state. Transfer policy has developed over the past couple decades to focus on transferable general education curricula; the system-wide recognition of A.A. and A.S. degrees; the development of transfer assurance guides for pre-major and major courses in specific programs of study and career and technical education; and more recently to the awarding of college credit for military training, experience, and coursework. In addition to these policies, Ohio has a well-developed technology infrastructure to support the exchange of electronic transcripts among public institutions, as well as online systems for institutions and students to easily identify course equivalencies.

It is also important to contextualize reverse transfer within Ohio's college completion efforts. Ohio has participated in multi-institutional or multi-state efforts such as Achieving the Dream, Complete College America, Completion by Design, and Project Win-Win. In addition, under Ohio's performance-based funding policy, institutions are increasingly being rewarded for student success rather than student enrollments.

Reverse Transfer Implementation Strategies

The development and implementation of reverse transfer policies and practice in Ohio can be characterized and organized around four strategies: (a) leadership; (b) common policy and process development; (c) leveraging existing assets and policies; and (d) sustainability.

LEADERSHIP

The Ohio Board of Regents (OBR) is the state coordinating board for higher education in Ohio and provides leadership for the development and implementation of reverse transfer under the CWID initiative. Through the CWID grant, a reverse transfer manager coordinates and manages daily grant activities. The project manager is instrumental in coordinating statewide efforts including leading monthly conference calls, facilitating webinar trainings, and visiting individual campuses to gather information to inform policy development.

POLICY DEVELOPMENT

Unlike some CWID states, reverse transfer was not legislated in Ohio, so from November 2012 through April 2013, the OBR engaged the public institutions participating in the CWID grant to develop a statewide policy framework for reverse transfer. In addition to input gathered through this process, policies were modeled after a reverse transfer pilot between Cuyahoga Community College and its regional university partners. Several key policy decisions were made to guide the implementation of reverse transfer. First, the number of credits required for a community college to award a degree, known as the residency requirement, varied among institutions. For the purposes of the grant period, the institutions agreed to use 20 credits as the

233

common residency requirement for reverse transfer. Second, the state agreed to common reverse transfer eligibility criteria. These criteria state that students must:

- meet the 20 credit residency requirement at an Ohio public community college;
- pursue a bachelor's degree and be enrolled at an Ohio public university;
- earn 45 cumulative college credits;
- have not previously earned an associate degree or higher; and
- have a GPA of 2.0 or higher.

This common set of eligibility requirements provided consistency across the state so institutions would be able to identify similarly eligible students. Third, a common memorandum of understanding (MOU) was developed to ensure common institutional practices and policies across institutions. For example, the MOU stipulated that community colleges would not require students to pay a graduation fee as part of the reverse transfer program. Fourth, guidance was provided on the interpretation of the Family Educational Rights and Privacy Act (FERPA) in the context of reverse transfer. This guidance suggested that universities should obtain consent via an "opt-in" model before transmitting students' transcripts to community colleges. A sample consent letter and student FAQs were developed and disseminated for institutions to obtain consent and to communicate and market reverse transfer to potentially eligible students. Finally, common report metrics were developed and defined to report back to OBR and to the external researchers.

These common policies were established early in the grant period and agreed upon by all participating institutions prior to implementation. A process flow chart and many sample policies and processes were released and disseminated as a result of these development efforts.

LEVERAGING EXISTING TECHNOLOGY ASSETS AND TRANSFER AND ARTICULATION POLICIES

The existing technology and policy infrastructure in Ohio provided a strong foundation for reverse transfer. The technology foundation allowed for efficient and automated transcript exchange and a strong course articulation system. The Ohio Articulation and Transfer Clearinghouse (ATC) is the state's platform to exchange electronic transcripts among Ohio state-assisted institutions. The ATC allows for the fully electronic exchange of transcripts using Extensible Markup Language (XML) such that no paper transcripts are required and electronic records are automatically read into institutional student information systems. The ATC also provides the transcript in alternative electronic formats if a community college chooses not to upload reverse transfer transcripts directly into the student information system.

Ohio also has a well-developed course equivalency system called the Course Equivalency Management System (CEMS). The CEMS is the foundation for course-to-course articulation among public institutions; it houses the course equivalency tables that allow institutions and students to easily identify course articulations within the OBR system. In addition to CEMS, a contract with Transferology provides course articulations for most public and private Ohio institutions, as well as many out-of-state institutions.

SUSTAINABILITY

The final strategy of Ohio's grant involved efforts to sustain reverse transfer by integrating the responsibilities of the grant project coordinator into the transfer and articulation division at the OBR. Because the grant funded the project coordinator and related activities, the OBR intentionally included the reverse transfer roles and responsibilities in an existing unit in the organization. The OBR is also working with institutions to determine the best way to sustain several policies such as the residency requirement, institutional roles and responsibilities, and graduation fee waivers.

Five Steps of Reverse Transfer Implementation

In early 2015, a paper released by Office of Community College Research and Leadership (OCCRL) outlined five steps of reverse transfer implementation and how states, systems, and institutions participating in the CWID initiative were optimizing reverse transfer. Optimization was defined as "policy and program change at any level—state, system, or institution—that yields the largest number of students who are eligible for and able to benefit from reverse transfer," without negatively impacting quality or overextending resources. These five steps of reverse transfer are: (a) student identification, (b) consent, (c) transcript exchange, (d) degree

audit, and (e) degree conferral and advising (Taylor and Bragg 2015).

STUDENT IDENTIFICATION

The Ohio Board of Regents uses the Higher Education Information system to apply the eligibility criteria and identify which students are potentially eligible for reverse transfer. The OBR then sends the list of potentially eligible students to the participating universities. Moving forward, the OBR is working with the National Student Clearinghouse to determine alternative options for generating an eligibility list that can be sent to community colleges so that the two-year schools provide leadership, in collaboration with universities, in their communications with students about reverse transfer.

CONSENT

As part of Ohio's opt-in consent process, the universities send a letter, endorsed by the university and the community college, to the list of potentially eligible students, inviting them to participate in reverse transfer. If a student agrees to participate, they sign a consent letter indicating that they permit the university to send their transcripts to the community college and allow the community college to confer the degree, should they meet all of the associate degree requirements.

TRANSCRIPT EXCHANGE

Once a student consents to participate in reverse transfer, the university sends their electronic transcript to the respective community college, and the community college student

235

information system reads the transcript. An electronic field added to the transcript exchange signals to the receiving community college that the transcript is for the purpose of reverse transfer.

DEGREE AUDIT

Once the community college receives the transcript, institutional degree audits assess the degree against existing associate degree requirements. Most community colleges use degree audit software to conduct the audit, but some colleges conduct a manual degree audit.

DEGREE CONFERRAL AND ADVISING

The final process involves conferring the associate degree to students who meet the degree requirements. For students who do not meet the degree requirements, most community colleges inform students of the credits and/or courses needed to complete the degree.

Preliminary Outcomes

Ohio and all states participating in Credit When It's Due continue to collaborate with researchers at the Office of Community College Research and Leadership to collect data on the impact of reverse transfer implementation efforts. The preliminary aggregate data provide a portrait of the initial impact of reverse transfer in Ohio during the first round of implementation that began in spring 2013. A total of 8,718 students were potentially eligible for reverse transfer with results available for 7,535 or 84 percent of students at the time of this publication (*see* Figure 11, on page 237). Of these 7,535 potentially eligible stu-

dents, the percentage of students who consented and agreed to participate in reverse transfer was approximately 19 percent, or 1,462 students. A total of 1,408 degree audits were conducted by the community colleges that resulted in the conferral of 594 associate degrees. Thus, of the 7,535 potentially eligible students for which results were available, approximately 8 percent received an associate degree.

Successes

Several key actions during the initial grant period provided a pathway for implementation by spring 2013. The Ohio Board of Regent's leadership around policy and process development ensured that all institutions were operating under a similar policy framework. Many policy issues previously discussed, such as the residency requirement, consent policy, and the fees associated with degree conferral, were addressed early in the grant period. Another success, which should not be understated, was the leveraging of transcript exchange and course equivalency technologies that allowed Ohio to quickly proceed with reverse transfer implementation using existing automated technologies.

Challenges

One challenge experienced by the state was the low opt-in consent rate. Nearly two thirds of potentially eligible students did not respond to the option to participate in reverse transfer. The average consent rate among the participating universities was 23 percent, but some institutions obtained consent rates of nearly

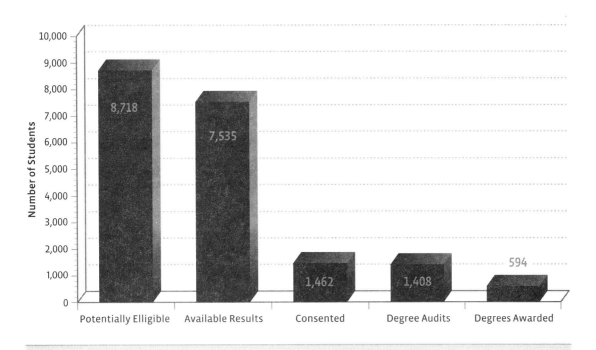

Figure 11. Outcomes of Ohio's First Round of Reverse Transfer Implementation

40 percent (Ohio State University) and as high as 53 percent (Shawnee State University).

The role of reverse transfer in the performance-based funding (PBF) context in Ohio constitutes both a success and a challenge. On the one hand, community colleges were encouraged to make the time to conduct degree audits because reverse transfer associate degrees could be factored into performance funding for degree completion. Like some other states with PBF policies, however, the way reverse transfer figures into the PBF formula in Ohio has not been treated uniquely from the general policy. Concerns have been raised about a fair funding distribution among multiple institutions that have served students. Questions about which institutions receive credit for reverse transfer associate degrees under a PBF policy need to be explored further.

Finally, the state lacks a systematic way to articulate upper-division courses back to the community college, a policy issue that has emerged in several states. Because reverse transfer involves transferring back large numbers of upper-division courses, many of which the community college does not offer, new articulations or substitutions often need to be created. Columbus State Community College reported that approximately 80 percent of the degrees conferred via reverse transfer required some type of new articulation or substitution, so the prospects of reverse transfer benefiting a larger number of students rests, in part, on new articulations.

Concluding Thoughts

Reverse transfer is an emerging policy issue in most states throughout the nation. Our unpublished analysis at the Office of Community College Research and Leadership shows that 15 states, many but not all of which are also Credit When It's Due (CWID) states, have legislative policy related to reverse transfer. In all but one state without legislative policy, we identified at least one or more postsecondary institution with a reverse transfer program. Given the widespread interest in and adoption of reverse transfer at the institutional and state levels, it is important to share the experiences and lessons from early adopters so other states and institutions can learn from these experiences. This chapter shared Ohio's CWID experience and highlighted factors that shaped and influenced reverse transfer implementation in Ohio, how reverse transfer works in Ohio, and preliminary outcomes based on data from the first round of implementation.

Although the CWID grant period had not yet ended when this chapter was written, several important issues emerge from Ohio's reverse transfer experience. First, the postsecondary governance and coordination structure in Ohio that provided coordination and leadership for the CWID project was an important implementation factor. Whereas the centralized nature of Ohio's postsecondary governance and coordination structure facilitated reverse transfer implementation efforts, many states do not share similar governance structures. If these states intend to pursue a statewide reverse transfer initiative, state leadership will likely be important to implementation efforts.

Second, reverse transfer implementation initiated an assessment of and conversation about several institutional policies such as residency requirements, graduation applications and fees, unique community college degree requirements, and new course substitutions, among others. Many, although certainly not all, of these institutional policies and practices are not legislated or mandated by states. As states and institutions proceed with reverse transfer, variation in these policies warrant a discussion about whether and how to standardize these policies among institutions within the state.

Third, Ohio's existing investment in technologies for exchanging electronic transcripts and for course articulation was clearly an asset in terms of automating steps of the reverse transfer process. States and institutions considering adoption of reverse transfer policies should consider an assessment of technology capacity for these functions, as well as consider new solutions such as those currently under development by the National Student Clearinghouse or private vendors such as Parchment and AcademyOne.

Fourth, although some technologies were an asset for Ohio, the methods used to obtain consent resulted in inconsistent consent rates among universities and an overall low consent rate. Some CWID states are leveraging existing processes or technologies to obtain consent, such as integrating consent into transfer student admission applications or integrating consent into students' university

238

registration portals. Ohio is considering additional options for consent as part of their sustainability strategy, and improvements in the overall consent rate could dramatically increase the number of reverse transfer associate degrees conferred.

Finally, it is important to reflect on how reverse transfer influences and intersects with existing transfer policies and other state completion policies. Precisely how reverse transfer will affect or be affected by existing and emerging transfer and completion policies is yet to be determined. However, states considering adoption of reverse transfer should analyze how reverse transfer policies intersect with performance-based funding policies or existing articulation and transfer policies, for example, and account for these factors in the design of their policies.

239

THE

TRANSFER HANDBOOK

PROMOTING
STUDENT
SUCCESS

CHAPTER NINETEEN

Facilitating Transfer Students' Transition to a Liberal Arts College

CHARLES HANNON
*Associate Dean of the Faculty and Professor of
Computing and Information Studies,
Washington & Jefferson College*

CHAPTER NINETEEN

Facilitating Transfer Students' Transition to a Liberal Arts College

Two phenomena have combined in recent years to make the student recruitment process at selective private liberal arts colleges more competitive than ever: The first is the decreasing U.S. public high school population. While some regions, such as the Southwest and Florida, are experiencing a population boom, others—particularly the northeastern states—are experiencing dramatic decreases. This has presented a particular challenge to mid-Atlantic colleges that historically have been considered "regional"; over the past five years, many of them have responded by adopting national student recruitment strategies.

The second phenomenon is the more recent economic recession and slow-growth recovery, which together have further diminished the supply of prospective students and have made parents more aware of their negotiating power in the admissions process. In this environment, college officials carefully examine their recruitment efforts, business costs, and fee structures. They are committed to enrolling freshman classes of comparable quality to previous years' but without "buying" them at an unsustainable discount.

The small liberal arts college where I serve as associate dean of the faculty has made significant changes to its efforts to attract and serve transfer students as part of its overall strategy to respond to these challenges. Washington & Jefferson College (W&J) has long welcomed transfer students, having enrolled an average of ten per year during the period from 2000 through 2010. But a concerted effort, begun in 2010, to increase to 40 the number of transfer students per year (roughly 15 percent of all new students annually by 2013–14) has resulted in a significant review of and rededication to the principles of a liberal arts education within the context of a difficult business imperative. This effort has required a "change management" philosophy based upon cooperation and collaboration amongst divisions of the college that traditionally have not worked together to accomplish shared goals. Most of all, it has required a deep understanding of the transfer experience from the point

243

of view of transfer students themselves, whose interests we serve and whose lives and futures we hope to help shape.

All corners of the campus expressed concern about the concerted effort to quadruple the number of transfer students matriculating at this traditional, residential liberal arts college. The admissions office was concerned about obstacles inherent in existing processes and policies that might result in transfer students enrolling elsewhere. Academic Affairs—to include the faculty we represent—was concerned about academic standards, about students succeeding in higher-level courses when they had taken foundational courses elsewhere, and about the increase in faculty workload due to evaluating transcripts and advising incoming students. And Student Life was concerned about additional resources and programming that would be required to effect a successful transition for these new students.

Evaluating Student Transcripts

The first and most significant change was in the evaluation of student transcripts. In the past, a transfer student applied to the College, submitted transcripts and clearance forms, and was accepted or rejected by admissions. Only if the student paid a $200 non-refundable deposit did admissions refer his transcripts to the registrar's office for evaluation, and the student to student life for orientation ("Nuts and Bolts"). This system had the advantage of ensuring that the registrar and department chairs spent time reviewing courses only of students who were committed to attending the College. But it had the

disadvantage of deferring for far too long an answer to transfer students' most important questions: Which courses will transfer, and how will they be counted toward general education and major requirements? After reviewing College procedures, we decided to refer to the registrar—and then to department chairs—the transcript of every student who submitted an application. Academic Affairs committed to conducting these evaluations in ten or fewer business days. Admissions still conducts an initial review and excludes applicants whom the College is certain not to accept, but all remaining applicants' transcripts are reviewed. This has significantly increased the amount of time the registrar and department chairs devote to this activity.

Reviewing transfer courses is time consuming and touches the core of our mission as a liberal arts college. In general, our policy is to accept all courses that are similar in kind to those we teach (or would teach) in our own curriculum. Thus, if a student takes HIS 105: History of U.S. II at another college, we want to credit it as HIS 206: 20th Century America, as the course is named in our curriculum. One goal (among others) is that we want to ensure that the student does not take what is essentially the same course twice. Alternatively, if a student takes a course elsewhere that does not have a direct equivalent on our campus—for example, HIS 213: 20th Century World History—we can evaluate it as similar to something we would teach (provided we had the resources to do so) and award "generic" credit for HIS 200. This process requires input from department chairs

244

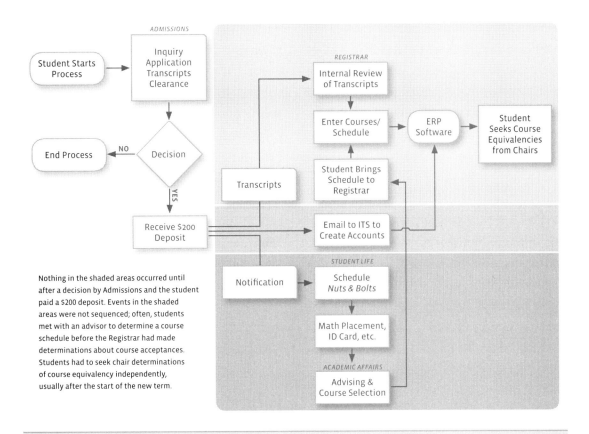

Nothing in the shaded areas occurred until after a decision by Admissions and the student paid a $200 deposit. Events in the shaded areas were not sequenced; often, students met with an advisor to determine a course schedule before the Registrar had made determinations about course acceptances. Students had to seek chair determinations of course equivalency independently, usually after the start of the new term.

Figure 12. Admissions and Registrar's Office Processes: Before

to ensure that equivalencies are correct and that we accurately identify courses we *cannot* accept—*e.g.*, those that are not similar in kind to courses we do—or would—teach.

The change in process from reviewing only the transcripts of matriculated students to reviewing the transcripts of all transfer applicants represents a significant workload increase for departments. It also appears to make us less efficient: Prior to the change, 100 percent of the students whose courses were reviewed by department chairs were already matriculated at the College. By fall 2011 (after the change was implemented), only 32 percent of

the students whose courses were reviewed ultimately matriculated. Yet the yield was much greater: 21 transfer students compared to 9 the previous year. For 2012–13, 29 students out of an applicant pool of 125 matriculated, representing a 23 percent yield. No one questions the value of the additional work, but it has been a significant increase for the registrar and department chairs nonetheless.

As we implemented this change, we also reviewed and revised our internal communication process regarding transfer students. Admissions now initiates a message chain by sending an email to the registrar to which

245

PDFs of student transcripts are attached. Academic Affairs is copied on this e-mail to signal the beginning of the process and to allow us to intervene as we deem necessary—for example, when a non-academic course should not transfer at all. Academic Affairs also determines whether courses that are not equivalent to any in our own curriculum yet and qualify for transfer can be designated as meeting our general education (humanities, social sciences, etc.) or skills (quantitative reasoning, oral communication, etc.) requirements.

The registrar then e-mails department chairs to request course equivalency designations; the emails specify whether any of the courses were taken online and indicate the student's intended major. This information can influence whether courses are counted toward the student's major. At W&J, department chairs have always had the discretion not to count online courses toward major requirements. Also, some departments require that certain courses be taken on campus, so information about the student's intended major aids the chairs of these departments in their decision making. For example, our Department of Economics and Business requires that ECN 101, ECN 102, and several other courses be taken on our campus; alternatively, the student must pass a recent final exam for the course in question in order for the other college's course to be considered equivalent. For non-business, economics, and accounting majors who will not be applying the course toward the respective W&J major, the course can count as equivalent (to ECN 101, for example). But for students intending

to major in one of these disciplines, the department chair will work more closely with them to plan their subsequent coursework.

After receiving the department chairs' responses, the registrar sends a summary of the course designations back to Admissions; copies are sent to Academic Affairs and Student Life. Admissions then can inform the prospective transfer student as to which courses will transfer and which requirements they will count toward. Although the process is laborious, it has become more efficient as the registrar has built a large database of previously evaluated courses. Now, *before* sending emails to department chairs, the registrar can determine whether a course has been evaluated previously. Ultimately, this is expected to reduce by more than half the number of courses sent to department chairs for review. Despite the extra effort that is required, the process is necessary to ensure that all stakeholders have the opportunity to apply their respective standards to courses being considered for transfer equivalency.

Nuts and Bolts

The summary email from the registrar that lists all course equivalencies per prospective transfer student is sent as a reply to the initial transcript email sent by the Admissions Office. This is important for the next step in the transfer student's journey: Nuts and Bolts, an on-campus event that is customized for each transfer student. The organizer of Nuts and Bolts schedules math placement tests for the student (unless the student has passed a calculus or higher-level math course prior to

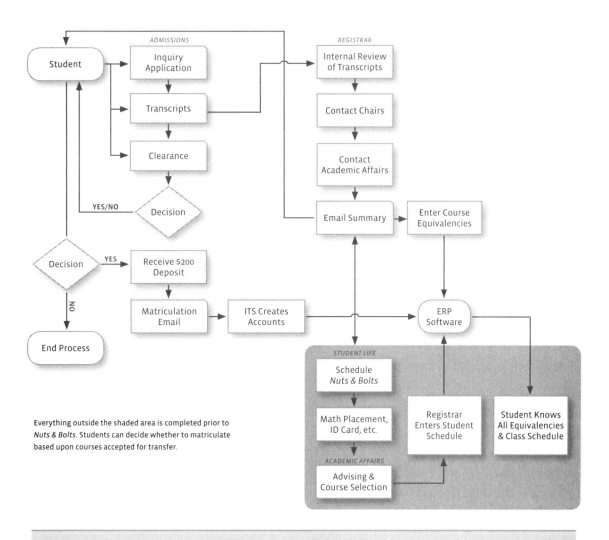

Everything outside the shaded area is completed prior to *Nuts & Bolts*. Students can decide whether to matriculate based upon courses accepted for transfer.

Figure 13. Admissions and Registrar's Office Processes: After

transferring to w&j, in which case the placement test is waived). The email chain thus helps the Nuts and Bolts organizer determine which orientation activities will be necessary for the student. The email chain is forwarded to the student's major advisor, thus enhancing her ability to help the student make immediate progress in the major.

Nuts and Bolts is another area where the evaluation of student transcripts as early in the

admissions process as possible has proven essential. Course equivalencies now are entered into our information system *before* the student arrives on campus for advising and course registration. In the past, this was seldom the case, with the result that advising was nearly blind: we would read transcripts, make our best guess as to course equivalencies, and then register the student in classes according to a "first do no harm" philosophy. Now, with a database

247

of equivalencies and designations, we can better place transfer students in courses that will help them progress toward graduation.

Until recently, the assistant dean for academic advising was responsible for all transfer student advising. However, beginning in summer 2012, transfer students who know their intended major (greater than 80 percent do) have been assigned an advisor within that major. Again, this change required additional work by departments. We were reluctant to ask that faculty commit to being available throughout the semester and the summer. But because everyone understood the overall goal and was committed to helping students make the right decisions as soon as they enrolled at the College, the change was adopted fairly readily. Summer advising is made less onerous by the fact that we are a small institution, and many faculty live within an easy commute.

Having students fully entered into the system prior to Nuts and Bolts has improved other aspects of their orientation. Our Information Technology Services (ITS) group cannot create a new student's email account, authorize his ID card, enter him into math placement exam systems, etc., until he is fully matriculated. Typically, several days elapse between student matriculation and Nuts and Bolts, so when new transfer students meet with financial aid or the business office, select their meal plan, obtain their ID cards, etc., everything can be associated with their account in our enterprise information system.

Other changes have further improved transfer students' transition to our campus. A new mentoring program under the aus-

pices of Student Life matches an upper-class W&J student with each new transfer student, usually by major. Often, the mentor is a student orientation leader who is familiar with issues common to new students. Our fall matriculation ceremony, originally conceived to welcome the new freshman class, has been revised to include all "new students"—matriculating freshmen, transfer students, and international students. For spring transfer and exchange students, a separate spring matriculation ceremony provides a similar welcoming experience; the ceremony's highlights include a presidential welcome, the distribution of College pins, and the signing of the mission statement. The spring event, though smaller, also includes transfer student mentors, faculty advisors, coaches—anyone who has been involved in helping the students transition to our campus. A few new events, such as a student excursion to nearby Pittsburgh and a fall dessert reception at the president's house, were scheduled in recognition of the fact that transfer students differ from other new students: They don't want to be treated like freshmen; they've "done that" already at their previous institutions, and they appreciate being treated as unique additions to the student population.

Room for Improvement

During the past two and a half years, we have met regularly to review changes to our transfer student procedures and to discuss ways in which to improve them further. One issue that remains to be addressed is the reserving of seats in courses for incoming transfer students. Transfer students typically need to enroll in courses both at the lower level (often to satisfy general education requirements) and at the upper level (to make progress in the major). This has not been a significant problem in the past, but our goal of increasing the number of transfer students to approximately 40 each year suggests that it might become one. A precedent for "preferential enrollment" does exist on campus in that incoming international exchange students typically are enrolled in courses after seniors have registered. The faculty have understood both that international students need to enroll in certain courses and that their presence is an important component of the campus's overall diversification efforts. However, most incoming transfer students matriculate at the College at a much later date—weeks or even months after freshmen and continuing students register for the following semester. Predictive analysis of past trends may help identify patterns in the courses that transfer students typically need so we can begin to reserve seats accordingly.

Another challenge pertains to language placement tests. W&J requires students to complete two semesters of a foreign language and uses an online test to determine the appropriate starting level. (Some students "test out" of this requirement by demonstrating proficiency.) Matriculating freshmen take the language placement tests during the summer; language faculty review the completed tests individually in order to make final placement determinations. This process helps prevent students from "registering down"—*i.e.*, enrolling in a lower-level language course de-

spite having studied the language for several years in high school. Because faculty review of placement tests is manual, it is difficult to meld it into the transfer student process, which has become a nearly year-round effort. Just as we identified a faculty member from each department who is willing to advise transfer students throughout the year—including during the summer—so we anticipate needing to approach the language faculty about designating someone from each language to support the language placement process for transfer students. Additional challenges are technical and workload-related: All new students—freshmen as well as transfers—need to be enrolled in the course site that is used to administer the language placement test. The College's ITS group manages this enrollment as a batch for incoming freshmen but would need to enroll transfer students manually well in advance of each student's Nuts and Bolts program. Although this seems a minor request, such additions to workload and routine can be difficult to implement.

Despite our best efforts to streamline enrollment processes for transfer students, it is inevitable that some transfer students will approach the College on very short notice—sometimes as late as the first week of classes. We do everything we can to facilitate these students' transition, but it is difficult to provide a comparably high level of service in such a compressed timeframe. Overall, however, the College's efforts to increase the numbers of transfer students while maintaining academic standards and the centrality of the liberal arts curriculum are paying off.

249

Alongside other efforts, such as the development of articulation agreements with local community colleges and advising guides written specifically for students at those colleges, we are facilitating students' transition to a four-year degree program with academic integrity and minimal loss of credits. Within the local context of our campus and curriculum and within the national context of a challenging economy and an increased need for a better-educated population, the extra effort required of everyone involved is being justified by tangible results.

250

APPENDIX A

Who Handles Transfer Articulation?[27]

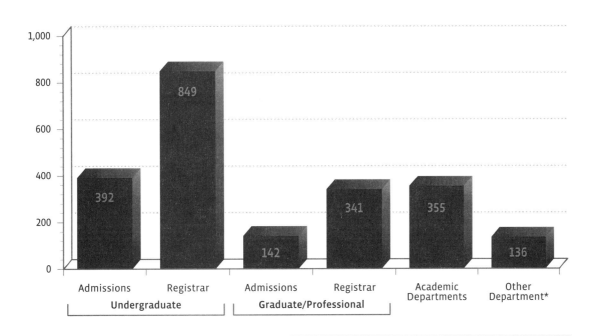

Figure 14. Department Responsible for Processing Transfer Credit Articulation

*Other departments listed by respondents included, but were not limited to:

Academic Advising
Academic Affairs
Academic Counseling
Academic Evaluations
Academic Services
Academic VP
Articulation Officer
Assessment Center
Counseling
Curriculum Dean
Dean Of Student Services

Degree Audit & Transfer Credit unit
Directors of Registration & Advising
Enrollment Management
Enrollment Services Processing
Center
Faculty
Financial Aid
Graduation Office
Institutional Research
International Admissions
Learner Services and Operations

Office of Transfer Services
Prior Learning Assessment
Provost's Office
Registrar High School
Residential Academic Services/Std.
Services
Student Services
Study Abroad
Transfer Articulation Center
Transfer Student Services
VP of Instruction

251

---

[27] Includes selected data from "60 Second Survey Results: Transfer Articulation Practices," an AACRAO survey of 1204 institutions in 38 countries conducted in October 2014.

Table 22. Transfer Articulation Responsibility by Department

	Undergraduate		Graduate/Professional		Department	
	Admissions	Registrar	Admissions	Registrar	Academic	Other
Data Entry Only	33%	21%	34%	40%	2%	16%
Data Entry and Equivalency Determination	55%	74%	46%	55%	9%	54%
Equivalency Determination Only, No Data Entry	12%	4%	21%	5%	90%	30%

252

APPENDIX B

Sample Articulation Agreement: Colorado Statewide Transfer Articulation Agreement

Statewide Transfer Articulation Agreement for a Bachelor's Degree in Business Between...

Colorado Public Community/Junior Colleges	&	Colorado Public Four-Year Institutions of Higher Education
Aims Community College		Adams State University[2]
Arapahoe Community College		Colorado Mesa University[2]
Colorado Mountain College[1]		Colorado State University-Ft Collins
Colorado Northwestern Community College		Colorado State University-Pueblo
Community College of Aurora		Fort Lewis College
Community College of Denver		Metropolitan State University of Denver
Front Range Community College		University of Colorado Boulder
Lamar Community College		University of Colorado Colorado Springs
Morgan Community College		University of Colorado Denver
Northeastern Junior College		University of Northern Colorado
Otero Junior College		Western State Colorado University
Pikes Peak Community College		
Pueblo Community College		
Red Rocks Community College		
Trinidad State Junior College		

[1] Colorado Mountain College also offers a four-year business degree; CMC is participating in this agreement as both a two-year and four-year degree-granting institution.
[2] Adams State University and Colorado Mesa University also offer two-year degrees; they are participating in this agreement as both two-year and four-year degree-granting institutions.

The purpose of a statewide articulation agreement is to identify the courses a student at a Colorado public community college must complete as part of an AA/AS degree to be guaranteed to be able to complete the designated baccalaureate degree program at any public four-year college and university (hereafter referred to as receiving institutions) that

253

offers that program within the minimum number of credits designated by the Colorado Commission on Higher Education.

The guarantees and limitations below describe the minimum requirements to which all participating institutions have agreed.

An appeal related to denial of transfer credits will follow the Colorado Commission on Higher Education student appeal process. An appeal may be filed at http://highered. colorado.gov/Academics/Complaints/.

Part One

Students who complete an AA/AS degree and the prescribed curriculum in the articulation agreement and are admitted (with no academic deficiencies that require additional coursework) to a receiving institution participating in this agreement are guaranteed the following:

- Junior standing with no more than 60 remaining credits to meet the graduation requirements for a baccalaureate degree in the degree program covered by this articulation agreement.
- Completion of the receiving institution's lower division general education requirements as defined by the gtPathways curriculum.
- The same graduation requirements as students who begin and complete this degree program at the receiving institution.

Part Two: Limitations

- Completion of the curriculum prescribed within this statewide articulation agreement does not guarantee admission to a

participating receiving institution. Students must meet all admission and application requirements at the receiving institution including the submission of all required documentation by stated deadlines.

- Only courses with grades of C- or higher are guaranteed to transfer.
- Admission to a receiving institution does not guarantee enrollment in a specific degree program. Some programs at receiving institutions have controlled entry due either to space limitations or academic requirements.
- The credit and course transfer guarantees described in this agreement apply to the specific degree program covered by this agreement. Receiving institutions will evaluate application of the courses designated in this agreement to other degree programs on a course-by-course basis.
- Students who wish to use credits awarded by exam, such as AP (Advanced Placement), or IB (International Baccalaureate), to fulfill specific course requirements are responsible for consulting with the institution to which they are considering transferring to determine whether the credits they have been awarded by exam meet the standards of the receiving institution for specific course equivalents.
- The receiving institution will accept all applicable credits earned within ten years of transfer to the receiving institution. Credits earned more than ten years earlier will be evaluated on a course-by-course basis.

Because of the limitations above, students must consult with the Office of Admissions

254

Table 23. Prescribed Curriculum

	Credit Hours	Community College Course No.	Course Title or Category
Required Courses that Fulfill General Education Requirements (37 Credit Hours)			
Communication	3	ENG 121	English Composition I
	3	ENG 122	English Composition II
Mathematics	4	MAT 121 *or* MAT 123	College Algebra *or* Finite Mathematics
	4	MAT 125	Survey of Calculus *or* a higher level Calculus course
Arts & Humanities	6		Two guaranteed transfer Arts & Humanities courses (GT-AH1, GT-AH2, GT-AH3, GT-AH4)
History	3		One guaranteed transfer History course (GT-HI1)
Social & Behavioral Sciences	3	ECO 201	Macro Economics
	3	ECO 202	Micro Economics
Natural & Physical Sciences	8		Two guaranteed transfer Natural & Physical Sciences courses (GT-SC1, GT-SC2)
Additional Required Courses (23 Credit Hours)			
	4	ACC 121	Accounting Principles I
	4	ACC 122	Accounting Principles II
	3	BUS 216	Legal Environment of Business
	3	BUS 115	Introduction to Business
	3	BUS 217	Business Communications and Report Writing
	3	BUS 226	Business Statistics
	3	COM 115	Speech
Total	**60**		

at the institution to which they are considering transferring.

Part Three: Prescribed Curriculum
(*See* Table 23.)

Addendum to Agreement
Students who do not complete an AA/AS degree can use the prescribed curriculum within a statewide articulation agreement as a common advising guide for transfer to all public institutions that offer the designated baccalaureate degree program.

Please note the following:

■ The guarantee that the number of credits required to graduate will be at the State-mandated minimum for this baccalaureate degree program applies only to students who complete the AA/AS degree and the complete curriculum prescribed in this agreement.

■ Students are guaranteed application of completed gtPathways courses within the curriculum prescribed in this agreement up to the established maximum in each category.

● Except in special cases (*e.g.,* the partial completion of a required sequence of courses or variation in the number of credit hours institutions award for course equivalents), students can expect that courses specified within the prescribed curriculum in this agreement that are successfully completed with a C- or higher will fulfill the relevant course requirements in the designated major.

● Receiving institutions will evaluate all courses other than those specified in this agreement on a course-by-course basis.

Students transferring without a completed AA/AS degree must consult with the Office of Admissions at the institution to which they are considering transferring to review the issues identified above and to make sure they meet all admission and application requirements at the receiving institution, including the submission of all required documentation by stated deadlines.

This agreement will remain in force until such time as the curriculum of the degree program changes or a participating institution requests reconsideration of the terms of the agreement.

Dated: April 1, 2011

COLORADO COMMUNITY COLLEGE SYSTEM

Printed Name

Signature

_____   _____

President   Chief Academic Officer

AIMS COMMUNITY COLLEGE

Printed Name

Signature

_____   _____

President   Chief Academic Officer

COLORADO MOUNTAIN COLLEGE

Printed Name

Signature

_____   _____

President   Chief Academic Officer

256

ADAMS STATE UNIVERSITY

Printed Name   _____   _____

Signature   _____   _____
                President   Chief Academic Officer

COLORADO MESA UNIVERSITY

Printed Name   _____   _____

Signature   _____   _____
                President   Chief Academic Officer

COLORADO STATE UNIVERSITY-FT COLLINS

Printed Name   _____   _____

Signature   _____   _____
                President   Chief Academic Officer

COLORADO STATE UNIVERSITY-PUEBLO

Printed Name   _____   _____

Signature   _____   _____
                President   Chief Academic Officer

FORT LEWIS COLLEGE

Printed Name   _____   _____

Signature   _____   _____
                President   Chief Academic Officer

METROPOLITAN STATE UNIVERSITY OF DENVER

Printed Name   _____   _____

Signature   _____   _____
                President   Chief Academic Officer

UNIVERSITY OF COLORADO BOULDER

Printed Name   _____   _____

Signature   _____   _____
                President   Chief Academic Officer

UNIVERSITY OF COLORADO COLORADO SPRINGS

Printed Name   _____   _____

Signature   _____   _____
                President   Chief Academic Officer

UNIVERSITY OF COLORADO DENVER

Printed Name

Signature

_____   _____
President   Chief Academic Officer

UNIVERSITY OF NORTHERN COLORADO

Printed Name

Signature

_____   _____
President   Chief Academic Officer

WESTERN STATE COLORADO UNIVERSITY

Printed Name

Signature

_____   _____
President   Chief Academic Officer

258

APPENDIX C

List of Statewide Articulation Agreements

State	URL
Alabama	stars.troy.edu
Alaska	www.alaska.edu/future/transfer-information/index.xml
Arizona	aztransfer.com
Arkansas	acts.adhe.edu
California	www.assist.org
Colorado	http://highered.colorado.gov/Academics/Transfers/gtPathways/curriculum.html
Connecticut	www.ct.edu/initiatives/tap
Delaware	www.dtcc.edu/programs
Florida	www.fldoe.org/academics/career-adult-edu/career-technical-edu-agreements/
Georgia	N/A
Hawaii	www.hawaii.edu/offices/app/aa/articulation/articulation.html
Idaho	www.boardofed.idaho.gov/public_col_univ/credit_transfer.asp, www.boardofed.idaho.gov/policies/documents/policies/iii/iiiv_articulation_and_transfer_1212.pdf
Illinois	www.itransfer.org
Indiana	www.transferin.net
Iowa	www.transferiniowa.org/pdf/lacts_2.pdf
Kansas	http://kansasregents.org/126-academic_affairs/transfer_articulation
Kentucky	www.knowhow2transfer.org
Louisiana	http://regents.louisiana.gov/wp-content/uploads/2014/02/Common-Course-Catalog-Feb-2014-2014-0212.pdf
Maine	www.maine.edu/transfer-students/, www.advantageu.me.edu/
Maryland	www.artsys.usmd.edu
Massachusetts	www.mass.edu/masstransfer/Students/AboutMassTransfer.asp

State	URL
Michigan	www.michigantransfernetwork.org
Minnesota	www.mntransfer.org
Mississippi	www.mississippi.edu/trnms/about/splash.aspx
Missouri	http://dhe.mo.gov/policies/credit-transfer.php
Montana	http://mus.edu/transfer/gened.asp
Nebraska	www.ncca.ne.gov/ncca/netransferinitiative.html
Nevada	N/A
New Hampshire	www.nhtransfer.org
New Jersey	http://njtransfer.org
New Mexico	http://admissions.unm.edu/future_students/transfer-course-equivalencies.html
New York	http://student.cuny.edu/cgi-bin/CourseGuide/Colleges.pl?STYLE=NEW
North Carolina	www.nccommunitycolleges.edu/academic-programs/comprehensive-articulation-agreement-caa
North Dakota	www.ndus.edu/employees/articulation-transfer/gerta-guides-request-form/
Ohio	www.ohiohighered.org/transfer/tag
Oklahoma	www.okhighered.org/transfer-students/course-transfer.shtml
Oregon	www.oregon.gov/ccwd/pdf/FreqDocs/ArticulationAgreementsReport2012.pdf
Pennsylvania	www.pacollegetransfer.com
Rhode Island	www.ritransfers.org
South Carolina	www.sctrac.org
South Dakota	www.sdbor.edu/services/academics/ARTICULATION/
Tennessee	www.tntransferpathway.org
Texas	http://statecore.its.txstate.edu
Utah	www.transferutah.org
Vermont	N/A
Virginia	www.schev.edu/students/transfer/default.asp
Washington	www.wsac.wa.gov/sites/default/files/TransferBrochure2011.pdf
West Virginia	N/A
Wisconsin	www.wisconsin.edu/transfer/
Wyoming	www.uwyo.edu/registrar/students/transfer_credit.html

260

APPENDIX D

WICHE Passport
Guidelines for Registrars

Interstate Passport Initiative
Recording and Tracking Passport Students
Guidelines for Registrars

The Interstate Passport Initiative is a grass-roots originated effort by academic leaders in the Western Interstate Commission for Higher Education (WICHE) states[1] to develop policies and practices supporting friction-free transfer for students between institutions in the WICHE region. Students who master all Learning Outcomes in the General Education block transfer Passport would not have to repeat academic work that addresses any of the Passport Learning Outcomes. This initiative proposes a set of related regional projects that would take place during an approximate five-year time span.

The first project, launched in October 2011, is *The Interstate Passport Initiative: Focusing on Learning Outcomes to Streamline Transfer Pathways to Graduation,* a pilot project funded for two years by the Carnegie Corporation of New York with the goal of determining the feasibility and the process of developing the Interstate Passport. This initial effort seeks to forge general education core block transfer agreements, based on the Essential Learning Outcomes, among 28 institutions in the five partner states: California, Hawaii, North Dakota, Oregon, and Utah.

The Essential Learning Outcomes—a quartet of targets that a college curriculum should aim to foster in students in order to prepare them for work, life, and strong citizenship—were developed by the Association of American Colleges and Universities' Liberal Education and America's Promise, known as LEAP, and are already being ad-

261

---

[1] States in the Western Interstate Commission for Higher Education (WICHE) Region: Alaska, Arizona, California, Colorado, Hawaii, Idaho, Montana, Nevada, New Mexico, North Dakota, Oregon, South Dakota, Utah, Washington, and Wyoming.

opted at a variety of institutions and some higher education systems.

During the two years of this first phase project, faculty will define the learning outcomes to be included in the general education core, registrars will determine how to indicate completion of the Passport block on the student's academic record, and registrars and institutional research officers will recommend methods to track the academic progress of Passport students. Subsequent stages of the Passport project will use the methodology established in the two-year pilot to incorporate learning outcomes from general education areas beyond the core into the Passport block, and to gather and analyze the tracking data on the academic progress of the Passport students.

The pilot partners are initially concentrating on the learning outcomes in the lower-division general education core because it is a common denominator among institutions, and so provides the best opportunity for the successful development of an interstate Passport during the two years of the pilot project. Faculty leaders in the pilot institutions have agreed that for this pilot project the scope of the general education core will consist of oral communication, written communication, and quantitative literacy.

The resulting regional block transfer agreement is expected to demonstrate a proof of concept for the development and implementation of a new transfer framework—one based on learning outcomes rather than courses and credits—that could streamline pathways to graduation by eliminating students' repetition of academic work. Future

phases of the project will incorporate additional learning outcomes into the Passport block and monitor the academic progress of Passport students.

WICHE serves as the project manager and fiscal agent. A Pilot State Facilitator has been appointed in each of the five partner states to lead the intrastate efforts and to collaborate in the interstate work to achieve a regional Passport agreement.

The Registrars' Role

In the spring of 2012, the Pilot State Facilitator in each of the partner states enlisted faculty and charged them with determining what constitutes achieving the Passport's selected learning outcomes at their institution and how it equates for transfer to/from other participating institutions. During the summer of 2012, a Passport Task Force on Student Tracking was assembled by convening selected registrars and institutional researchers from the pilot institutions and others in the West. This Task Force was asked to develop methods for the two tracking requirements of the pilot project:

- Ways for a sending institution to signify on a student's record that he or she has achieved the learning outcomes in the Interstate Passport Gen Ed Core Block so that this requirement is recognized as fulfilled by a participating receiving institution.
- Ways for participating receiving institutions to track Passport student success and compare it with that of students transferring without the Passport and with native students. Receiving institutions would

send reports to sending institutions to use in their continuous improvement work.

In undertaking this work, the Task Force was informed by background information related to the transcript and student record from the American Association of Collegiate Registrars and Admissions Officers (AACRAO). According to AACRAO, the transcript is an extract of a student's record which reflects his or her academic performance at an institution. Items considered essential for inclusion on a transcript are academic activities that result in credits, grades, and credentials, such as degrees. AACRAO distinguishes between a database and a transcript, indicating that a database may contain many items which are either optional or not recommended for inclusion on the transcript (*AACRAO 2011 Academic Records and Transcript Guide*).

Guiding Principles and Assumptions

The Student Tracking Task Force worked within the following parameters established by the Passport Advisory Board, the Pilot State Facilitators and their faculty representatives:

- The Passport will be a GE block transfer framework based on LEAP learning outcomes, not courses and credits.
- The Passport GE Block will roll out in a number of stages as the faculty from Passport institutions adds more learning outcomes, either singly or as additional blocks. The first version will be a proof of concept.
- The first version of the Passport will include the lower division general education core learning outcomes associated with written communication, oral communication, and quantitative literacy.

- The number of courses and credits required to achieve a version of the Passport will vary from one institution to another. *For example, a student may achieve the first version of the Passport at Institution A with nine credits. Although 12 credits would be required of native students at Institution B, a student from Institution A could transfer with the Passport and meet all the general education core requirements. S/he may be required to take an additional three credits to graduate or meet some other requirement, but not in general education core.*

- Students may achieve the Passport in different ways at different institutions. These may include course completion, test scores, eportfolio and/or other ways deemed appropriate by the Passport institution's faculty.

- The number of institutions participating in the Passport Initiative will grow as this new transfer model wins acceptance and more learning outcomes are included in the block.

- The solutions must work across different student information systems and work for both paper and electronic student records. They may require minor customization for different platforms.

- The solutions should be simple and easy to implement. They should not require vendor modifications at this time.

- The notations on the student's record will make sense to registrars at non-Passport institutions.

263

Recommendations

The Task Force makes the following recommendations responding to the two objectives for recording and tracking Passport students.

OBJECTIVE 1:
SHOW ON A TRANSCRIPT THAT LEARNING OUTCOMES HAVE BEEN MET.

Recommendation 1: Institutions indicate that a student has achieved the Passport by *choosing to use one or more of the following options* as preferred by the registrar:

- Adding a comment on the transcript using a standard format.
- Posting a pseudo course on the transcript.
- Creating an additional record to accompany a transcript.

Observations: In choosing one or more of the options above, the Task Force suggests that registrars consider the following advantages and potential issues.

- *Comment:* A comment can be added to the transcript to let a transcript processer know about the Passport, when it was achieved, and where to find additional information about it.

  ADVANTAGES
  - Easily read by transcript evaluators reviewing paper transcripts.
  - Easy to post manually.
  - By making the comments self-explanatory, the transcript key will not need to be modified.

- Institutions choosing this option could easily move to one of the other options later.
- An automated process can be created to identify the learning objectives and then add the comment (and/or add the pseudo course) to the transcript.
  - ▷ Utah State, a Passport institution, has volunteered to write a script for its Banner system to identify the learning objectives and add a comment. It will share this program with other Banner institutions.
  - ▷ Because this would be written as a separate program it should not be an issue as upgrades are done to the Banner application. This will not be a modification to Banner; it will be a separate process that accesses the Banner Oracle database.
  - ▷ The program will have the following sections:
    - ▷ As part of the "end of term" process, it would check to see if the student has already acquired the passport and, if not, test to see if the criteria are met. [This will have the most differences among institutions. USU will document its criteria well so that it can be modified to meet individual institutional requirements. Initially, the criteria may be limited to courses, but as academic leaders identify other criteria (such as test scores, portfolios, experi-

ential learning), the program can be modified to include these.]

▷ This section will add a comment to the transcript. This should be the same for all Banner schools, but the comment itself could be modified if needed.

POTENTIAL ISSUES

▶ Difficult to query for reporting.
▶ Conversion to other formats could be problematic.
▶ May be limited to one line of text at some institutions.
▶ If not automated, may be time consuming to post and prone to human error.

● *Pseudo Course:* A pseudo course can be added to the academic history to indicate achievement of the Passport. Institutions not using EDI or XML based transactions would not be required to use the pseudo course.

ADVANTAGES

▶ An automated process can be created to identify the learning objectives and then add the pseudo course to the transcript.
▶ May be used to automate some functionality at some institutions, *e.g.,* equivalency tables or degree audit.
▶ Easily used for reporting purposes.
▶ Institutions choosing this option could easily move to one of the other options later.
▶ Could work with EDI and EXL transcript exchange.

▶ This method would enable receiving institutions to load pseudo courses directly into their SIS to be processed against their articulation rules.

POTENTIAL ISSUES

▶ Not identified as good record keeping practice by many institutions.
▶ May not be allowed under many institutional faculty policies.
▶ May not be easily automated at many institutions or require additional programming support.
▶ Could be confusing to transcript recipients who are not Passport institutions, *e.g.,* businesses and grad schools, etc.
▶ If only the pseudo course is used, the transcript key will need to explain the meaning of the course and give a web reference.
▶ May require the transcript key to be updated and official transcript paper be reprinted.

● *Supplementary Record:* An additional record can be created to accompany a transcript sent to Passport Institutions.

ADVANTAGES

▶ Banner institutions could create another level or PeopleSoft another career or transcript type to send an additional transcript recording all Passport outcomes.
▶ A participating institution could perform the system-set up to automate and share it with other institutions.

265

▶ Could be sent with the transcript to Passport institutions only, thus not creating additional questions or confusion for the reader.

▶ Could be manually produced by institutions who do not wish to create an additional level, career, or transcript.

▶ Provides for the fewest possible conflicts with faculty policy at pilot institutions.

▶ Would work with EDI and XML transcript exchange.

▶ Space for the description would not be as limited as on a regular transcript.

▶ Easily seen and understood by transcript evaluators.

▶ Will be easy to discontinue if process changes or Passport discontinues.

POTENTIAL ISSUES

▶ Some institutions may not want to create an additional level or transcript.

▶ This process would be somewhat manual, but may eventually be able to be automated based on the type of information system.

▶ The names of institutions participating in the Passport would have to be coded into the systems and updated to indicate sending the special transcript.

▶ A second level transcript may require a lot of work by institutions.

▶ Institutions choosing this option could not move to one of the other options later without a lot of difficulty.

Recommendation 2: Comments on the transcript regarding the Passport be posted in the standard format including the version of the Passport, the date it was achieved by the student, and the website where more information is available as shown in the following example:

WICHE Passport Phase 1
Oral and Written Communications; and Quantitative Literacy
July 19, 2012 (date Passport achieved)
See www.wiche/edu/passport/registrar for details

Recommendation 3: A standard title for the pseudo course that will work for all institutions—identical to the first line of the standard comment—be used to identify the Passport and its version. (Note: Banner allows a maximum of 29 characters for a course title. Example: WICHE Passport Phase I)

● The title will not conflict with actual courses. It would have zero credits and a P grade.

● Other considerations in developing the pseudo course:

▶ Where the pseudo course fits alphabetically in the catalog listings. It may be good to have it first or last (ZZZ for example).

▶ Special characters should be avoided.

▶ Careful consideration must be given to the prefix and the course number as some institutions may use 3 digits and others 4 digits.

▶ It would be best to add this as an institutional course in the semester that the criteria are met. This allows tracking students before receiving the passport vs. after receiving the passport. By adding it

266

as an institutional course, the receiving institution knows which institution issued the passport.

▶ The title of the course should be consistent with all institutions and should be descriptive. Example might be "WICHE Passport Phase I."

Recommendation 4: For subsequent versions of the Passport, the (1) comment, (2) pseudo course, and (3) supplementary record should be named in a consistent fashion.

Recommendation 5: Institutions participating in the Passport project include information about it in their student catalog.

Recommendation 6: WICHE provide information for registrars on its website defining the Passport, what constitutes each version and its date range, and a list of participating institutions and the date they were approved for Passport status.

Recommendation 7: Passport partners raise awareness about the Passport by making presentations at AACRAO and other conferences and by sending emails to registrars.

OBJECTIVE 2:
TRACKING PASSPORT STUDENTS FOR
CONTINUOUS IMPROVEMENT OF
PARTICIPATING INSTITUTIONS.

Observations: In developing its recommendations, the Task Force made the following observations:

A receiving institution will see a comment and/or a pseudo course, or a supplementary transcript from the sending institution. Regardless of how the Passport is noted, the receiving institution can enter a pseudo course in the transfer work from the sending institution. Those using EDI/XML can have the course entered automatically.

Using a pseudo course to record a passport from another institution allows the receiving institution to note the sending institution that awarded the Passport and the semester it was awarded. A pseudo course in transfer work does not have the same issues of having a pseudo course that is an institution-based course. That is, there is not a need to have something in the institution catalog about the course and there does not need to be an entry on the transcript key.

This method will provide all of the information to do comparisons of graduation rates, GPA, and other statistics: comparing students with the Passport and those without the Passport. Registrars can also do the reports by the sending institution and can compare the results from the various sending institutions, as well as to those of native students. They can also do reports comparing students that transfer from the various institutions who have completed the Passport vs. those who transfer without completing the Passport. They can also track students' success up to the point they get the Passport and their progress after getting the Passport. All the information needed to produce reports will be available and the reporting process

267

will be similar to that currently used for various cohorts.

Recommendation 1: Request academic leadership, in consultation with their institutional research staff, specify

- Information they want included in the institutional reports.
- How frequently the reports should be run and shared.

- Information they want included in aggregate reports published on the WICHE site.

Recommendation 2: Reconvene the Task Force to

- Create templates for the various reports.
- Develop guidelines for the reporting and sharing process.

APPENDIX E

Joint Statement on the Transfer and Award of Credit

The following set of guidelines has been developed by the three national associations whose member institutions are directly involved in the transfer and award of academic credit: the American Association of Collegiate Registrars and Admissions Officers, the American Council on Education, and the Council for Higher Education Accreditation. The need for such a statement came from an awareness of the growing complexity of transfer policies and practices, which have been brought about, in part, by the changing nature of postsecondary education. With increasing frequency, students are pursuing their education in a variety of institutional and extrainstitutional settings. Social equity and the intelligent use of resources require that validated learning be recognized wherever it takes place.

The statement is thus intended to serve as a guide for institutions developing or reviewing policies dealing with transfer, acceptance, and award of credit. "Transfer" as used here refers to the movement of students from one college, university, or other education provider to another and to the process by which credits representing educational experiences, courses, degrees, or credentials that are awarded by an education provider are accepted or not accepted by a receiving institution.

Basic Assumptions

This statement is directed to institutions of postsecondary education and others concerned with the transfer of academic credit among institutions and the award of academic credit for learning that takes place at another institution or education provider. Basic to this statement is the principle that each institution is responsible for determining its own policies and practices with regard to the transfer, acceptance, and award of credit. Institutions are encouraged to review their policies and practices periodically to assure that

269

they accomplish the institutions' objectives and that they function in a manner that is fair and equitable to students. General statements of policy such as this one or others referred to should be used as guides, not as substitutes, for institutional policies and practices.

Transfer and award of credit is a concept that increasingly involves transfer between dissimilar institutions and curricula and recognition of extrainstitutional learning, as well as transfer between institutions and curricula with similar characteristics. As their personal circumstances and educational objectives change, students seek to have their learning, wherever and however attained, recognized by institutions where they enroll for further study. It is important for reasons of social equity and educational effectiveness for all institutions to develop reasonable and definitive policies and procedures for acceptance of such learning experiences, as well as for the transfer of credits earned at another institution. Such policies and procedures should provide maximum consideration for the individual student who has changed institutions or objectives. It is the receiving institution's responsibility to provide reasonable and definitive policies and procedures for determining a student's knowledge in required subject areas. All sending institutions have a responsibility to furnish transcripts and other documents necessary for a receiving institution to judge the quality and quantity of the student's work. Institutions also have a responsibility to advise the student that the work reflected on the transcript may or may not be accepted by a receiving institution as

bearing the same (or any) credits as those awarded by the provider institution, or that the credits awarded will be applicable to the academic credential the student is pursuing.

Interinstitutional Transfer of Credit

Transfer of credit from one institution to another involves at least three considerations:

- the educational quality of the learning experience which the student transfers;
- the comparability of the nature, content, and level of the learning experience to that offered by the receiving institution; and
- the appropriateness and applicability of the learning experience to the programs offered by the receiving institution, in light of the student's educational goals.

ACCREDITED INSTITUTIONS

Accreditation speaks primarily to the first of these considerations, serving as the basic indicator that an institution meets certain minimum standards. Users of accreditation are urged to give careful attention to the accreditation conferred by accrediting bodies recognized by the Council for Higher Education Accreditation (CHEA). CHEA has a formal process of recognition which requires that all accrediting bodies so recognized must meet the same standards. Under these standards, CHEA has recognized a number of accrediting bodies, including:

- regional accrediting commissions (which historically accredited the more traditional colleges and universities but which now accredit proprietary, vocational-technical, distance learning providers, and single-purpose institutions as well);

- national accrediting bodies that accredit various kinds of specialized institutions, including distance learning providers and freestanding professional schools; and
- professional organizations that accredit programs within multipurpose institutions.

Although accrediting agencies vary in the ways they are organized and in their statements of scope and mission, all accrediting bodies that meet CHEA's standards for recognition function to ensure that the institutions or programs they accredit have met generally accepted minimum standards for accreditation.

Accreditation thus affords reason for confidence in an institution's or a program's purposes, in the appropriateness of its resources and plans for carrying out these purposes, and in its effectiveness in accomplishing its goals, insofar as these things can be judged. Accreditation speaks to the probability, but does not guarantee, that students have met acceptable standards of educational accomplishment.

COMPARABILITY AND APPLICABILITY

Comparability of the nature, content, and level of transfer credit and the appropriateness and applicability of the credit earned to programs offered by the receiving institution are as important in the evaluation process as the accreditation status of the institution at which the transfer credit was awarded. Since accreditation does not address these ques-

tions, this information must be obtained from catalogs and other materials and from direct contact between knowledgeable and experienced faculty and staff at both the receiving and sending institutions. When such considerations as comparability and appropriateness of credit are satisfied, however, the receiving institution should have reasonable confidence that students from accredited institutions are qualified to undertake the receiving institution's educational program. In its articulation and transfer policies, the institution should judge courses, programs, and other learning experiences on their learning outcomes and the existence of valid evaluation measures, including third-party expert review, and not on modes of delivery.

ADMISSIONS AND DEGREE PURPOSES

At some institutions there may be differences between the acceptance of credit for admission purposes and the applicability of credit for degree purposes. A receiving institution may accept previous work, place a credit value on it, and enter it on the transcript. However, that previous work, because of its nature and not its inherent quality, may be determined to have no applicability to a specific degree to be pursued by the student. Institutions have a responsibility to make this distinction, and its implications, clear to students before they decide to enroll. This should be a matter of full disclosure, with the best interests of the student in mind. Institutions also should make every reasonable effort to reduce the gap between credits accepted and credits applied toward an educational credential.

The following additional criteria are offered to assist institutions, accreditors, and higher education associations in future transfer decisions. These criteria are intended to sustain academic quality in an environment of more varied transfer, assure consistency of transfer practice, and encourage appropriate accountability about transfer policy and practice.

Balance in the Use of Accreditation Status in Transfer Decisions

Institutions and accreditors need to assure that transfer decisions are not made solely on the source of accreditation of a sending program or institution. While acknowledging that accreditation is an important factor, receiving institutions ought to make clear their institutional reasons for accepting or not accepting credits that students seek to transfer. Students should have reasonable explanations about how work offered for credit is or is not of sufficient quality when compared with the receiving institution and how work is or is not comparable with curricula and standards to meet degree requirements of the receiving institution.

Consistency

Institutions and accreditors need to reaffirm that the considerations that inform transfer decisions are applied consistently in the context of changing student attendance patterns (students likely to engage in more transfer) and emerging new providers of higher education (new sources of credits and experience to be evaluated). New providers and new attendance patterns increase the number and type of transfer issues that institutions will address, making consistency even more important in the future.

Accountability for Effective Public Communication

Institutions and accreditors need to assure that students and the public are fully and accurately informed about their respective transfer policies and practices. The public has a significant interest in higher education's effective management of transfer, especially in an environment of expanding access and mobility. Public funding is routinely provided to colleges and universities. This funding is accompanied by public expectations that the transfer process is built on a strong commitment to fairness and efficiency.

Commitment to Address Innovation

Institutions and accreditors need to be flexible and open in considering alternative approaches to managing transfer when these approaches will benefit students. Distance learning and other applications of technology generate alternative approaches to many functions of colleges and universities. Transfer is inevitably among these.

FOREIGN INSTITUTIONS

In most cases, foreign institutions are chartered and authorized to grant degrees by their national governments, usually through a Ministry of Education or similar appropriate ministerial body. No other nation has a system comparable with voluntary accreditation

272

as it exists in the United States. At an operational level, AACRAO's Office of International Education Services can assist institutions by providing general or specific guidelines on admission and placement of foreign students or by providing evaluations of foreign educational credentials.

Evaluation of Extrainstitutional and Experiential Learning for Purposes of

TRANSFER AND AWARD OF CREDIT

Transfer and award of credit policies should encompass educational accomplishment attained in extrainstitutional settings. In deciding on the award of credit for extrainstitutional learning, institutions will find the services of the American Council on Education's Center for Adult Learning and Educational Credentials helpful. One of the Center's functions is to operate and foster programs to determine credit equivalencies for various modes of extrainstitutional learning. The Center maintains evaluation programs for formal courses offered by the military and civilian organizations such as business, corporations, government agencies, training providers, institutes, and labor unions. Evaluation services are also available for examination programs, for occupations

with validated job proficiency evaluation systems, and for correspondence courses offered by schools accredited by the Distance Education and Training Council. The results are published in a Guide series. Another resource is the General Educational Development (GED) Testing Program, which provides a means for assessing high school equivalency.

For learning that has not been evaluated through the ACE evaluation processes, institutions are encouraged to explore the Council for Adult and Experiential Learning (CAEL) procedures and processes.

USES OF THIS STATEMENT

Institutions are encouraged to use this statement as a basis for discussions in developing or reviewing institutional policies with regard to the transfer and award of credit. If the statement reflects an institution's policies, that institution may wish to use these guidelines to inform faculty, staff, and students.

It is also recommended that accrediting bodies reflect the essential precepts of this statement in their criteria.

American Association of Collegiate Registrars and Admissions
    Officers [signed 9/28/01]
American Council on Education [signed 9/28/01]
Council for Higher Education Accreditation [signed 9/28/01]

273

REFERENCES

AACRAO. *See* American Association of Collegiate Registrars and Admissions Officers.

Adelman, C. 1999. *Answers in the Tool Box: Academic Intensity, Attendance Patterson, and Bachelor's Degree Attainment.* U.S. Department of Education. Retrieved from: <www2.ed.gov/pubs/Toolbox/>.

American Association of Collegiate Registrars and Admissions Officers. 2004. *The College Transfer Student in America: The Forgotten Student.* Washington, D.C.

———. 2007. *Accreditation Mills.* Washington, D.C.

———. 2014. Helping Veterans Succeed: A Handbook for Higher Education Administrators. Washington, D.C.

American Association of Community Colleges. 2014. *2014 Fact Sheet.* Retrieved Aug. 5 from: <www.aacc.nche.edu/AboutCC/Pages/fastfactsfactsheet.aspx>.

American Council on Education. 2014. *ACE Transfer Guide: Understanding Your Military Transcript and ACE Credit Recommendations.* Washington, D.C. Available at: <www.acenet.edu/news-room/Pages/Transfer-Guide-Understanding-Your-Military-Transcript-and-ACE-Credit-Recommendations.aspx>.

Anderson, G., J.C. Sun, and M. Alfonso. 2006. Effectiveness of statewide articulation agreements on the probability of transfer: A preliminary policy analysis. *The Review of Higher Education.* 29: 261–291.

———. 2006. Rethinking cooling out at public community colleges: An examination of fiscal and demographic trends in higher education and the rise of statewide articulation agreements. *Teachers College Record.* 108(3): 422–451.

Ang, T., and D. Molina. 2014. From access to graduation: Supporting post-9/11 Undergraduate Student Veterans. *Higher Education Today.* Retrieved Dec. 22, 2014 from: <http://higheredtoday.org/2014/11/10/from-access-to-graduation-supporting-post-911-undergraduate-student-veterans/>.

Appalachian State University. 2014. Office of Transfer Services. Retrieved Sep. 3 from: <http://transfer.appstate.edu/>.

Astin, A.W. 1993. *What Matters in College? Four Critical Years Revisited.* San Francisco: Jossey-Bass.

Baker, S.J. 2014. *Role of Transfer Students in Meeting College Completion.* Annapolis MD: Department of Legislative, Office of Policy Analysis. Retrieved Aug. 6 from: <http://mgaleg.maryland.gov/pubs/budgetfiscal/2015fy-budget-docs-operating-HEPB1-Higher-Education-Policy-Briefing-Transfer-Students.pdf>.

Baum, S., and J. Ma. 2013. *Trends in College Pricing 2013.* New York: College Board.

Bautsch, B. 2013. *State Policies to Improve Student Transfer.* Washington, D.C.: National Conference of State Legislatures. Retrieved from: <www.ncsl.org/documents/educ/student-transfer.pdf>.

Berger, J.B., and G.D. Malaney. 2001. Assessing the Transition of Transfer Students from Community Colleges to a University. Presented at the Annual Conference of the National Association of School Psychologists. Seattle, WA.

Bess, J.L., and J.R. Dee. 2008. *Understanding College and University Organization: Theories for Effective Policy and Practice* v. 2. Sterling, VA: Stylus.

Bishop, G. 2013. Want to play at a different college? O.K., but not there or there. *The New York Times.* June 8. Retrieved from: <www.nytimes.com/2013/06/08/sports/ncaafootball/college-coaches-use-transfer-rules-to-limit-athletes-options.html>.

Blaylock, R.S., and M.J. Bresciani. 2011. Exploring the success of transfer programs for community college students. *Research and Practice in Assessment.*(6): 43–61.

Bohn, S., B. Reyes, and H. Johnson. 2013. *The Impact of Budget Cuts on California's Community Colleges.* San Francisco: Public Policy Institute of California. Retrieved from: <www.ppic.org/main/publication.asp?i=1048>.

California State Department of Education. 1960. *A Master Plan for Higher Education in California: 1960–1975.* Sacramento, CA: Liaison Committee of the State Board of Education and The Regents of the University of California, California State Department of Education. Retrieved from: <www.ucop.edu/acadinit/mastplan/mp.htm>.

Cate, C.A. 2014. *Million Records Project: Research from Student Veterans of America.* Student Veterans of America, Washing-

275

ton, D.C. Available at: <www.studentveterans.org/images/Reingold_Materials/mrp/download-materials/mrp_Full_report.pdf>.

Choy, S. 2002. *Findings from the Condition of Education 2002: Nontraditional Undergraduates.* Washington, D.C.: National Center for Education Statistics. Retrieved Jan. 1, 2015 from: <http://nces.ed.gov/pubs2002/2002012.pdf>.

Chronicle of Higher Education. 2014. On Leadership: Freeman A. Hrabowski III, University of Maryland-Baltimore County. Video interview by Sara Lipka. Retrieved Aug 7 from: <http://chronicle.com/article/Video-What-It-Takes-to-Help/147511/>.

City University of New York. 2014. *Pathways.* Retrieved from: <www.cuny.edu/news/publications/pathways.pdf>.

Clemetsen, B. 2009. Building effective community college/university partnerships. In *Applying SEM at the Community College,* edited by B. Bontrager and B. Clemetsen, 67–80. Washington, D.C.: American Association of Collegiate Registrars and Admission Officers.

College Board. 2011. *Improving Student Transfer from Community Colleges to Four-Year Institutions: The Perspective of Leaders from Baccalaureate-Granting Institutions.* Retrieved from: <http://advocacy.collegeboard.org/sites/default/files/11b3193transpartweb110712.pdf>.

Community College of the Air Force 2014–16 Catalog. Available at: <www.au.af.mil/au/barnes/ccaf/catalog/2014cat/2014_2016_General_catalog.pdf>.

Contomichalos, S. K. 2014. Issues and obstacles for lateral transfer students to selective colleges. *Journal of College Admission.* Fall.

Council for Higher Education. 2005. Transfer of credit: Taking a fresh look or continuing the controversy? *Inside Accreditation with the President of CHEA.* 1(4). Retrieved from: <http://chea.org/ia/IA_110405.htm>.

Davies, T.G., and K. Casey. 1999. Transfer student experiences: Comparing their academic and social lives at the community college and university. *College Student Journal.* 33(1): 60–71.

Davis, J., and K. Bauman. 2013. *School Enrollment in the United States: 2011 Population Characteristics.* Retrieved September 13, 2014 from: <www.census.gov/prod/2013pubs/p20–571.pdf>.

De los Santos, A., Jr., and I. Wright. 1990. Maricopa's swirling students: Earning one-third of Arizona State's bachelor's degrees. *Community, Technical, and Junior College Journal.* 60(6): 32–34.

Department of Veterans Affairs. VA Campus Toolkit Handout. Retrieved Dec. 15, 2015 from: <www.mentalhealth.va.gov/studentveteran/docs/ed_todaysStudentVets.html>.

Dowd, A., J. Cheslock, and T. Melguizo. 2008. Transfer access from community colleges and the distribution of elite higher education. *The Journal of Higher Education.* Retrieved from: <http://cue.usc.edu/tools/Dowd.Cheslock.Melguizo_%20Transfer%20Access%20to%20Elites_JHE%20in%20press_pages%20proofs.pdf>.

Dundar, A. 2014. The New Transfer Marketplace Student Mobility and Transfer: Patterns and Success Outcomes. National Student Clearinghouse Research Center. Presentation at the Transfer Solutions through Cross-Organization Alignment Convening, July 28. Denver, CO.

Ekal, D., and P.M. Krebs. 2011. Reverse-transfer programs reward students and colleges alike. *Chronicle for Higher Education.* June 19. Retrieved from: <http://chronicle.com/article/Reverse-Transfer-Programs/127942/>.

Ellis, M.M. 2013. Successful community college transfer students speak out. *Community College Journal of Research and Practice.* 37(2): 73–84.

Embry-Riddle Aeronautical University. n.d. *Credit: Transfer, Military, Time Limits, and Advanced Standing* (web page). Available at: <http://catalog.erau.edu/worldwide/student-services-academic-affairs/credit/>.

———. n.d. *Military and Veterans* (web page). Available at: <http://daytonabeach.erau.edu/military/>.

Flaga, C.T. 2006. The process of transition to community college transfer students. *Community College Journal of Research and Practice.* 30: 3–19.

Gard, D.R., V. Paton and K. Gosselin. 2012. Student perceptions of factors contributing to community-college-to-university transfer success. *Community College Journal of Research and Practice.* 36 (11): 833–848.

Glass, J.C., and A.R. Harrington. 2002. Academic performance of community college transfer students and "native" students at a large state university. *Community College Journal of Research & Practice.* 26(5): 415–430.

Goldrick-Rab, S. 2007. *Promoting Academic Momentum at Community Colleges: Challenges and Opportunities.* New York: Community College Research Center, Teachers College, Columbia University.

Goldrick-Rab, S., and F.T. Pfeffer. 2009. Beyond access: Explaining socioeconomic differences in college transfer. *Sociology of Education.* 82(2): 101–125. Retrieved from: <http://soe.sagepub.com/content/82/2/101>.

Gonzalez, J. 2012. A Third of Students Transfer Before Graduating, and Many Head Toward Community Colleges. *The Chronicle of Higher Education.* February 28. Retrieved from: <http://chronicle.com/article/A-Third-of-Students-Transfer/130954/>.

Gordon, E.J. 2014. "Do I have to take this class?" Nontraditional students' attitudes toward and perceptions of a required effective learning course. *The Journal of Continuing Higher Education.* 62(3): 163–172. Retrieved Dec. 22, 2014 from: <www.tandfonline.com/doi/pdf/10.1080/07377363.2014.956029>.

Grubb, W.N. 2006. Like, what do I do now? The dilemma of guidance counseling. In, *Defending the Community College Equity Agenda,* edited by T. Bailey and V.S. Morest. Baltimore: The Johns Hopkins University Press.

Handel, S.J. 2007. Second chance, not second class: A blueprint for community-college transfer. *Change:* 38–45.

———. 2010. Silent partners in transfer admissions. *The Chronicle of Higher Education.* Retrieved from: <http://chronicle.com/article/Silent-Partners-in-Transfer/124514/>.

———. 2011. Improving student transfer from community colleges to four-year institutions: The perspective of leaders from baccalaureate-granting institutions. New York: College Board. Available at: <www.jkcf.org/assets/1/7/Perspective_of_Leaders_of_Four-Year_institutions.pdf>.

———. 2013. *Transfer as Academic Gauntlet: The Student Perspective.* New York, NY: The College Board. Retrieved Aug. 30 from: <http://media.collegeboard.com/digitalServices/pdf/advocacy/policycenter/transfer-academic-gauntlet-student-perspective-report.pdf>.

Handel, S.J., and R. Williams. 2012. *The Promise of the Transfer Pathway: Opportunity and Challenge for Community College Students Seeking the Baccalaureate Degree.* New York: The College Board.

Hanna, D.E. 2003. Building a leadership vision: Eleven strategic challenges for higher education. *Educause Review.* (38): 24–34.

Herrera, A., and D. Jain. 2013. Building a transfer-receptive culture at four-year institutions. *New Directions for Higher Education*, no. 162.

Herrmann, E., E. Schroeder, B. Boss, D. Schultz, and S. Alberts. 2013. *NAIA Academic Study Report.* Kirksville, MO: Center for Applied Statistics and Evaluation.

Hills, J.R. 1965. Transfer shock: The academic performance of the junior college transfer. *Journal of Experimental Education.* 33(Spring): 201–216.

Horn, L. 2009. *On Track to Complete? A Taxonomy of Beginning Community College Students and Their Outcomes 3 Years After Enrolling: 2003–04 through 2006* (NCES Publication No. 2009–152). Washington D.C.: National Center for Education Statistics.

Horn, L. J., and C. D. Carroll. 1996. *Nontraditional Undergraduates: Trends in Enrollment from 1986 to 1992 and Persistence and Attainment Among 1989-90 Beginning Postsecondary Students* (NCES Publication No. 97-578). Washington, D.C.: National Center for Education Statistics. Retrieved Dec. 31, 2014 from: <http://nces.ed.gov/pubs/web/97578a.asp>.

Horn, L., and P. Skomsvold. 2012. *Community College Student Outcomes 1994–2009* (NCES Publication No. 2012–253). Washington D.C.: National Center for Education Statistics.

Horn, L. and S. Nevill. 2006. *Profile of Undergraduates in U.S. Postsecondary Education Institutions: 2003–04, with a Special Analysis of Community College Students* (NCES Publication No. 2006184). Washington, D.C.: National Center for Education Statistics. Retrieved February 7, 2014 from: <http://nces.ed.gov/pubsearch/pubsinfo.asp?pubid=2006184>.

Hosick, M.B. 2013. Division I student-athletes show progress in graduation success rate. *National Collegiate Athletic Association (NCAA).* October 24. Retrieved from: <www.ncaa.com/news/ncaa/article/2013–10–24/division-i-student-athletes-show-progress-graduation-success-rate>.

Hossler, D., D. Shapiro, A. Dundar, M. Ziskin, J. Chen, D. Zerquera, and V. Torres. 2012. *Transfer and Mobility: A National View of Pre-degree Student Movement in Postsecondary Institutions* (Signature Report No. 2). Herndon, VA: National Student Clearinghouse Research Center.

Hostetter, S. 2007. Transfer credits and accreditation (Letters to the Editor). *The Chronicle Review.* 53(35).

Hussar, W. J., and T. M. Bailey. 2013. *Projections of Education Statistics to 2021.* Washington, D.C.: National Center for Education Statistics. Retrieved Aug. 6 from: <www.nces.ed.gov/pubs2013/2013008.pdf>.

Ignash, J.M., and B.K. Townsend. 2000. Evaluating state-level articulation agreements according to good practice. *Community College Review.* 28(3): 1–21.

———. 2001. Statewide transfer and articulation policies: Current practices and emerging issues. In *Community Colleges: Policy in the Future Context*, edited by B.K. Townsend and S.B. Twombly. Westport, CT: Ablex Publishing.

Jacobs, B.C. 2004. Introduction & overview. In *The College Transfer Student in America: The Forgotten Student*, edited by B.C. Jacobs, B. Lauren, M.T. Miller, and D.P. Nadler (pp. i-iv). Washington, D.C.: American Association of Collegiate Registrars and Admissions Officers.

Jain, D., A. Herrera, S. Bernal, and D. Solórzano. 2011. Critical race theory and the transfer function: Introducing a transfer

receptive culture. *Community College Journal of Research and Practice.* 35(2): 252–266.

Kadlec, A., J. Immerwahr, and I. Gupta. 2014. *Guided Pathways to Student Success: Perspectives from Indiana College Students and Advisors.* Indiana Commission for Higher Education.

Keathley, M. 2012. In praise of senior citizen students. *Best Colleges Online* (blog). January 26. Retrieved from: <www.bestcollegesonline.com/blog/2012/01/26/in-praise-of-senior-citizen-students>.

Kinser, K., and B.A. Hill. 2011. *Higher Education in Tumultuous Times: A Transatlantic Dialogue on Facing Market Forces and Promoting the Common Good.* Washington, D.C.: American Council on Education.

Kisker, C.B., R.L. Wagoner, and A.M. Cohen. 2012. Elements of effective transfer associate degrees. *New Directions for Community Colleges.* 160: 5–11. San Francisco, CA: Jossey-Bass.

Kolowich, S. 2013. American Council on Education recommends 5 MOOCs for credit. *The Chronicle of Higher Education.* February 7. Retrieved from: <http://chronicle.com/article/American-Council-on-Education/137155/>.

Kortesoja, S. L. 2009. Postsecondary Choices of Nontraditional-age Students: Non-credit Courses or a Credential Program? *Review of Higher Education.* Retrieved Jan. 2, 2015 from: http://search.proquest.com.ezproxy.libproxy.db.erau.edu/docview/220851966/fulltext?accountid=27203.

Kuh, G.D., J. Kinzie, J.H. Schuh, and E.J. Whitt. 2005. *Student Success in College: Creating Conditions That Matter.* San Francisco: Jossey-Bass.

Kuh, G.D., J. Kinzie, J.A. Buckley, B.K. Bridges, and J.C. Hayek. 2006. *What Matters to Student Success: A Review of the Literature.* National Postsecondary Education Cooperative. Available at: <http://nces.ed.gov/npec/pdf/kuh_team_report.pdf>.

Laanan, F.S., S.S. Starobin, and L.E. Eggleston. 2010. Adjustment of community college students at a four-year university: Role and relevance of transfer student capital for student retention. *Journal of College Student Retention.* 12 (2): 175–209.

Ling, T.J. 2006. *The Relation of Self Variables to Transfer Student Success as Measured by Academic, Psychological, and Career Functioning.* (Unpublished masters thesis). (ED491812)

Lumina Foundation. 2012. Foundations help 12 state partnerships expand associate degree completion for students transferring from community colleges to universities [Press release]. October 10. Retrieved from: <www.luminafoundation.org/newsroom/news_releases/2012-10-10.html>.

Mangan, K. 2014. When students transfer, credits may not follow. *The Chronicle of Higher Education.* Retrieved from: <http://chronicle.com/article/When-Students-Transfer/148425/>.

Marling, J. 2013. Navigating the new normal: Transfer trends, issues, and recommendations. *New Directions for Higher Education.* Wiley Online Library.

Maryland Association of Community Colleges. 2013. *College and Career Readiness and College Completion Act of 2013.* May 2013 Regional Meeting presentation. Annapolis. Retrieved from: <www.mdacc.org/PDFs/Publications/Special%20Reports/SB740_Regional_Meeting_Presentation.pdf>.

McBain, L. 2012. *From Soldier to Student II: Assessing Campus Programs for Veterans and Service Members.* Washington, D.C.: American Association of State Colleges and Universities.

McCormick, A. 2003. Swirling and double-dipping: New patterns of student attendance and their implications for higher education. In *Changing Student Attendance Pat-*

terns: *Challenges for Policy and Practice, New Directions for Higher Education*, no. 121, edited by J. King, E. Anderson and M. Corrigan. San Francisco: Jossey-Bass.

McCormick, A.C., and Carroll, C.D. 1997. *Transfer Behavior Among Beginning Postsecondary Students: 1989–94*. Washington, D.C.: National Center for Education Statistics. Retrieved from: <http://nces.ed.gov/pubs97/97266.pdf>.

McDonough, P.M. 1997.*Choosing Colleges: How Social Class and Schools Structure Opportunity*. Albany, NY: State University of New York Press.

Millard, M. 2014. Students on the move: How states are responding to increasing mobility among postsecondary students. *Transfer and Articulation*. May. Education Commission of The States. Retrieved from: <www.ecs.org/clearinghouse/01/12/29/11229.pdf>.

Monaghan, D.B., and P. Attewell. 2015. The community college route to the bachelor's degree. *Educational Evaluation and Policy Analysis*. 37: 70–91.

Moore, C., and N. Shulock. 2011. *Sense of Direction: The Importance of Helping Community College Students Select and Enter a Program of Study*. Sacramento, CA: California State University, Sacramento, Institute for Higher Education Leadership and Policy. Retrieved from: <www.csus.edu/ihelp/PDFs/R_Sense_of_Direction.pdf>.

Mullin, C.M. 2012. Transfer: An indispensable part of the community college mission (Policy Brief 2012–03PBL). Washington D.C.: American Association of Communication Colleges.

Napolitano, J. 2013. *Remarks to The Regents of the University of California*. November 13. Oakland, Office of the President, University of California. Retrieved from: <http://ucop.edu/president/public-engagement/remarks-to-regents-nov-2013.html>.

National Association of Independent Colleges and Universities. 2003. *Twelve Facts That May Surprise You About Private Higher Education*. Washington, D.C.: NAICU.

National Association of Intercollegiate Athletics. 2013a. *Legislative Brief: Recruiting Rules for Coaches*. May 14. Retrieved from: <www.naia.org/ViewArticle.dbml?SPSID=730210&SPID=124108&DB_LANG=C&DB_OEM_ID=27900&ATCLID=207652961>.

———. 2013b. *Legislative Brief: 24/36-Hour Rule, Part 3: The Progress Rule*. April 18. Retrieved from: <www.naia.org/ViewArticle.dbml?SPSID=730210&SPID=124108&DB_LANG=C&DB_OEM_ID=27900&ATCLID=209470154>.

———. 2013c. *Institutional Credit Hours and Remedial Courses*. August 8. Retrieved from: <www.naia.org/ViewArticle.dbml?SPSID=730210&SPID=124108&DB_LANG=C&DB_OEM_ID=27900&ATCLID=208997560>.

———. 2014. *24/36-Hour Rule, Part 1: The Basics*. March 5. Retrieved from: <www.naia.org/ViewArticle.dbml?SPSID=730210&SPID=124108&DB_LANG=C&DB_OEM_ID=27900&ATCLID=209427034>.

National Center for Education Statistics. 2011. *Six-Year Attainment, Persistence, Transfer, Retention, and Withdrawal Rates of Students Who Began Postsecondary Education in 2003–04*. Retrieved Feb. 6 from: <http://nces.ed.gov/pubs2011/2011152.pdf>.

National Conference of State Legislatures. 2014. *Performance-Based Funding for Higher Education*. Retrieved Aug. 5 from: <www.ncsl.org/research/education/performance-funding.aspx>.

National Postsecondary Education Cooperative. *Information Required to Be Disclosed Under the Higher Education Act of 1965: Suggestions for Dissemination*. Retrieved from: <http://nces.ed.gov/pubs2010/2010831rev.pdf>.

National Student Clearinghouse. 2012a. *Transfer & Mobility: A National View of Pre-Degree Student Movement in Postsecondary Institutions*. Retrieved from: <www.studentclearinghouse.info/signature/2/NSC_Signature_Report_2.pdf>.

———. 2012b. *Reverse Transfer: A National View of Student Mobility from Four-Year to Two-Year Institutions*. Retrieved from: <www.studentclearinghouse.info/signature/3/NSC_Signature_Report_3.pdf>.

———. 2012c. *Snapshot Report: Degree Attainment*. Retrieved from: <http://nscresearchcenter.org/wp-content/uploads/SnapshotReport8-GradRates2-4Transfers.pdf>.

———. 2013. *Baccalaureate Attainment: A National View of the Postsecondary Outcomes of Students Who Transfer from Two-Year to Four-Year Institutions*. Available at: <http://nscresearchcenter.org/wp-content/uploads/SignatureReport5.pdf>.

———. 2014a. *Snapshot Report: First-Year Persistence and Retention Rates by Starting Enrollment Intensity: 2009–2012*. Retrieved from: <http://nscresearchcenter.org/snapshotreport-persistenceretention14/>.

———. 2014b. *Snapshot Report: Degree Attainment*. Retrieved July 17 from: <http://research.studentclearinghouse.org>.

———. 2014c. *Snapshot Report: Mobility*. Retrieved July 17 from: <http://research.studentclearinghouse.org>.

Nite, C. 2012. Challenges for supporting student-athlete development: Perspectives from an NCAA Division II athletic department. *Journal of Issues in Intercollegiate Athletics*. 5: 1–14. Retrieved from: <http://csriiia.org/documents/puclications/research_articles/2012/JIIA_2012_5_1_1_14_Challenges_for_Supporting_Student-Athlete_Development.pdf>.

Noel-Levitz. 2013. *The Attitudes of Second-Year College Students*. Retrieved from: <www.noellevitz.com/papers-research-higher-education/2013/2013-report-the-attitudes-of-second-year-college-students>.

NSC. *See* National Student Clearinghouse.

Ott, A.P., and B.C. Cooper. 2014. Transfer credit evaluations: How they are produced, why it matters and how to serve students better. *College and University*. 89(4):14–25. Retrieved from: <www.readperiodicals.com/201407/3473949051.html>.

Pascarella, E.T. and P.T. Terenzini. 2005. *How College Affects Students: A Third Decade of Research* (Vol. 2). San Francisco, Jossey-Bass.

Pennington, R. 2006. Rethinking grade transfer shock. Examining its importance in the community college transfer process. *Journal of Applied Research in Community College*. 14(1): 19–33.

Peter, K., and C.D. Carroll. 2005. *The Road Less Traveled? Students Who Enroll in Multiple Institutions* (NCES Publication No. 2005–157). Washington, D.C.: National Center for Education Statistics.

Poisel, M.A., and S. Joseph. 2011. *Transfer Students in Higher Education: Building Foundations for Policies, Programs, and Services that Foster Student Success*. Monograph Series No. 54. Columbia, SC: National Resource Center for the First-Year Experience and Students in Transition.

Prescott, B.T., and P. Bransberger. 2012. *Knocking at the College Door: Projections of High School Graduates* (eighth edition).